Gaining Cultural Competence in Career Counseling

SECOND EDITION

Kathy M. Evans, Ph.D. and Aubrey L. Sejuit, Ph.D.

National Career Development Association

Copyright 2021 by the National Career Development Association
305 North Beech Circle
Broken Arrow, OK 74012

No part of this book may be reproduced, stored in a retrieval system, or transmitted in any form or by any means, electronic, mechanical, photocopying, recording, or otherwise without prior permission of the National Career Development Association.

Printed in the United States of America

Library of Congress Cataloging-in-Publication Data

Names: Evans, Kathy M., author. | Sejuit, Aubrey L., author.
Title: Gaining cultural competence in career counseling / Kathy M. Evans, University of South Carolina, Aubrey L. Sejuit, Limestone University
Description: Second edition. | Broken Arrow : National Career Development Association, [2020] | Includes bibliographical references and index. | Summary: "This book is designed as a supplement to textbooks used in career development courses as well as a resource for career counselors and practitioners encountering an increasingly diverse clientele. Using a career perspective, this text synthesizes the competencies recommended to career counselors and practitioners by the National Career Development Association, the Association for Multicultural Counseling and Development, and the Counselors for Social Justice. It offers both theoretical and practical approaches to increase the likelihood that counselors-in-training and career professionals can successfully integrate career, multicultural, and social justice competencies into their practice"-- Provided by publisher.
Identifiers: LCCN 2020041274 (print) | LCCN 2020041275 (ebook) | ISBN 9781885333643 (paperback) | ISBN 9781885333643 (adobe pdf)
Subjects: LCSH: Cross-cultural counseling. | Counselor and client. | Cultural competence. | Vocational guidance--Vocational guidance.
Classification: LCC BF636.7.C76 E93 2020 (print) | LCC BF636.7.C76 (ebook) | DDC 158.3--dc23
LC record available at https://lccn.loc.gov/2020041274
LC ebook record available at https://lccn.loc.gov/2020041275

NCDA opposes discrimination against any individual based on age, culture, disability, ethnicity, race, religion/spirituality, creed, gender, gender identity and expression, sexual orientation, marital/partnership status, language preference, socioeconomic status, or any other personal characteristic not specifically relevant to job performance. (Approved by the NCDA Board – October 2016)

PREFACE

For career professionals to be considered proficient, they must demonstrate competence not only in career development but also in multicultural sensitivity and social justice. Unfortunately, these competencies are typically taught separately making it difficult for career professionals to integrate these skills into their practice once they have completed their training. When career professionals fail to synthesize these competencies, they are likely to approach clients from a one-size-fits-all perspective that is detrimental to their marginalized clients (Sue et al., 1998). In *Gaining Cultural Competence in Career Counseling*, it is our goal to assist career professionals and career counseling students in synthesizing and implementing these competencies.

What is New in the Second Edition

The number of years that have passed since publishing the first edition (Evans, 2008) called for substantial updating of the material here. Thankfully, there have been many positive changes and social justice movements in those intervening years that are reflected in the chapters. However, after this manuscript was written, but before it was published, both nation-wide and world-wide protests occurred to stress the need for social justice and have been referred to here in a nascent way. Also in this edition, most chapters include new activities and/or new scenarios. Not only is new research included but the language has been updated as well. The biggest change in this second edition is the addition of the chapter on career counseling with children and adolescents, a population that is under-represented in the research literature on career development but well represented among the clientele of career professionals working in schools.

Content and Organization

This book is divided into two parts. The first part is comprised of four chapters that focus on the foundational skills for effective counseling across cultures. It is important that career professionals engage in some introspection before delving into specific skills for culturally competent career counseling. The information and activities in these first few chapters assist readers in reflecting on oppression and what it means in their lives. The second part of the book integrates those multicultural competencies with specific career and social justice counseling competencies. It is crucial for career professionals and those preparing for the profession to master the multicultural skills presented in the first part of the book before moving ahead to the applications addressed in the second part. Following is a more specific guide to each chapter.

Chapter 1 – The Importance of Culturally Competent Career Counseling. The first chapter sets the tone for the rest of the book, beginning with a provocative scenario that helps readers understand the definition of multiculturalism employed in this book. The chapter highlights the various reasons why multicultural counseling is important, introduces the original Association for Multicultural Counseling and Development (AMCD) multicultural counseling competencies endorsed by the American Counseling Association (ACA; included in abbreviated form in Appendix A) and the National Career Development Association (NCDA) Minimum Competencies for Multicultural Career Counseling and Development (included in its entirety in Appendix B), discusses via illustrated examples how the ethical codes of the ACA, NCDA, and American Psychological Association (APA) speak to the importance of multiculturalism, and begins the process of synthesizing the AMCD and NCDA and social justice competencies. Later in the text, the new Social Justice Multicultural Counseling Competencies will be introduced and integrated into the total picture of culturally competent career counseling.

Chapter 2 – Awareness of Your Own Cultural Heritage. This chapter leads readers through an exploration of their own cultural heritages through a discussion of the dominant American culture, and a study of the definitions of cultural relativism, worldview, and value orientation. Readers are introduced to the Racial/Cultural Identity Development Model, and the White Racial Identity Model. The chapter provides a wide variety of exercises to facilitate the independent self-exploration of cultural heritage.

Chapter 3 – Exploring Your Own Values and Biases. For some readers, this may be the book's most emotionally challenging chapter, for it encourages career professionals and those training for the profession to uncover their own biases, and to consider how these biases manifest themselves in stereotyping, prejudice, racism and oppression, and privilege. As in Chapter 2, plentiful exercises facilitate reader self-exploration. Once biases are identified, career professionals are encouraged to determine ways in which their biases may impact their work with clients who differ from them.

Chapter 4 – Awareness of the Client's Worldview. This final foundational chapter of the book asks readers who have just explored their own cultures and own biases to step outside of themselves and focus on the worldviews of clients. By doing this, career professionals and trainees can better understand the client's history, degree of cultural mistrust, cultural expectations and values, difference from others within his or her cultural group, and racial/cultural identity development status. The chapter then relates these factors to the client's career counseling experience and concludes with an overview of current sociopolitical issues that affect client worldviews and attitudes toward work today, such as affirmative action, the current state of LGBT and women's rights, the Americans with Disabilities Act, and the current situation with regard to poverty and welfare.

Chapter 5 – Using Career Development Theories. As a first step in the application of multicultural skills explored in the first half of the book, the second half commences with a discussion of the effectiveness of various career development theories, in terms of multicultural application. This chapter analyzes the traditional career theories, including Parson's trait and factor theory, Super's career development theory, Holland's career theory of personality types and environments, and Krumboltz's social learning theory of career development. Also discussed are current theories that more strongly represent diversity, such as the social cognitive career theory, post-modern approaches and recent career counseling process models specifically designed for multicultural groups.

Chapter 6 – Multiculturally Competent Career Counseling Skills. Beginning with a review of the NCDA and AMCD competencies, this chapter integrates the career and multicultural competencies in a clear and straightforward manner. The integration is followed by a close examination of the synthesis of career and multicultural competencies in practice. Each of eight stages of career counseling is examined in detail, with an ongoing case study woven throughout the discussion to illustrate real-world applications.

Chapter 7 – Cultural Competence in Assessment. This chapter discusses the strengths and limitations of existing career assessments—such as interest inventories, aptitude tests, and personality inventories—and provides suggestions for the appropriate selection, administration, and interpretation of standardized tests with multicultural populations. In addition, the chapter explores various cultural and environmental factors that may affect assessment outcomes, such as values and beliefs, race/ethnicity/sexual orientation/gender, cultural/racial identity, acculturation and language, socioeconomic status, community, and racism and discrimination. As a means of concretizing the discussion, a single case is followed throughout the chapter.

Chapter 8 – Culturally Competent Career Counseling with Children and Adolescents. This chapter strays from the general format of this text by focusing on one population: K-12 students. The chapter was added to this second edition because of the great need to start the career process early with children from marginalized groups. Children from these groups have been known to have (a) early foreclosure on careers, (b) the most interference from society (e.g., discrimination, stereotyping), (c) an over-representation among the poor (d) the least exposure to or access to career choices (e) scores lower than their non-marginalized peers on standardized assessments and (f) lower graduation rates. All of these issues present challenges for career planning for culturally diverse children and adolescents.

Chapter 9 – Social Action in Career Practice. Understanding and applying multiculturalism in a career counseling context has been the focus of the book up to this point. This chapter takes multicultural career counseling to the next logical step, one that is not often discussed in career textbooks. It advocates moving from reacting to the occupational oppression of marginalized individuals to acting, that is, making positive changes to the social systems in order to reduce occupational oppression in the future. The chapter introduces the importance of social justice and the Advocacy Competencies endorsed by the American Counseling Association (included in Appendix D).

Special Features

We have included a number of special features in this book to supplement the discussion and promote active learning, the end result of which we hope will be enhanced actual career practice with culturally diverse clients. The special features are as follows:

- **Exercises:** Most chapters, particularly those in the first portion of the book where the focus is on the development of multicultural skills, include extensive exercises to help readers internalize the chapter content. Readers are encouraged to use their own notebook or journal to compile responses to the exercises.
- **Real-World Examples and Scenarios:** Included in all of the chapters to bring to life the abstract concepts being discussed.
- **"Final Thoughts" and "Review/Reflection Questions":** Included to reinforce key chapter material before moving on to the next chapter.
- **References:** Each chapter concludes with a list of works cited within the chapter, enabling readers to explore various topics even further.

References

Evans, K. (2008). *Gaining cultural competence in career counseling.* Boston, MA: Lahaska Press.

Sue, D. W., Carter, R. T., Casas, J. M., Fouad, A., Ivey, A. E., Jensen, M., LaFromboise, T., Manese, J. E., Ponterotto, J. G. & Vasquesz-Nutall, E. (1998). *Multicultural counseling competencies: Individual and organizational development.* Thousand Oaks, CA: Sage Publications.

TABLE OF CONTENTS

Preface iii

Chapter 1   The Importance of Culturally Competent
            Career Counseling.. 1

Chapter 2   Awareness of Your Own Cultural Heritage 17

Chapter 3   Exploring Your Own Values and Biases 41

Chapter 4   Awareness of the Client's Worldview 67

Chapter 5   Using Career Development Theories 91

Chapter 6   Multiculturally Competent Career Counseling Skills 117

Chapter 7   Cultural Competence in Assessment 147

Chapter 8   Culturally Competent Career Counseling with
            Children and Adolescents 177

Chapter 9   Social Justice Career Counseling 193

Appendix A AMCD Cross-Cultural Competencies 211

Appendix B NCDA Minimum Competencies for Multicultural
            Career Counseling and Development..................... 215

Appendix C School Counselor Multicultural Competence Checklist 218

Appendix D Advocacy Competencies............................... 220

Subject Index 226

Name Index 232

Author Bios 240

CHAPTER 1

The Importance of Culturally Competent Career Counseling

Mary Speaks, a 25-year-old, single, European American woman has been a career counselor for five months at a nonprofit organization in the southeastern region of the United States that offers a variety of counseling services to the community. Mary is proud of her multicultural competence in working with people of color, who make up 40% of her client load. Recently, she received a folder for a new client-- a 38-year-old European-American married man, Joe, who was out of work due to a factory closing. He had two children and a wife who works at a retail chain store. Mary was surprised to see that, at his age, Joe still had not completed high school. Her agency provides a three-year federal grant to assist low-income, displaced workers to retrain and reenter the workforce. This man was Mary's first White client eligible for assistance through this grant.

When Mary first met Joe, it appeared to her as if he had not bathed in some time. The t-shirt he was wearing barely covered his ample abdomen and, to her horror, a Confederate flag was emblazoned on the front. Mary could not take her eyes off the t-shirt during the first 10 minutes of the session. The client spoke loudly and often interrupted her when she spoke. He called her "honey" in almost every sentence, and often challenged the information she gave him. When Mary informed Joe that the agency required that all participants enroll in a GED program, the client replied, "Well, honey you just let them know that I ain't gonna do that. I'll be damned if I'm gonna sit in some classroom with a bunch of niggers and spics like you got in that waiting room. I just wanna get into one of them apprenticeship programs – what they told me you had here, and I don't want to waste no time doing that *#! GED." This statement made Mary so angry that she could hardly stand to stay in the same room with the man. She thought he was a rude, arrogant, racist – a real redneck; however, she just bit the inside of her mouth and continued with the interview. Questions and probes became fewer and fewer until it was time for the session to end.

Mary had never disliked a client so much, and she was surprised at her raw emotion with him. She did not see how she could continue working with him and told her peer supervisor that she was tempted to "haul off and smack him." Mary thought it was in the best interest of the client to refer him to another counselor. She personally did not see how the agency could take on such a client.

The Importance of Culturally Competent Career Counseling

In the above scenario, Mary has met a new challenge to her multicultural sensitivity as a counselor. Mary had previously assumed that multiculturalism only involved being sensitive to and accepting of people who were racially different from her. Even though Mary and her new client were of the same racial heritage, there were cultural and class differences that were significant enough to ignite extreme anger in her. Mary fell victim to what Pederson (1984) identified as "one of the 10 most frequently encountered examples of cultural bias" in counseling (p. 64), and that is presuming that she was fully aware of all her culturally biased assumptions. As Mary learned, when she encountered someone who, though of the same race, was from a completely different world in terms of class and culture, counselors need to be continuously aware of their biases and prejudices in order to be sensitive to clients from all types of backgrounds. Mary's client, though obviously and reprehensively racist and sexist, was also under-educated and poor—aspects of the client that were overshadowed in Mary's mind by his prejudices which prevented her from considering his qualifications to receive agency services. To avoid overlooking areas of bias such as those described above, most practitioners, educators, and researchers embrace a more inclusive definition a multicultural counseling (Arredondo et al., 1996; Das, 1995; Sue et al., 1998). In this text, we, too, use a broad definition of multicultural counseling that includes not only race, culture, and ethnicity, but also gender, sexual orientation, physical ability, age, and class. Our definition of multicultural counseling is not so broad as to say that all counseling is multicultural. Nevertheless, in a counseling relationship, the potential for differences between the persons involved are considerable and require that counselors undergo special training to be effective.

You are reading this book to strengthen your career counseling skills to work with people who are different from you. It is our wish that by reading this book, you will become more competent and more confident in handling issues of multiculturalism and diversity. This chapter will introduce you to the reasons why multicultural and social justice counseling skills are necessary, then generally describe multicultural, social justice and career counseling competencies that will be examined more closely in subsequent chapters and, finally discuss the importance of ethics in the multicultural career counseling setting.

Why Multicultural Counseling?

For years now, the counseling and psychology literature has forecast the impact of the growth in ethnic minority populations in the United States on the helping professions. As of this writing, we have come face-to-face with the reality of diversity. The United States is populated by so many different groups of people today that it has become difficult for the government to classify and count them all in the census. The U.S. Census Bureau has gone from listing only two categories for race in 1962 to listing 15 categories in 2010, with the option of identifying with more than one group (U.S. Census Bureau, 2011). In the 2010 census, 28% of the respondents indicated that they were "of a race other than White only" and 3% reported more than one racial group membership. The fastest growing populations between the 2000 census and the 2010 census was the Hispanic/Latino with an increase of 43%. In fact, in April 2018, the U.S. Census Bureau reported that the estimated Hispanic population (regardless of race) made up 18% of the population, Whites (non-Hispanic) 60.7%, African Americans 13.4%, Asian/Asian American 5.5%, and American Indian 1.3% (U.S. Census Bureau, 2017). Although racial differences are only part of the story as far as multicultural counseling competence is concerned, these numbers give us some insight into the enormity of the cultural difference issues.

The following vignette, from a European American female community college career counselor, further illustrates the importance of multicultural career counseling in a real-world context:

I remember the first time I realized the importance of my multicultural training. It was a day in early August and things were really picking up in our office just before the start of the semester. My first client was a young European American mother of three whose husband had been laid off from a construction job. The couple did not know when or if he would find employment again. She needed to find a higher paying job than her minimum-wage position at a restaurant. When she left, I saw a disabled African-American male college graduate who was looking to find a technical career where he would make a lot more money than his current position paid. I also saw an Asian American female high school senior who was distraught because she wanted to attend a community college for specific career training as a veterinary technician but her parents were adamant that she attend a prestigious four-year college nearby. My last client of the day was a 30-year-old lesbian Latina. Her current career was as a fourth-grade teacher, but she was afraid she would lose her job when she revealed her sexual orientation. She didn't feel up to a fight with her school board over her sexuality so she wanted to prepare for an alternative career.

I never thought that I would see so many people who differed from me so significantly. I certainly never fathomed that it would happen in one day. I was thankful that day that I was able to meet most of the needs of my clients, but I felt I could do more with some of them. The experience reminded me that I would need to continue to educate myself about cultural and other differences and explore my own biases and prejudices.

Research shows that ethnic minority clients appreciate and respond well to multicultural content in counseling. Such content helps to build counselor credibility and is linked to the clients' willingness to continue in counseling

The Importance of Culturally Competent Career Counseling

and positive working relationships (Burkard, Knox, Groen, Perez & Hess, 2006; Chang & Yoon, 2011; Maxie, Arnold, & Stephenson, 2006; Thompson & Jenal, 1994). Conversely, counseling that avoids multicultural issues has proved to be detrimental. In their research, Thompson and Jenal (1994) found that ethnic minority clients and counselors who avoided the topic of race during counseling tended to become disengaged during the counseling process. In a more recent study, Zhang and Burkard (2008) found that White counselors were perceived to be more credible and had a better working alliance with their ethnic minority clients when they addressed racial issues. To increase multicultural counseling competence and to meet the needs of ethnic minority groups, counselor preparation programs have offered multicultural counseling training for decades. Today, programs accredited by the American Psychological Association (APA) and the Council for the Accreditation of Counseling and Related Educational Programs (CACREP) must include coursework containing multicultural competencies (American Psychological Association, 2017; Council for Accreditation of Counseling and Related Educational Programs, 2015).

It is agreed that multicultural training is imperative, however, the merits of training that consists of a single course versus an infusion of multicultural content throughout the curriculum has been debated (Falicov, 1995; Ridley, Espelage, & Rubinstein, 1997; Tomlinson-Clark & Wang, 1999). Celinska and Swazo (2016) offered support for the effectiveness of one course. They found that when a single course was offered, students were more open to diversity than those who attended programs that infused multicultural curriculum into all the courses. On the other hand, critics of the one-course strategy believe that if the course depends heavily on written materials rather than experiential learning, students will be unable to acquire deeper levels of understanding of cultural differences. For instance, Sue and Sue (2016) and others (Ridley et al., 1997) have suggested that when students receive a purely intellectual treatment of multicultural counseling, they fail to appreciate the sociopolitical context of the clients' lives. They need to have more than an intellectual understanding of oppression, discrimination, and racism. Though Sammons and Speight (2008) support the infusion of multicultural curricula, because they found more positive changes in students with this kind of training, they suggest that the optimum training should include a multicultural course along with an infusion of multicultural content and experience in the rest of the curriculum. This training should continue through practicum and internship. According to Celinska and Swazo (2016), Cates and Schaefle (2009) found that when multicultural training is infused in practicum, students had "a greater increase in perceived multicultural awareness, knowledge and skill throughout the course" (Celinska & Swazo, 2016, p. 6). This suggestion was supported by Vespia, Fitzpatrick, Fouad, Kantamneni and Chen (2010) whose national survey of career counselors led them to conclude that counselors' self-perceptions of their competence were not supported by external ratings of their behavior. To be multiculturally competent, the trainees must internalize this information. They need to read about it, experience it, and hear about it in every class as well as apply the skills in practicum and internship settings.

Although most counselor training programs offer courses in multicultural counseling and career development, there is no reason to assume that career development professionals have been trained to combine their multicultural and career development skills. Many currently available career development texts used by instructors and graduate training programs often devote only a single chapter to multicultural issues or special populations (Evans & Larrabee, 2002). Similarly, multicultural counseling texts rarely contain information related to career development (Evans & Rotter, 2000). In 1993, the issue of raising the multicultural career counseling competence level of counselor trainees was addressed in a special edition of the *Career Development Quarterly*. While much has been written about career counseling of diverse populations in the decades since the publication, there is little evidence of specific training in multicultural career counseling. Given that multicultural counseling and career counseling are taught separately, there are a few opportunities for synthesis. This failure to synthesize knowledge and skills is especially worrisome when students' practicum and internship experiences do not include diverse clientele and a multiculturally trained supervisor. The worst-case scenario when synthesis does not occur, is that a counselor will approach culturally different clients from an ethnocentric, monocultural, one-size-fits-all perspective. Such a counselor would not vary career counseling processes or techniques with clients regardless of their race, ethnicity, religion, age, or sexual orientation; and the client may suffer as a consequence (Sue et al., 1998). The goal of this text is to help counselors discover ways to bring together their skills in career counseling with those of multicultural counseling. We believe a blending of the multicultural, social justice and career counseling competencies will accomplish this goal.

Multicultural Competencies

The first attempt to formalize multicultural competencies was made by the APA division of counseling psychology, committee on cross-cultural competencies (Sue et al., 1982). The committee, led by Derald Wing Sue, published the first list of 11 multicultural counseling competencies. These competencies have become the foundation of subsequent competency statements that have been continually approved by counseling organizations (Ponterotto, Fuertes & Chen, 2000; Sue et al., 1998). Derald Sue also headed the competency writing committee of the Association for Multicultural Counseling and Development (AMCD), a division of the American Counseling Association (ACA). He was given the task to further develop the original 11 competencies. This refinement of the competencies was published in 1992 and included 31 different competencies (Sue et al., 1992). These competencies have been endorsed by two divisions of APA (17 and 45) and six divisions of ACA: the Association for Counselor Education and Supervision (ACES); the Association for Adult Development and Aging (AADA); the American School Counselor Association (ASCA); the Association of Gay, Lesbian, and Bisexual Issues in Counseling (AGLBIC); the Association for Specialist and Group Work (ASGW); the International Association of Marriage and Family Counseling (IAMFC). The AMCD and APA's Society for Counseling Psychology have continued to update the competency statements. When the competencies were criticized for being too vague to be included in the accreditation standards for counselors, Arredondo et al. (1996) tackled the enormous task of operationalizing them. In the resulting document, each competency was broken down into several explanatory statements that describe the specific behaviors counselors need to master in order to achieve multicultural competence. The authors also included strategies for achieving those competencies. (See Appendix A for an abbreviated version of the AMCD Cross Cultural Competencies.)

The competencies Arredondo and colleagues proposed (1996) outline three dimensions of personal identity, which take into account not only racial and cultural differences in people, but also other differences that are important in people's lives. The outline assigns a separate letter designation to each of the three dimensions. The A dimension includes "characteristics that serve as a profile for all people" (p. 47) and includes those characteristics that are predetermined in people—age, gender, culture, ethnicity, race, and language. The B dimension includes those aspects of a person's identity that may be influenced by the A dimension or by history and experience. They include: educational background, geographic location, relationship status, religion, work experience, and hobbies and recreation. The C dimension encompasses those characteristics that are universal but may affect individuals differently, such as historical, political, and sociocultural events.

> The model communicates several premises (a) that we are all multicultural individuals; (b) that we all possess a personal, political, and historical culture; (c) that we are affected by sociocultural political environmental and historical events; and (d) that multiculturalism also interacts with multiple factors of individual diversity (Arredondo et al., 1996, p. 3)

Arredondo and colleagues (1996) suggest that all three dimensions must be addressed in counseling and that to address two of the dimensions and not the third would undermine the counseling relationship. Counselors who tend to ignore the C dimension, for instance, even though they can communicate their acceptance of cultural differences, may miss important client issues. For example, a Christian counselor who is seeing an Arab Muslim client may be accepting of their differences but if the counselor does not address the effects of negative U.S. sentiments toward Arabs and Muslims on the client during counseling, the client may think the topic is forbidden, thereby creating a barrier in the relationship.

In 1998, Sue and a joint committee of the Society for Counseling Psychology and the Society for the Psychological Study of Ethnic Minority Issues further expanded the competencies to include multicultural organizational competence. The APA's most recent effort to update the multicultural competencies was published by the American Psychological Association in 2017 in the form of *Multicultural Guidelines: An Ecological Approach to Context, Identity and Intersectionality* (American Psychological Association [APA], 2017). There were significant changes from the original competencies. The new document takes a broader view of multiculturalism and was "conceptualized from a need to reconsider diversity and multicultural practice within professional psychology... with intersectionality as a primary purview" (APA, 2017, p. 6). While the guidelines concentrate on multiple identities and the intersectionality of these identities, APA has also developed separate guidelines for working with specific groups (e.g., race, gender, transgender, GLB, people with disabilities, older clients and those with age-related cognitive problems).

The AMCD competencies have been updated as well. In 2003, the work in the previous document was extended to include case studies and practical examples, organizational plans, and more recent research findings (Roysircar, Sandhu, & Bibbins, 2003). More recently, the competencies were changed significantly to include social justice competencies as well (Ratts et al., 2016). These new competencies will be discussed in detail in Chapter 9, Social Justice Career Counseling. The new Multicultural and Social Justice Counseling Competencies (MSJCC) incorporate the original multicultural counseling competencies developed by Arredondo et al. (1996) and added in social justice competencies as well. The increased focus on social justice may be the result of the work of critics such as Vera and Speight (2003), who suggested that the multicultural counseling competencies (MCC) failed to attend issues of social justice, and societal change agents. According to Arredondo and Perez (2003), "social justice has always been the core of the multicultural counseling competency movement" (p. 282). Nevertheless, in 2016, Ratts, Singh, Nassar-McMillan, Butler, & McCollough published the MSJCC to

> revise and update the MCC to address current practices and future needs of the counseling profession and related fields... describe guidelines for developing multicultural and social justice competency for the counseling profession as it relates to accreditation, education, training, supervision, consultation

research, theory, and counseling practice [and]...merge the multicultural and social justice counseling constructs and literature. (p. 30)

Career Counseling Competencies

Because this book is not just about multicultural competencies but, more specifically about multicultural competencies needed in a career counseling setting, it is vital to understand career counseling competencies in conjunction with multicultural competencies. The career counseling competencies referred to in this book are those that were created, refined, and disseminated by the National Career Development Association (NCDA). Under its previous name, the National Vocational Guidance Association (NVGA), this organization completed the first set of career counseling competencies in 1981 (National Vocational Guidance Association [NVGA], 1982). The goal was to define the counselor's role in career counseling. The document describes these competency areas – general counseling, information, individual and group assessment, management and administration, implementation, and consultation. The original publication of those competencies was aimed specifically at professional counselors at or above the master's level and they made a significant statement regarding the minimum skills professional counselors needed to acquire if they wish to engage in career counseling. Over time, the competencies became the basis for accreditation and certification of career counselors (Engels et al., 1995). The NCDA has continued to update and review career counseling competencies. In 1991, NCDA updated the competency areas and broadened them. Not only were new categories added, but also the existing categories were refined to include minimum skills. The five new categories included career development theory, special populations, supervision, ethical and legal issues, and research and evaluation (Herr, Cramer & Niles, 2004). In 1997, the competency statements were further refined. Subcategories were renamed, and technology was added as a new category. Each of the competency statements identified specific skills and knowledge base needed (National Career Development Association [NCDA], 1997).

In 2009, NCDA replaced the 1997 competencies with the *Minimum Competencies for Multicultural Career Counseling and Development* (see Appendix B). These new competencies were designed for all career practitioners so that

> promotion and advocacy of career development for individuals is ensured regardless of age, culture, mental/physical ability, ethnicity, race, nationality, religion/spirituality, gender, gender identity, sexual orientation, marital/partnership status, military or civilian status, language preference, socioeconomic status, any other characteristics not specifically relevant to job performance.

(NCDA, 2020, p. 1)

The 2009 competencies are less specific than those described in the 1997 edition but they still cover each of the previous categories with just a couple of changes—the special populations category was no longer needed since the competencies were aimed at multicultural expertise; consultation now includes coaching and performance improvement, and skills replaced the general counseling category.

Career professionals are likely to hold membership in a number of organizations that match their on-the-job goal behaviors. Ethical codes of each of these organizations requires members to adhere to a certain standard of behavior regarding treatment of culturally diverse groups. These ethical codes have evolved to the point that they include greater commitment to multiculturalism. Although the American Psychological Association's current ethical standards were originally approved in 2002, there have been two revisions, the latest of which was approved in 2016 (APA, 2017); the National Career Development Association updated its code in 2015 (NCDA, 2015); and the American Counseling Association (ACA, 2014) has made its most recent changes in 2014. The issue of ethical behavior with diverse groups is addressed in each of these ethical codes. The codes for the ACA, APA, and NCDA may be found on the website of the respective organizations.

The NCDA Code of Ethics

In the introduction of Section A, The Professional Relationship, the NCDA Code of Ethics states,

> Career professionals actively attempt to understand the diverse cultural backgrounds of the individuals they serve. Career professionals also explore their own cultural identities and how these affect their values and beliefs about the working relationship. Career professionals are encouraged to contribute to society by devoting a portion of their professional activity to services for which there is little or no financial return "pro bono publico." (p. 3)

In addition, Section A.2.c states:

> Career professionals communicate information in ways that are both developmentally and culturally appropriate. Career professionals use clear and understandable language when discussing issues related to informed consent. When clients have difficulty understanding the language used by career professionals, ar-

rangements may be made (e.g., helping to locate a qualified interpreter or translator) to ensure comprehension by clients. (p. 4)

The preamble to the ACA Code of Ethics (2014) lists its professional values which include: "honoring diversity and embracing a multicultural approach in support of the worth, dignity, potential, and uniqueness of people within their social and cultural contexts"; and "promoting social justice" (p. 3). The ACA Code of Ethics (2014) also assigns one standard to the appropriate behavior for multicultural counseling in Section A.2.c. Developmental and Cultural Sensitivity.

Ethical codes have traditionally been designed to provide minimum standards of professional behavior in a particular field. Typically, adherence to the ethical guidelines leads to behavior that exceeds legal requirements. There are times when this does not happen and laws are passed or interpreted by the courts which spark the creation of new ethical guidelines. An example of this is the inclusion of ethical guidelines addressing exceptions to confidentiality to the ACA code after the ruling on the 1976 case *Tarasoff v. Regents of the University of California*. In this case the university was held liable because the counselor (by reason of confidentiality) did not warn the victim that the client was going to harm her.

Conversely, there are times when laws are passed which actually violate ethical codes. This is what happened in 2016 when the state of Tennessee passed a law allowing counselors to refuse to work with LGBTQ clients for moral reasons and prohibiting clients to sue counselors for rejecting them (Almasy, 2016). ACA thought this law was such a violation of its counseling ethics that it moved its annual conference from Nashville, TN to San Francisco, CA (American Counseling Association, 2016).

When counselors have questions in which clear answers cannot be found in the ethical guidelines, both the NCDA and ACA recommend not only discussing the problem with professionals of like qualifications and membership of the same professional organization, but also to follow a systematic ethical decision-making model. Ethical decision-making models are designed to help professionals decide whether or not the dilemma they face (a) is an ethical issue, (b) involves two conflicting ethical principles, and/or (c) has a potential for bias. All decision-making models help professionals determine a course of action. The NCDA publication, *A Case Study Approach to Ethics in Career Development*, 2nd ed., offers a look at nine common components of ethical decision-making models, as well as guided reflection steps to use when examining ethical cases. ACA provides a model on its website: https://www.counseling.org/knowledge-center/ethics/ethical-decision-making. A tool for ethical decision-making which is designed to work with diverse populations is the Intercultural Model of Ethical Decision Making (IMED; Luke, Goodrich, & Gilbride, 2013).This model is unique in that it focuses on the cultural, religious and worldview factors related to ethical dilemmas professionals may encounter. However, if for any reason a counselor is still unsure about the appropriate action, further consultation with another professional or consultation with the professional organization itself would be the best course.

Ethical Dilemma Exercises

Four career counseling ethical dilemmas are presented here. Read each dilemma and decide on the applicable ethical codes from the organization that you are most likely to have a membership, e.g., NCDA, ACA… Using a decision-making model of your choice, describe how you believe career professionals should proceed if they or someone else questions whether or not they will be in violation of the ethical code. Respond in your notebook or journal.

Dilemma 1. *Caroline is a 34-year-old White female employment counselor working with a 23-year-old African American male client who has recently been incarcerated. She set up an interview for the client, but he reported that he did not get the job. Caroline was very upset because she had been told that this employer was open to hiring individuals with non-violent criminal records. After her client left, Caroline called the employer to inquire about why her client was not hired. Caroline explained that the client was released early for exhibiting good behavior while he was incarcerated, completed his GED while in prison, and that he had a critically ill mother he would be helping to support as well as two young children. She asked the employer if he would please reconsider.*

Cite the specific ethical code in question.

Actions to be taken given the decision-making model you used.

Dilemma 2. *Brian is a 56-year-old African-American male employee assistance counselor who has been assigned a large number of clients who have recently been displaced from their jobs. They will each receive six weeks of severance pay as well as six sessions of career counseling to help them find a new job. Most of the clients are Latinos or Latinas and Native Americans – both males and females. Because the task is so overwhelming, he decides to maximize his time and minimize his effort on individual cases. He has recently completed a workshop on how to do a group interpretation of a career inventory, so he will give all the clients an interest inventory and personality inventory to take home and complete. Because the group is diverse, he feels he should know where they stand in terms of ability, so he will administer a paper and pencil intelligence test at the first session. Brian will call the group back together when the results from the testing come in and provide a group interpretation of the entrance inventory, personality inventory, and intelligence test. He will follow up with any individuals* *who just do not get it.*

Cite the specific ethical code in question.

Actions to be taken given the decision-making model you used.

Dilemma 3. *Isabel, a 20-year-old Puerto Rican college student, has been referred by her mother to Maria, a career counselor at Isabel's college. Maria and Isabel's mother were college roommates, so Isabel's mother is grateful for a close family friend to trust completely and help her daughter make major life decisions regarding her future career. Maria is happy to see Isabel, and after they have worked together for a few weeks, receives an invitation from Isabel to attend a family gathering. Isabel says that her mother wants to use this occasion to thank Maria for all her work with her daughter. Isabel is most anxious for Maria to come and will not take no for an answer. Maria agrees to go, but first discusses confidentiality again with Isabel. Maria reminds Isabel that it is her intent to respect Isabel's wishes as to what to tell her family about the counseling process and what not to tell.*

Cite the specific ethical code in question.

Actions to be taken given the decision-making model you used.

Dilemma 4. *Jessie is a White female, heterosexual career counselor who is new to a community agency that serves adolescents. Due to a loss of a staff member, Jessie is assigned to work with the LGBTQ youth at the agency. Jessie is proud of her multicultural training and, though she has never worked with LGBTQ clients before, she feels confident that she can do the job. Her first client is a 17-year-old lesbian, Karder, an emancipated youth who reports to Jessie that she was just wait-listed for a job training program and that the waiting list was at least a year long. Karder bursts out in tears saying she doesn't know what she is going to do. First, her parents throw her out because she is a lesbian and now she doesn't have a way to support herself. Jessie puts her arm around Karder, who is sobbing uncontrollably, and says that she will call the agency and get Karder reconsidered. She tells Karder not to worry. As Karder calms down, Jessie telephones the agency and talks to the director about Karder's situation.*

Cite the specific ethical code in question.

Actions to be taken given the decision-making model you used.

Synthesizing Multicultural Competencies and Career Counseling Competencies

The most recent NCDA competencies are a synthesis of the previous AMCD and NCDA competency statements. Prior to this revision, Ward and Bingham

(1993) offered ideas for synthesizing these skills through a multicultural career counseling checklist (see Appendix C), which was an excellent beginning to blending the two sets of competencies. The goal of the checklist is to help career professionals assess their ability to assist a client who differs from them in terms of preparation, assessment, working relationship, cultural challenges, and cultural strengths. The multicultural competencies will be covered in more detail in Chapter 2, "Awareness of Your Own Cultural Heritage" and Chapter 3, "Exploring Your Own Values and Biases." Chapter 4, "Awareness of the Client's Worldview" will also cover one of the career counseling competencies, "diverse populations." To gain multicultural competence, it is very important to have done the work in these next three chapters before moving ahead to the rest of the book.

References

Almasy, S. (2016). Tennessee governor signs 'therapist bill' into law. *CNN Politics.* Retrieved from https://www.cnn.com/2016/04/27/politics/tennessee-therapist-bill/index.html

American Counseling Association. (2014). *ACA code of ethics 2014.* Retrieved from https://www.counseling.org/knowledge-center/ethics

American Counseling Association. (2016). *The American Counseling Association will not hold its annual conference and expo in Tennessee.* Retrieved from https://www.counseling.org/news/updates/2016/05/10/the-american-counseling-association-will-not-hold-its-annual-conference-expo-in-tennessee

American Psychological Association. (2017). *Ethical principles of psychologists and code of conduct.* Retrieved December 15, 2018 from https://www.apa.org/ethics/code/index

Arredondo, P., & Perez, P. (2003). Expanding multicultural competence through social justice leadership. *The Counseling Psychologist, 31,* 282-289.

Arredondo, P., Toporek, R., Brown, S. P., Jones, J., Locke, D. C., Sanchez, J., & Stadler, H. (1996). Operationalization of the multicultural counseling competencies. *Journal of Multicultural Counseling and Development, 24,* 42-78.

Burkard, A., Knox, S., Groen, M., Perez, M., & Hess, S. (2006). European American therapist self-disclosure in cross-cultural counseling. *Journal of Counseling Psychology, 5,* 15-25.

Cates, J. T., & Schaefle, S. E. (2009). Infusing multicultural training into practicum. *Journal of Counseling Research and Practice, 1*(1), 32-41.

Celinska, D., & Swazo, R. (2016). Multicultural curriculum designs in counselor education programs: Enhancing counselors-in-training openness to diversity. *The Journal of Counselor Preparation and Supervision, 8*(3). http://dx.doi.org/10.7729/83.1124

Chang, D. F., & Yoon, P. (2011). Ethnic minority clients' perceptions of the significance of race in cross-racial therapy relationships. *Psychotherapy Research, 21*(5), 567-582.

Council for the Accreditation of Counseling and Related Educational Programs. (2015). Retrieved from http://www.cacrep.org/wp-content/uploads/2018/05/2016-Standards-with-Glossary-5.3.2018.pdf

Das, A. K. (1995). Rethinking multicultural counseling: Implications for counselor education. *Journal of Counseling and Development, 74,* 45-52.

Engels, D. W., Minor, C. W., Sampson, J. P., & Splete, H. H. (1995). Career counseling specialty: History, development, and prospect. *Journal of Counseling and Development, 74,* 134-138.

Evans, K. M., & Larrabee, M. J. (2002). Teaching the multicultural counseling competencies and revised career counseling competencies simultaneously. *Journal of Multicultural Counseling and Development, 30,* 21-39.

Evans, K. M., & Rotter, J. C. (2000). Multicultural family approaches to career counseling. *The Family Journal, 8,* 67-71.

Falicov, C. J. (1995). Training to think culturally: A multidimensional comparative framework. *Family Process, 34,* 363-388.

Herr, E. L., Cramer, S. H., & Niles, S. G. (2004). *Career guidance and counseling through the lifespan: Systematic approaches.* Boston, MA: Pearson Education, Inc.

Makela, J. P., & Perlus, J. G. (2017). *A case study approach to ethics in career development,* 2nd ed. Broken Arrow, OK: National Career Development Association.

Maxie, A., Arnold, D., & Stephenson, M. (2006). Do therapists address ethnic and racial differences in cross-cultural psychotherapy? *Psychotherapy: Theory, Research, Practice, Training, 43,* 85-98.

National Career Development Association. (1997). Career counseling competencies Retrieved from https://ncda.org/aws/NCDA/pt/sd/news_article/37798/_self/layout_ccmsearch/true

National Career Development Association. (2015). *2015 NCDA code of ethics.* Retrieved from https://www.ncda.org/aws/NCDA/asset_manager/get_file/3395

National Career Development Association. (2020). *Minimum competencies for multicultural career counseling and development.* Retrieved from https://ncda.org/aws/NCDA/pt/fli/12508/true

National Vocational Guidance Association. (1982, September). *Vocational/career counseling, competencies approved by the board of directors,* Falls Church, VA: Author.

Pedersen, P. B. (1984). Levels of intercultural communication using the rehearsal demonstration model. *Journal of Non-White Concerns in Personnel and Guidance, 12*(2), 57-68.

Ponterotto, J. G., Fuertes, J. N., & Chen, E. C. (2000). Models of multicultural counseling. In S. D. Brown & R. W. Lent (Eds.), *Handbook of counseling psychology* (3rd ed., pp. 639-669). Hoboken, NJ: John Wiley & Sons, Inc.

Ratts, M. J., Singh, A. A., Nassar-McMillan, S., Butler, S. K., & McCullough, J. R. (2016). Multicultural and social justice counseling competencies: Guidelines for the counseling profession. *Journal of Multicultural Counseling and Development, 44*(1), 28-48.

Ridley, C. R., Espelage, D. L., & Rubinstein, K. J. (1997). Course development in multicultural counseling. In D. B. Pope-Davis & H. L. K. Coleman (Eds.), *Multicultural counseling competencies: Assessment, education, and training, and supervision* (pp. 131-158). Thousand Oaks, CA: Sage Publications.

Roysircar, G., Sandhu, D. S. & Bibbins, V. E., Sr. (Eds.). (2003). *Multicultural competencies: A guidebook of practices*. Alexandria, VA: Association for Multicultural Counseling and Development.

Sammons, C., & Speight, S. (2008). A qualitative investigation of graduate-student changes associated with multicultural counseling courses. *The Counseling Psychologist, 36*(6), 814-838.

Sue, D. W., Arredondo, P., & McDavis, R. J. (1992). Multicultural competencies/standards: A pressing need. *Journal of Counseling and Development, 70*(4), 477-486.

Sue. D. W., Bernier, J. B., Durran, M., Feinberg, L., Pedersen, P., Smith, E., & Vazquez-Nuttall, E. (1982). Position paper: Cross-cultural counseling competencies. *The Counseling Psychologist, 10*, 45-52.

Sue, D. W., Carter, R. T., Casas, J. M., Fouad, A., Ivey, A. E., Jensen, M., LaFromboise, T., Manese, J. E., Ponterotto, J. G., & Vazquez-Nuttall, E. (1998). *Multicultural counseling competencies: Individual and organization development*. Thousand Oaks, CA: Sage Publications.

Sue, D. W. & Sue, D. (2016). *Counseling the culturally diverse: Theory and practice* (7th edition). Hoboken, NJ: John Wiley & Sons.

Thompson, D. E., & Jenal, S. T. (1994). Interracial and intraracial quasi-counseling interaction when counselors avoid discussing race. *Journal of Counseling and Development, 41*, 484-491.

Tomlinson-Clark, S., & Wang, V. O. (1999). A paradigm for racial-cultural training in the development of counselor cultural competencies. In M. S. Kiselica (Ed.), *Prejudice and racism during multicultural training*. Alexandria, VA: American Counseling Association.

U.S. Census Bureau. (2011). *Overview of race and hispanic origin: 2010: 2010 census briefs*. Retrieved from https://www.census.gov/prod/cen2010/briefs/c2010br-02.pdf

U.S. Census Bureau. (2017). *Quick facts*. Retrieved from https://www.census.gov/quickfacts/fact/table/US/PST045217

Vera, E. M., & Speight, S. L. (2003). Multicultural competence, social justice, and counseling psychology: expanding our roles. *The Counseling Psychologist, 31*(3), 252-272.

Vespia, K. M., Fitzpatrick, M. E., Fouad, N. A., Kantamneni, N., & Chen, Y. L. (2010). Multicultural career counseling: A national survey of competencies and practices. *The Career Development Quarterly, 59*(1), 54-71.

Ward, C. M., & Bingham, R. P. (1993). Career assessment of ethnic minority women. *Journal of Career Assessment, 1*, 246-257.

Zhang, N., & Burkard, A. W. (2008). Client and counselor discussions of racial and ethnic differences in counseling: An exploratory investigation. *Journal of Multicultural Counseling and Development, 36*(2), 77-87.

CHAPTER 2

Awareness of Your Own Cultural Heritage

My instructor assigned us to write a paper on our culture, so I decided to order one of those DNA tests so I could have a good idea of my culture. The results show that I am 50% Irish, 25% Scottish, 16% Italian, and 9% German. I always knew we were Irish because there is Irish on both my mom's and my dad's side but, other than our name, there isn't really anything particularly Irish about us. I'm thinking I should look up those other groups to figure out just what my culture really is. I didn't think this would be so hard to figure out.

The idea that everyone has a culture was initially debated by White career counselors-in-training. Students would typically say that they did not think they had a culture (Helms, 1984); however, in recent years, that has been less problematic especially with easily accessible ancestry databases and the advent of publicly available DNA testing. Individuals who did not identify with any specific White ethnic group (Irish, Italian, German, and so forth) are finding their ancestors and are connecting more with their roots, but there still seems to be some confusion about the differences among ethnicity, nationality, and culture. That confusion may be caused by the fact that the definitions of culture tend to vary from narrow to broad. Narrowly defined, culture is limited to ethnicity, language, ideology, nationality, and religion. Pedersen (1999) offers his broad definition of culture: "the total way of life of a people including their interpersonal relations as well as their attitudes" (p.7). Similarly, Arredondo and colleagues (1996) define culture as "patterns of learned thinking and behavior of people communicated across generations through traditions, language, and artifacts" (p.40). Pedersen (1999) also states that broader definitions of culture are becoming more accepted and provide for greater application of culture to all counseling relationships. Regardless of how one defines it, students soon learn that everyone does indeed have a culture.

Once culture has been adequately defined, it does not take long for formerly culture-confused career professionals and students to feel comfortable exploring their own cultures. Investigation of one's culture involves identifying with the common language, history, philosophy of life, traditions, concept of family and kinship, work, governance, education, communication styles, and religion of

Awareness of Your Own Cultural Heritage

one's group. It also involves exploring demographic variables such as gender, age, geography, and socioeconomic status.

Several authors have pointed out that all cultures are learned, shared, and dynamic (Gollnick & Chinn, 1994; Pedersen, 1994, 1999). Culture must be taught to others in order to survive; more than one person or family must adhere to the beliefs and traditions and culture must change and adapt as the world changes. Cultural lessons begin in childhood when children are socialized to the norms of the culture in which they live (Gollnick & Chinn, 1994). Children learn the language, cultural policies, appropriate behavior, role expectations, sex roles, and acceptable occupations for their culture. These lessons come from family members, family friends, teachers, clergy, and other powerful adults within the culture.

Although cultural learning begins at an early age, it continues into adulthood. Our cultural values, beliefs, behaviors, and so forth are natural to us after years of training (Gollnick & Chinn, 1994). The lessons become internalized to the point where "we often confuse biological and cultural heritage" (p. 14). This confusion has led to debates as to whether psychological and other characteristics such as intelligence are the result of nature (biological) or nurture (social/environmental). Such debates will continue, but what is important for career professionals to remember is that everyone is socialized into a culture. Gollnick and Chinn (1994) call this process enculturation. Though our culture defines a great part of our identity, it does not influence our genetic makeup.

Because we internalize our culture so completely, we are often unaware of cultural influences in our lives. There are several activities included in this chapter that may be helpful to anyone who is doubtful about his or her cultural heritage.

Exercises for Unearthing Your Culture

Exercise 1: A Different World

This is an imagery exercise that should be done in a quiet spot where you will not be interrupted. Begin by taking two or three deep breaths—inhaling your nose and exhaling through your mouth. Relax your body and clear your mind of all extraneous thoughts. Have someone read or record the instructions for this visualization.

Imagine that when you woke up this morning, you were in a different world. In this world, no one looks like you or speaks your language. None of the foods you like are available. In fact, you do not even recognize the food that you have been given. You notice that the rituals the people practice (you think the rituals may be religious) are completely foreign, as are the strange ways the people move their faces to express emotions. Their manner of speaking seems hostile and rude to you.

How does it feel to be in such a strange environment? What will you miss most from your old world while living in this new world? Would you miss being able to communicate most? Or would you miss the people who look like you? The food? Customs and rituals? Being able to read people? Write your thoughts in your notebook or journal.

For many, this imagery exercise is one of the quickest and easiest ways to recognize one's culture. Many career professionals find that the exercise helps them to get a better understanding of the importance of their way of life. They also realize that there are others whose way of life may differ and whose values, expectations, and traditions may seem strange to them. As such, it helps them develop empathy for those who are not members of their own cultural group.

Exercise 2: Where I'm From

George Ella Lyon (n.d.) wrote a poem several years ago entitled "Where I'm From" and it is an excellent example of exploring the cultural influences in her life. She has a website where she encourages other people to create their own poems about their lives. In this exercise, you will go to her website http://www.georgeellalyon.com/where.html, read her poem, and complete your own poem. There are also several templates for the "Where I'm From" poem on the Internet.

Exercise 3: Recording Values and Traditions

Write an essay in your notebook or videotape a message to your children or to young people in your family. Discuss what you learned from your family and significant adults in your culture about race, gender, religion, traditions, traditional foods, your geographic region, education, sexual orientation, manners, socioeconomic status, and powerful individuals. In addition, you may want to write about the origins of your family history in the United States. If your family immigrated, write about what the immigration was like. How did they adjust to the United States?

Exercise 4: A Cultural investigation

A very fruitful strategy for exploring your own culture is to investigate it as if you are from a different culture from your own. McGrath and Axelson (1999) and Parker (1998) recommend a cultural interview in which you ask people who identify as members of your culture specific questions about its characteristics. McGrath and Axelson (1999) as well as Haley (1990) suggest you start by interviewing your oldest relative. You will need to tease out characteristics that are representative of the whole culture as opposed to those characteristics that are unique to your own family. Here are some questions that you may want to include (questions are adapted from McGrath & Axelson, 1999, p. 52):

- How would you describe your family culture?
- Is the traditional culture still intact or has it changed greatly? How?
- Is there still a cultural community?
- What are your family's attitudes toward its culture?
- What occupations did your ancestors hold? Are those occupational choices typical of your culture?
- What are your family's attitudes toward work and vocation?

After the interview is over, reflect on it by answering the following questions of yourself (questions adapted from McGrath & Axelson, 1999, p. 53):

- Are you living up to your family of origin's expectations? How or how not?
- Are you living up to your family's cultural expectations? How or how not?
- What do you think a person of another culture (pick one) would think of your culture as you have "discovered" it?

The Dominant American Culture

Until recent years, the diverse groups that have immigrated to the United States during its history have all been expected to leave behind the cultures from their countries of origin and adopt an "American" culture common to all. This "melting pot" metaphor was prevalent for most of the history of the United States; however, the metaphor became more problematic during and after the Civil Rights movement when the world could see that all Americans were not included in the melting pot. In fact, the American landscape was more akin to a "salad" or a "mosaic" of different parts existing side by side than to a blended melting pot. Initially, those Americans who were visibly different from the dominant group were, more often than not, legally forbidden to blend in with others. For example, prior to the Civil Rights legislation, there were laws in many Southeastern states that segregated people of color (most especially, African Americans) from Whites in public places. People of color were also forbidden to marry Whites in many states. This type of separation limited the exposure of Whites to other racial and cultural groups; however, members of these visibly different groups (African Americans, Asian Americans, Hispanics, and Native Americans) were consistently exposed to the dominant U.S. culture.

Following the definitions of culture outlined earlier in this chapter, the dominant U.S. culture is based on White European American values and can be characterized as follows: the predominant language is Standard English, the government is a republic, the family is nuclear, religion is Protestant Christianity, basic education (K-12) is free, "American" foods are hot dogs (or hamburgers) and apple pie, the predominant socioeconomic group is the middle class, and the most prized values are rugged individualism and the belief in meritocracy. Because culture is learned, individuals who were born in the United States are familiar with these cultural elements (Sue & Sue, 2016). The dominant U.S. culture is like an umbrella that covers all the other cultural groups in the country. It is important, therefore, to understand the dominant U.S. culture because it has undoubtedly been intertwined into the internal culture of many people—career professionals and their clients as well.

Cultural groups other than the dominant U.S. culture, however, may value languages different from English, believe in the extended family, prefer other foods, be predominantly from lower classes, and/or believe in collectivism (valuing the group over the individual). How much an individual internalizes the U.S. culture is dependent on the individual, the number of years the person has lived in the United States, the strength of the individual's other cultural characteristics (from the person's country of origin, or cultural or racial group), and the consequences for adopting U.S. culture (rewards or punishments).

Acculturated individuals identify "with the attitudes, behaviors, and values of the predominant microculture" (Lee, 1995, p. 12). The more an individual's own acculturation lags or exceeds that of his or her family, the more family conflict there is, and the more isolated the individual may become. At the same time, the more an individual resembles people from the dominant cultural group (middle class, Protestant, European American), the more likely it is that he or she will enjoy a privileged status in society. U.S. society is geared toward meeting the needs and desires of the dominant group to the extent that the dominant group has unearned advantages or privileges. A more in-depth discussion of privilege occurs in Chapter 3.

Cultural Relativism and Worldview

Two critical concepts have emerged from the study of multicultural counseling. The first is "cultural relativism" and the second is "worldview."

Cultural Relativism

Cultural relativism is the belief that everything is subjective and that nothing can be considered outside the context in which it exists (Ridley, Liddle, & Li, 2001).

In other words, we must always take into account a person's culture when we observe any behavior. For example, let us consider what it means to be suspicious of someone. To be suspicious of someone means different things in different cultures, and at the same time it also means different things to individuals who are members of the same culture. A member of a marginalized group (such as Native Americans) may distrust or be suspicious of anyone outside that group; however, specific tribes may be accepting of selected non-Native Americans. In cultural relativism, the context (i.e., the individual's culture, subculture or even the individual's perception of the culture) is the primary consideration. While cultural relativism has been criticized by some as being too broad a concept to be useful in counseling, it sets the stage for career professionals to consider not only the differences among groups but, also the difference within groups.

Worldview

The concept of worldview has become a staple in multicultural training and counseling. Essentially, "worldview" denotes one's beliefs about the world and one's relationship to the world. Sire's (1976) definition of worldview is "the presuppositions and assumptions we hold about our world" (p. 17). Sue and Sue (2016) suggest that worldview is inclusive of cultural factors such as values and expectations along with personal factors such as thoughts, attitudes, and beliefs. In other words, worldview is shaped by cultural socialization (in which we learn acceptable behaviors, beliefs, and attitudes) as well as personal experiences and the meaning people take from worldviews of others.

Locus of control/responsibility. Sue (1978) and Sue and Sue (2016) describe individual worldviews via two cognitive concepts that are independent of one another—locus of control and locus of responsibility. According to Sue and Sue (2016), locus of control and locus of responsibility can be either internal or external. Individuals with an internal locus of control believe that they have control over themselves and their behaviors (e.g., I am the captain of my ship) while individuals with an external locus of control believe that outside forces, such as luck and fate control their beliefs and behaviors (e.g., I cannot help it; I am just so unlucky). Individuals with an internal locus of responsibility are likely to claim responsibility for their actions (e.g., I apologize; It was my fault things did not work out the way we wanted) while individuals with an external sense of responsibility are likely to place blame on others for their actions (e.g., See what you made me do!).

Sue and Sue (2016) have illustrated how individuals are likely to fall into one of four combinations of these worldviews with a grid of four quadrants (see Figure 2.1). Quadrant 1 is characteristic of the dominant American perspective

Figure 2.1

Locus of Control/Responsibility: The Four Quadrants

		LOCUS OF RESPONSIBILITY	
		INTERNAL	EXTERNAL
LOCUS OF CONTROL	INTERNAL	Quadrant 1 *Internal* locus of control and *internal* locus of responsibility	Quadrant 4 *Internal* locus of control and *external* locus of responsibility
	EXTERNAL	Quadrant 2 *External* locus of control and *internal* locus of responsibility	Quadrant 3 *External* locus of control and *external* locus of responsibility

Adapted from "Eliminating cultural oppression in counseling: Toward a general theory" by D. W. Sue, 1978, *Journal of Counseling Psychology, 25*, p. 422. Copyright 1978 by the Journal of Counseling Psychology.

and the other three are characteristic of minority (or marginalized) groups. For example, a person with an internal locus of control and an internal locus of responsibility is likely to have a worldview that is consistent with the dominant U.S. society. Individuals with an external locus of control and internal locus of responsibility (Quadrant 4) are people who feel marginalized because they believe in the dominant culture's view of things and at the same time blame themselves and those within their own cultural group for not realizing the American dream. Individuals with an external locus of control and an external locus of responsibility (Quadrant 3) would say "I am not okay and society is not okay" (Axelson, 1999). According to Sue and Sue (2016) individuals in the third quadrant have acquired a learned helplessness perspective. These individuals believe that they are not in control of what happens in their lives and that they are not responsible for what happens to them either. They believe that the barriers that have been erected to keep them from succeeding are too difficult to break down, so they give up. This is also referred to as learned helplessness. The persons in Quadrant 2 have an internal locus of control and an external locus of responsibility and are the healthiest marginalized individuals in terms of world view. These individuals believe that they are okay, but the system is not (Axelson, 1999). These individuals know that they have control of their own behaviors and beliefs, but they also know that there are forces beyond their control that are responsible for some of their problems. Racism, discrimination, and oppression are real to these individuals, but they do not internalize negative impressions of their racial or cultural groups.

> **Locus of control/responsibility exercise.** The first part of this exercise if for you to determine which worldview you tend to identify with most? In your notebook, write a brief rationale stating why you think this is your worldview.
>
> Identify at least one fictitious character from your reading, television, or movies who represents each of the four worldviews that Sue and Sue (2016) have identified. For example—what character would you say has an internal locus of control but an external locus of responsibility? Write at least one sentence in your notebook explaining why you have identified the characters in this way.

Value orientation. In 1961, Kluckhohn and Strodtbeck began a study that compared the cultural values of five diverse groups in the United States. The groups were the Navajo Indians, Spanish Americans, Texas homesteaders, Zuni (Pueblo) Indians and Mormons. As a result of this intensive ten-year study, Kluckhohn and Strodtbeck (1961) found differences in five value orientations: human nature, human activity, time orientation, social relationships, and relationship to nature. Each of these value orientations was broken into three possible viewpoints. For time orientation, the viewpoints were past, present, and future; for human activity, the viewpoints were being, being-in-becoming, and doing; for social relationships the viewpoints were linear, collateral, and individualistic; for relationship with nature, the viewpoints were subjugation, harmony, and mastery; and for human nature, the viewpoints were that people were inherently good, bad, or neutral.

Different cultural groups weighed in differently on each of the value orientations and viewpoints. For example, Sue and Sue (2016) noted that while Puerto Ricans typically value a present time focus, European Americans value a future time focus. The dominant European American view of activity leaned toward doing, while other cultures valued just being. Ibrahim (1991) applied to counseling the value orientations and viewpoints from Kluckhohn and Strodtbeck's (1961) study to create a multicultural counseling assessment instrument. According to Ibrahim (1991), the different viewpoints within the value orientations can lead to conflict in counseling situations. Therefore, it is important for career professionals to identify the cultural values they adhere to and those they reject. Further, if career professionals reject any of their own group's cultural values, this may influence counseling situations in which the client is someone from the same culture, but does not reject that value. To assist career professionals in determining their worldview and to help career professionals determine the worldview of their clients, Ibrahim and Kahn (1984; 1987) developed the Scale to Assess Worldview. Ibrahim and Kahn (1987) describe their scale as one that assesses "beliefs, values, time, and assumptions on…views of human nature, interpersonal relationships, nature, time, and activity" (p. 163).

An individual rates his or her level of agreement with an item on a scale of 1-5 (strongly agree to strongly disagree). One item example provided by Ibrahim and Kahn (1987) is "Human beings are a combination of good and evil" (p. 167). In career counseling, it is important to remember that value orientation in terms of work situations varies from one culture to the next. European Americans, African Americans, and Asian Americans all value the "doing" orientation of human activity. European Americans value doing for individual achievement of success. Asian Americans value doing that achieves honor and fulfills family and cultural expectations, and African Americans value doing activities that overcome barriers to achieving success (Sue & Sue, 2016). On the other hand, Native Americans and Latinos/as value the being-in-becoming orientation of human activity. This means that they believe that doing is not as important as living in harmony with the universe, achieving serenity, and valuing individuals for existing (being), not for what they have achieved. Understanding one's own worldview as well as that of others is an essential skill for a culturally competent career professional.

You may wish to complete the following exercise which utilizes Kluckhohn and Strodtbeck's (1961) value orientations, to examine your own worldview more closely.

> **Value orientations exercise: one-minute papers.** This is an exercise that can help you understand your worldview, specifically your value orientation. Write a brief essay on each of the topics listed below. Spend no more than one minute writing each essay.
>
> 1. What is your view of human nature? Are people innately good, bad, or neutral? Explain why.
> 2. What is your most valued human activity (doing, being-in-becoming, or self-growth)?
> 3. From what point of view do you focus on time? Is it more important to focus on the past and learn from history? Or is it more important to enjoy the moment that you are in rather than the past or future? Or is it more important to look to the future and plan for a better tomorrow?
> 4. What do you believe is the best relationship between humans and nature? Should humans try to assert power over nature and control it? Should people live in harmony with nature? Or should humans accept the fact that they have no control over nature?
> 5. What should relationships among humans be like? Should they be linear (some people leading others)? Or should they be collateral (meaning that groups should work together to solve problems)? Or should they be individualistic (meaning that each person should be self-sufficient)?

Using the interpersonal cultural grid. Pedersen (1994, 2000) co-designed a sophisticated model for understanding worldview—the Interpersonal Cultural Grid (Hines & Pedersen, 1980). The Interpersonal Cultural Grid provides a way to assess "an individual's personal-cultural orientation in a particular situation through attention to his or her behavior and its meaning" (Pedersen, 1994, p.135). To assess worldview, you may wish to complete the following exercises. Pedersen indicates that investigating the origins of your own values when doing a particular activity reflects your own enculturation and socialization.

> **Pedersen's Interpersonal Cultural Grid.** Using Pedersen's Interpersonal Cultural Grid, you will be able to plot your personal cultural orientation by examining social system variables such as nationality, religion, social status, and affiliations with others, as well as other variable, such as gender, age, and physical ability.
>
> Step 1. Choose an activity that you wish to analyze, such as writing a letter of application for a job. Describe in detail how you would go about writing that letter.
>
> Step 2. Identify the outcomes you expect from this activity. For example, you may expect to write a letter that will be good enough to get you an interview, represent you in a good light, keep your name in circulation, or help you move forward in your career.
>
> Step 3. Explore the personal values that accompany your expectations, such as valuing yourself as an employee, recognizing your own achievements, and appreciating your own abilities.
>
> Step 4. Examine the origins of these values. Did you get them from your family, your culture, your experience, etc.? If your letter reflects certain values, for instance, doing a job well or working hard, where do these values come from—your family and culture, your experiences, or some other source?

Unfortunately, many of the skills traditionally taught in counseling programs do not take into consideration multiple worldviews, and this lack of adjustment for different cultures may be the cause of premature termination of ethnic minority clients (Sue & Sue, 2016). More about the worldviews of specific groups is addressed in Chapter 4. A very important part of one's worldview is one's racial/cultural identity, which is considered in the next section.

Within Group Differences

One criticism of multicultural sensitivity training is career professionals end up failing to appreciate the differences between individuals from the same ethic minority group. They might erroneously conclude that every individual within a particular group has similar experiences, expectations, values, beliefs, and behaviors. More recently, emphasis has been given to within-group differences through the study of racial/cultural identity development models. Sue and Sue (2016) have credited both their own and other newer racial/cultural identity development models (which will be discussed in more detail next) with helping career professionals to acknowledge and recognize within-group differences among ethnic minority groups. Sue and Sue (2016) also state that knowledge of racial/cultural identity development models helps to decrease premature termination of counseling by racial/cultural minority clients because career professionals are more aware of possible client reactions to counseling. Therefore, career professionals can offer intervention strategies that are more appropriate to the client's stage of racial/cultural identity development. Sue and Sue (2016) point out that racial identity models acknowledge the "sociopolitical influences in shaping identity…[incorporating] the effects of racism and prejudice [oppression] upon the identity transformation of their victims" (p. 359).

In addition to helping career professionals understand their clients better, racial/cultural identity development models provide career professionals with a theoretical framework for understanding their own racism, prejudice, and privilege. The goal of multicultural education is essentially to assist career professionals in developing a positive racial/cultural identity of their own. A positive racial/cultural identity entails valuing one's own race, without making denigrating comparisons between one's own race and that of others (Helms, 1984).

Racial/cultural identity theories helped to explain racism from the "target's" perspective. "Target" is the term used by social psychologists to describe those groups who are the targets for prejudice and racism (Swim, Cohen, & Hyers, 1998). William Cross (1971) was one of the pioneers of racial/cultural identity theory building, and in his article entitled "The Negro to Black Conversion Experience" he explored how African Americans moved from being self-depreciating, self-hating "Negroes" to self-accepting, group-appreciating "Blacks." (Cross' article was written prior to the wide usage of the term "African American"). Cross' model offered a description of the coping strategies African Americans used to survive in a racist society. He argued that some of these coping mechanisms are psychologically healthy and self-promoting, while others are destructive and self-deprecating. In contrast to Cross' target-centered theory, the newer racial/cultural identity development models explain not only how marginalized group members view themselves, but also how racial/cultural minorities move from negative coping strategies to those that are more positive. In short, these models show how individuals who are oppressed develop a positive view of themselves and their race over time. As a result, racial/cultural identity development models have assisted career professionals in understanding not only how marginalized clients view themselves, but also how the influence of oppression and racism impact that view.

Since 1971, models of racial/cultural identity development have been designed for African Americans, (Hall, Cross & Freedle, 1972; Jackson, 1975; Vontress, 1971), Hispanics (Ferdman & Gallegos, 2012; Ruiz, 1990), Native American Indians (Horse, 2001), Asian Americans (Kim, 2012), biracial/multiracial individuals (Poston, 1990), women (Downing & Roush, 1985; McNamara & Rickard, 1989), gays and lesbians (Cass, 1979), and people with disabilities (Olkin, 1999). While most of these models were developed for specific ethnic or cultural groups, some models are more inclusive and may address people of any ethnicity or culture (Atkinson, Morten & Sue, 1989, 1998; Helms, 1995; Sue & Sue, 2003). For instance, Helms (1995) developed her People of Color model after much research on White and Black models. Her model addresses the racial identities of all the major racial minority groups in the United States—Asian, African, Latinx and Native Americans. Helms' model "is a derivative and integration of aspects of Cross' (1971) Negro-to-Black conversion model, Atkinson and colleagues' (1989) Minority Identity Development model, and Erikson's collective identity model, with some influence from Kohut's (1971) self-psychology" (Helms & Cook, 1999, p. 86).

Racial/Cultural Identity Development of Marginalized Groups

While there are strengths and weaknesses in all the identity models, the Sue and Sue (1990, 1999) model will be used for discussion here. This model was originally developed by Atkinson, Morten, and Sue (1978, 1989) and was named the Minority Identity Development model. Sue and Sue (1990, 1999) later decided to develop a more inclusive model of identity development. Rather than focus on one ethnic minority group exclusively, their Racial/Cultural Identity Development model (R/CID) can be used across cultures and includes European Americans, especially those who identify as members of oppressed groups, such as women, sexual minorities, those living poverty, and people with disabilities (Sue & Sue, 1990, 1999).

The R/CID model, though developed in 1999, is more comprehensive than the other racial/cultural identity models (Helms, 1995; Cross & Vandiver, 2001; Worrell, Cross, Vandiver, 2001) in that not only can it be used with clients from many marginalized groups, it can also be used with White clients (Sue & Sue, 2016). It may be used by marginalized career professionals to determine their own identity development; and it may help them understand how clients who are different from them may perceive them as career professionals. While the model does not predict client behaviors, it helps career professionals understand those behaviors.

The five stages of the R/CID model are Conformity, Dissonance, Resistance, Introspection, and Integrative Awareness. Familiarity with the attitudes that accompany the stages can help career professionals develop strategies for working effectively with individuals who have such attitudes.

Conformity Stage. During the Conformity Stage, individuals carry a negative view of self and they do not consider race to be an important factor in their lives. They disparage other oppressed groups as well as their own. In fact, individuals at this stage only appreciate the dominant White European American group. For example, Maria, a Puerto Rican female made the following comment:

Joey told me that I was lucky because I was bilingual and could get a job anywhere. I hate that he just assumed that I speak Spanish because I am Puerto Rican. I asked him "Did you ever hear me speak Spanish? Do I speak with a Spanish accent?" I speak better English than most of them, and when I get to work, I expect the people I work with to know how to speak English—I don't understand why people think they should get a job in this country without knowing how to speak English.

Dissonance Stage. Stage 2 is called the Dissonance Stage because individuals at this stage have discovered that discrimination and oppression, which they once denied, does exist, and they are conflicted about it. They are still self-deprecating about their own race/culture, but they see some merit within their own group. Their new knowledge about oppression also makes them conflicted in their views of other oppressed groups. Individuals at this stage begin to question the dominant group—sometimes appreciating it and sometimes disapproving of it. For example, a high school student in her school counselor's office stated the following:

I saw this program on TV last night about how people who have ethnic sounding names can't get jobs. I'm glad my parents gave me an American name, but if they named me Ashanti and I was qualified for the job, what difference should it make what my name is? Maybe it's because employers have to think about how their customers would react to someone's name if it is different. I still don't think it is fair.

Resistance and Immersion Stage. At the Resistance Stage, people are rejecting of the dominant culture and angry because of the oppression their people have suffered. They hold the dominant group, White European Americans, responsible for all their own groups' problems and all things associated with the dominant group are rejected.

During Immersion, individuals may feel guilty about their previous rejection of their own group but become joyous about their racial/cultural heritage. Their connection with other oppressed groups is primarily focused on joining with them to defeat the oppressor.

For example, an African American elementary school teacher said the following:

We have to get more African American counselors in the schools, because these White counselors are keeping Black children in special education classes and ruining their chance to have a decent life. We need to get into the schools and take care of our own to stop this educational genocide.

Introspection Stage. Individuals at the Introspection Stage begin to doubt the extremity of the "we are all good, they are all bad" stance of the Resistance and Immersion Stage. These individuals think that there are probably two sides to the issue of oppression. At this stage, individuals begin to pull away from the group position, and they are eager to learn about oppression from other oppressed groups, while choosing acceptable members of the dominant group to trust. Although they have begun to appreciate aspects of the dominant society, they still worry about selling out their own people (Sue & Sue, 2016). For example,

Brooklyn, an African American college student was active in protests over the government's handling of immigrants. She was especially angry when she found out that a friend of hers from the middle east could not return to school because of the ban on immigrants from Muslim countries. Most of the organizers of this protest are White and Brooklyn is impressed with their commitment to the cause; however, she hesitated getting involved with the protest for fear that her friends would think she was abandoning their concerns as Black students to follow what they believe are insincere White people just looking to get noticed.

Integrative Awareness Stage. Finally, individuals achieve a positive racial/cultural identity when they reach the Integrative Awareness Stage. They appreciate themselves as racial/cultural beings, their own group, and other groups. They understand and empathize with the stages of racial identity development of others. As far as the dominant group is concerned, they have not reverted to the conformity stage in their appreciation but, instead they choose to trust individuals from the dominant group who are also engaged in combating oppression. For instance, Mei-ling, an Asian American woman who participated on a search committee for her department, said the following to a Japanese American colleague who was passed over for a promotion:

Tamiko, I understand how angry you became when you discovered that you did not get the promotion. I understand that you and a group of employees are formally protesting the decision to promote a White woman over you when you have worked here longer. While it may appear to have been a decision based on race, I assure you that as an Asian American woman, I did everything I could to ensure that we exploited all of our resources when recruiting minorities for that position. I am certain that every minority applicant was thoroughly considered. I don't blame you for wanting to protest but I assure you that I confronted the committee on the issue of race throughout the hiring process. I feel confident that a fair decision has been made.

White Racial Identity Development

While the racial/cultural identity models promote understanding oppression from the target's point of view, White racial identity models help further understanding of oppression from the perspective of privilege. Several models of White racial identity have been created (Carney & Kahn, 1984; Hardiman, 1982; Helms, 1984, 1990, 1994, 1995; Rowe, Bennett, Atkinson, 1994; Terry, 1977). There are even models of racial identity for White career professionals (Gallardo & Ivey, 2014; Ponterotto, Utsey, & Pedersen, 2006). Each was developed to increase understanding of White dominance, racism, discrimination, and/or privilege. Hardiman (1982) conducted a qualitative study of White Americans and discovered that these individuals go through five stages of development before they reach a level of racial/cultural consciousness that is non-racist. The Rowe, Bennett, and Atkinson (1994) model is somewhat different from the Hardiman model in that it (a) does not propose a developmental stage model but, describes types of racial consciousness between which individuals can move, and (b) it divides people into two categories—those whose positive racial identity has been "achieved" and those whose positive racial identity has been "unachieved." In another study, Ponterroto, Gretchen, and Utsey (2002) and Sabnani and colleagues (1991) concentrate on the racial/cultural identity development of counselors-in-training, and they provide training suggestions that will promote growth and development in their counseling students.

Helms' (1984) White racial identity model will be outlined here, as it is the most sophisticated, well known, widely researched (and perhaps most controversial) model for White racial identity development to date. Helms contends that because of the perception that stages are static, and unchangeable, she decided to use the word "status" instead of "stages" in her identity development model. According to Helms, this was necessary to "encourage mental health workers who use racial identity models to conceive of the process of development as involving dynamic evolution rather than static personality structures or types" (Helms & Cook, 1999, p. 84). In other words, the word "status" reflects the process by which White individuals respond to race-based information. While the simplest status always develops first, White individuals have the potential to develop the other statuses as they mature. The status that receives the most reinforcement is likely to become dominant. Listed below are the White Racial Identity (WRI) status levels as devised by Helms.

Awareness of Your Own Cultural Heritage

Contact Status. The Contact Status is the one in which most Whites begin their journey toward positive racial/cultural identity. During this status, individuals deny that race is important or that racism exists. They are unaware of race privilege, they accept current race relations as they are, and they avoid racial issues in general. For example, a White career professional in the Contact Status might say:

I believe in person-centered counseling, and if I am accepting and respectful of my clients, I don't see why I need to learn anything specific about their culture or about multicultural counseling. I've never had a client dislike me because I'm White.

Disintegration Status. The Disintegration Status occurs when White individuals have been confronted with the reality of oppression and they are forced to choose between former misinformed beliefs and morality. If they continue to support oppression through denial of its existence, they are condoning mistreatment of fellow human beings; however, they most likely will not know how to handle the situation effectively. For example, a White career professional in the Disintegration Status might say:

I'm very frustrated about the attrition rate of ethnic minority clients in our drop-out prevention program. Nothing we do seems to be working, but I don't have a clue what does work. Maybe we just need to hire more minority career professionals who can do the job with clients more effectively.

Reintegration Status. In the Reintegration Status, White individuals retreat back to their own racial group and denigrate other racial groups. Individuals in this status have typically experienced such anxiety and pain while in the Disintegration Status they seek relief via traditional justification for oppression, thus relinquishing their own responsibility for it. For example, a person in the Reintegration status might say something blatantly racist and seek justification for it from another person, such as:

Look, I've tried to train some of those Black workers, but they just don't get it. I don't know why they let people like that into this company anyway. You know Jack's cousin couldn't get a job here, but they hire all the Blacks on Affirmative Action.

Pseudo-Independence (P-I) Status. Individuals at the P-I Status have developed an intellectual understanding of oppression and identify with non-oppressive Whites. Helms and Cook (1999) describe this status as an "intellectual commitment to one's own socioracial group" (p. 92). During P-I, Whites are most accepting of those oppressed group members who are most like themselves, and they are committed to helping those who are dissimilar to themselves to learn how to assimilate. For example, someone in the P-I status might say:

I had a wonderful Latina in my office this morning. She says that she wants to be a doctor and she has really good grades, so she can do it. The problem is that she has such a heavy accent, I'm not sure how well she will do at the university level. I'm going to see if I can get her into one of the speech classes that they have at the community college—you know the ones that help you speak Standard English and get rid of your accent. I'm sure she'll do great in it because she is so young.

Immersion Status. In the Immersion Status, White individuals attempt to redefine their Whiteness. They search for the truth regarding oppression and immerse themselves in this topic. For example, a White female law student in the Immersion status might say:

I know that this university must be discriminating against ethnic minorities because there are so few here as compared to other law schools. I've gotten together with a couple of students to research the admissions criteria. It will help me to understand why I was accepted and why African American applicants, like my friend Julie, who is brilliant, were not.

Autonomy Status. Individuals at Autonomy Status level have reached the most advanced level of White racial identity. Not only have they accepted and embraced their own racial group, but they also understand and reject unearned privileges of race and avoid people who are racist and otherwise oppressive. For example, someone in the Autonomy Status might say:

I had a White male client today who was really hurting. He says that he was let go from his job, but a younger, less experienced Asian American employee was retained. He is so bitter about all racial groups. It is going to be a challenge to work with him, but I think I saw a glimmer of hope when I asked him if there had ever been any people of color he liked and he said yes. I'm going to need some support with this one because it has been a very long time since I have even been exposed to someone who was so racist.

Developing a Positive Racial Identity

Sue and Sue (2016) outlined a seven-step process to be applied to White European Americans who are developing their White identity. They include:

1. Naivete phase: Curiosity about race that occurs during childhood while learning the superiority of being White
2. Conformity phase: Lack of awareness of one's own race and belief that all people, regardless of race have the same values and norms; the phrase "people are people" is often used at this phase
3. Dissonance phase: Still wanting to believe that all people are equal but faced with evidence that there are racial differences; sudden awareness

of one's own racist thoughts and behaviors as well as the racism in the broader society; feeling shame, guilt and overwhelmed about how to solve the problem

4. Resistance and Immersion phase: Confronts own racism; develops the awareness of the pervasiveness of racism in the United States; begins to develop negative feelings about being White and may develop a "paternalistic protector role or the overidentification with another minority group" (Sue & Sue, 2016, p. 410)

5. Introspective phase: Begins to reexamine one's Whiteness; begins to accept one's Whiteness and one's own participation in oppression; tries to answer the question of what it means to be White and what it means to be a cultural being

6. Integrative Awareness phase: Understands one's racial group and all the social and political implications of one's race and develops a non-racist identity; values multiculturalism by appreciating other racial/cultural groups and participating in efforts to overcome racism

7. Commitment to Anti-racist Action phase: Involved in social action from pointing out individual racist behaviors of friends, relatives, and co-workers to broaden social justice advocacy in the larger society to the point that one may lose friends and alienate family members but make connections with non-Whites and like-thinking Whites.

Certainly, everyone who reads about racial identity development would like to believe that he or she has reached the highest level of development; however, most people who take a closer look at their attitudes and behaviors may find that their racial identity attitudes are not quite as developed as they would like. Faced with this dilemma, career professionals can find a great many ideas and exercises to help in developing a positive racial identity (Arredondo et al., 1996; Helms, 1992; Parker, 1998; Sabnani, Ponterroto & Borodowsky, 1991). An excellent source for exploring White racial identity development is Helms' (1992), *A Race is a Nice Thing to Have: A Guide to Being a White Person or Understanding the White Persons in Your Life*. Sue and Sue (2016) listed five principles to promote a non-racist White identity.

1. Learn about people of color from sources within the group
2. Learn from healthy and strong people of the culture
3. Learn from experiential reality
4. Learn from constant vigilance of your biases and fears
5. Learn from being committed to personal action against racism. (Sue & Sue, 2016, pp. 415-417)

Activities for developing a positive racial identity. You may also want to try some growth exercises. Choose the status that you feel most describes your attitudes/beliefs. Completing the activities will help you move along to the next status level.

Conformity Stage/Contact Status. Do research on oppression by reading diaries, autobiographies, and historical accounts written by members of your own racial/cultural group. For example, European Americans should read autobiographies and biographies of Whites who both opposed and approved of slavery to have a greater understanding to the times and evolution of slavery (e.g., William Lloyd Garrison, Lucretia Mott, Jefferson Davis).

Dissonance Stage/Disintegration Status. Research the history of the racial/cultural groups that are not your own. Read the literature of other groups as written by members of those groups, including both their popular publications (e.g., magazines) and novels. Take field trips to visit museums devoted to the lives of other cultural groups. Begin reading on White privilege and talk to others about how it affects you.

Resistance Stage/Reintegration Status. Read research articles on racial/cultural identity development models. Pay special attention to those articles that discuss the emotional characteristics and effects of the various developmental stages/statuses. Read literature (novels, poetry, essay, autobiographies, biographies, etc.) on the effects of racism and oppression on all groups—not just the target group. When reading biographies/autobiographies of/by individuals involved in anti-oppression work, try to determine where those individuals would fall in the racial/cultural identity development model.

Pseudo-Independent Status (No Parallel under R/CID model). Write about your own experiences as a White person. Keep a journal of your feelings when you are in a racially/culturally mixed environment. Develop closer relationships with People of Color so that you can honestly talk about your feelings about race and racial differences. Realize when you are comfortable and uncomfortable around People of Color but, make efforts to leave your comfort zone so that you can add to your knowledge about others.

Immersion Status (No Parallel under R/CID). Find a role model who has moved through the stage/status you are trying to get through. Join clubs and organizations of people who are devoted to making positive changes in racial/cultural relationships. Read about the journeys of others who have fought racism and oppression—especially those who are members of your own racial or cultural group.

Introspection Stage (No Parallel under WRI). The confusion about whether all Whites (men, heterosexuals, able-bodied, etc.) are bad may be remedied by getting more information. Reading biographies and histories about White abolitionists and civil rights workers, male feminists, and heterosexual friends of gays, lesbians, bisexual and transgender individuals would be very helpful at this stage. Locating such individuals who are active in winning rights for oppressed people and talking with them about their commitment to the causes of social justice may go a long way toward transcending this stage.

Autonomy Stage/Internalization Status. Increase your exposure to a variety of racial and cultural groups. Research and become an active participant in organizations designed to promote social advocacy and anti-oppression.

Diversity/Intersectionality

To become multiculturally competent means not only understanding cultural diversity, but also understanding that within every cultural group there is diversity including, but not limited to, gender, age, sexual orientation, disability, social class, religion, and nationality. Depending on where a client falls within these areas of diversity will also contribute to an individual's level of privilege in U.S. society. Those who are privileged are typically those who hold the dominant social group memberships (Adams & Zuniga, 2016). In the United States, the privileged groups include males, adults, heterosexuals, able-bodied, middle class, Protestants, and native-born citizens.

Final Thoughts about Racial Identity and Culture

Awareness of one's own race and culture is the first step towards multicultural competence. Too often, it is a step that is skipped or glossed over. It is a great deal more difficult to have an appreciation and respect for the cultures of others when one has no appreciation for one's own culture. Falender, Shafranske, and Falicov (2014) found that the career professionals' readiness to begin multicultural training for some competencies was related to their racial identity. Ottavi, Pope-Davis, and Dings (1994) in their research on White counseling students, found that students' racial/cultural identity was significantly related to their perceptions of their own multicultural counseling competence. The authors recommended, therefore, that racial/cultural identity development needs to be a significant part of training new career professionals. Knowing the importance of your own cultural values and beliefs prepares you for the challenges you will face when you encounter clients with different cultural values and beliefs.

REVIEW/REFLECTION QUESTIONS

1. Given the readings and exercises you have completed in this chapter; how would you now describe your culture to someone? How does this definition compare to how you would have described your culture before reading the chapter?

2. Cultural value orientations (worldviews) are very important in the lifestyles of both client and career professional. What would be some of the challenges in working with career clients whose value orientations differ from the dominant culture regarding time, human activity, and relationship with the world?

3. Racial/Cultural identity development is an essential concept for the culturally competent career professional to understand. How would you describe racial/cultural identity to someone who has never heard of the concept? What would you emphasize as the most important aspect of racial/cultural identity to career professionals?

References

Adams, M., & Zuniga, X. (2016). Core concepts for social justice education. In M. Adams, L. A. Bell, D. J. Goodman, & K. Y. Joshi (Eds.), *Teaching for diversity and social justice* (3rd ed. pp. 95-130). New York, NY: Routledge.

Arredondo, P., Toporek, R., Brown, S. P., Jones, J., Locke, D.C., Sanchez, J., & Stadler, H. (1996). Operationalization of the multicultural counseling competencies. *Journal of Multicultural Counseling and Development, 24,* 42-78.

Atkinson, D. R., Morton, G., & Sue, D. W. (1989). A minority identity development model. In D. R. Atkinson, G. Morten, & D. W. Sue (Eds.), *Counseling American minorities* (pp. 35-52). Dubuque, IA: Brown.

Atkinson, D. R., Morten, G., & Sue, D. W. (1998). *Counseling American minorities.* Dubuque, IA: Brown.

Axelson, J. A. (1999). *Counseling and development in a multicultural society.* Pacific Grove, CA: Brooks/Cole Publishing Company.

Carney, C. G., & Kahn, K. B. (1984). Building competencies for effective cross-cultural counseling: A developmental view. *The Counseling Psychologist, 12,* 111-119.

Cass, V. C. (1979). Homosexual identity formation: A theoretical model. *Journal of Homosexuality, 4,* 219-235.

Cross, W. E. (1971). The Negro-to-Black conversion experience: Toward a psychology of Black liberation. *Black World, 20,* 13-27.

Downing, N. E., & Roush, K. O. (1985). From passive acceptance to active commitment: A model of feminist identity development for women. *The Counseling Psychologist, 13,* 695-709.

Falender, C. A., Shafranske, E. P., & Falicov, E. J. (2014). *Multiculturalism and diversity in clinical supervision*. Washington, DC: American Psychological Association.

Ferdman, B. M., & Gallegos, P. V. (2012). Latina and Latino ethnoracial identity orientations: A dynamic and developmental perspective. *New perspectives on racial identity development: Integrating emerging frameworks, 2*, 51-80.

Gallardo, M. E., & Ivey, A. (2014). What I see could be me. In M. E. Gallardo (Ed.), *Developing cultural humility* (pp. 223-363). Thousand Oaks, CA: Sage.

Gollnick, D. M. & Chinn, P. C. (1994). *Multicultural education in a pluralistic society*. New York, NY: Merrill.

Haley, A. (February, 1990). *Exploring your heritage*. Paper presented at the College of William and Mary, Williamsburg, VA.

Hall, W. S., Cross, W. E., & Freedle, R. (1972). Stages in the development of Black awareness: An exploratory investigation. In R. L. Jones (Ed.), *Black Psychology* (pp. 156-165). New York, NY: Harper & Row.

Hardiman, R. (1982). *White identity development: A process-oriented model for describing the racial consciousness of White Americans*. Unpublished doctoral dissertation, University of Massachusetts, Amherst.

Helms, J. E. (1984). Toward a theoretical explanation of the effects of race on counseling: A Black and White model. *The Counseling Psychologist, 12*, 153-165.

Helms, J. E. (1990). *Black and White racial identity: Theory, research, and practice*. New York, NY: Greenwood Press.

Helms, J. E. (1992). *A race is a nice thing to have: A guide to being a White person or understanding the White persons in your life*. Topeka, KS: Content Communications.

Helms, J. E. (1994). Racial identity and other "racial" constructs. In E. J. Trickett, R. Watts, & D. Birman (Eds.), *Human Diversity* (pp. 285-311). San Francisco, CA: Jossey-Bass.

Helms, J. E. (1995). An update of Helms' White and people of color racial identity models. In J. G. Ponterotto, J. M. Casas, L.A. Suzuki, & C. M. Alexander (Eds.), *Handbook of multicultural counseling* (pp. 181-191). Thousand Oaks, CA: Sage.

Helms, J. E., & Cook, D. A. (1999*). Using race and culture in counseling and psychotherapy: Theory and process*. Needham Heights, MA: Allyn & Bacon.

Hines, A., & Pedersen, P. (1980). The cultural grid: Matching social system variables and cultural perspectives. *Asian Pacific Training Development Journal 1*, 5-11.

Horse, P. G. (2001). Reflections on American Indian identity. In C. Wijeyesinghe, & B. W. Jackson (Eds.), *New perspectives on racial identity: A theoretical and practical anthology* (pp. 91-107). New York, NY: New York University Press.

Ibrahim, F. A. (1991). Contribution of cultural worldview to generic counseling and development, *Journal of Counseling and Development, 70*, 13-19.

Ibrahim, F. A., & Kahn, H. (1984). *Scale to Assess Worldview (SAWV)*. Unpublished document.

Ibrahim, F. A., & Kahn, H. (1987). Assessment of world views. *Psychological Reports, 60*, 163-176.

Jackson, B. (1975). Black identity development. *Journal of Educational Diversity, 2*, 19-25.

Kim, J. (2012). Asian American identity development theory. In C. Wijeyesinghe, & B. W. Jackson (Eds.), *New perspectives on racial identity: A theoretical and practical anthology* (pp. 138-160). New York, NY: New York University Press.

Kluckhohn, F. R., & Strodtbeck, F. L. (1961). *Variations in value orientations*. Evanston, IL: Row Patterson, & Co.

Kohut, H. (1971). *Analysis of the self*. New York, NY: International University Press.

Lee, D. (1995). School counseling and cultural diversity: A framework for effective practice. In C. C. Lee (Ed.), *Counseling for diversity: A guide for school counselors and related professionals* (pp. 3-17). Needham Heights, MA: Allyn & Bacon.

Lyon, G. E. (n.d.). *George Ella Lyon, my story*. Retrieved from http://www.georgeellalyon.com/about.html

McGrath, P., & Axelson, J. A. (1999). *Accessing awareness and developing knowledge: Foundations for skill in a multicultural society*. Pacific Grove, CA: Brooks/Cole Publishing.

McNamara, K., & Rickard, K. M. (1989). Feminist identity development: Implications for feminist therapy with women. *Journal of Counseling and Development, 68*(2), 184-189.

Olkin, R. (1999). *What psychotherapists should know about disability*. New York, NY: Guildford.

Ottavi, T. M., Pope-Davis, D. B., & Dings, J. G. (1994). Relationships between White racial identity attitudes and self-reported multicultural counseling competencies. *Journal of Counseling Psychology, 41*, 149-154.

Parker, W. M. (1998). *Consciousness-raising: A primer for multicultural counseling* (2nd ed.) Springfield, IL: Charles C. Thomas.

Pedersen, P. (1994). *A handbook for developing multicultural awareness* (2nd ed.). Alexandria, VA: American Counseling Association.

Pedersen, P. (1999). *Multiculturalism as a fourth force*. Philadelphia, PA: Brunner/Mazel.

Pedersen, P. (2000). *Hidden messages in culture-centered counseling*. Thousand Oaks, CA: Sage.

Ponterotto, J. G., Gretchen, D., & Utsey, S. O. (2002). A revision of the multicultural counseling awareness scale. *Journal of Multicultural Counseling and Development, 30*(3), 153-180.

Ponterotto, J. G., Utsey, S. O., & Pedersen, P. B. (2006). *Preventing prejudice: A guide for counselors and parents*. Thousand Oaks, CA: Sage.

Poston, W. S. (1990). The biracial identity development model: A needed addition. *Journal of Counseling and Development, 69,* 152-155.

Ridley, C. R., Liddle, M. C. U., Li, L. C. (2001). Ethical decision-making in multicultural counseling. In J. G. Ponterotto, J. M. Casas, L. A. Suzuki, & C. M. Alexander (Eds.), *Handbook of multicultural counseling* (2nd ed., pp.16-188). Thousand Oaks, CA: Sage Publications.

Rowe, W., Bennett, S. K., & Atkinson, D. R. (1994). White racial identity models: A critique and alternative proposal. *The Counseling Psychologist, 22,* 129-146.

Ruiz, A. S. (1990). Ethnic identity: Crisis and resolution. *Journal of Multicultural Counseling and Development, 18,* 29-40.

Sabnani, H. B., Ponterotto, J. G., & Borodowsky, L. G. (1991). White racial identity development and cross-cultural counselor training: A sage model. *The Counseling Psychologist, 19,* 76-102.

Sire, J. (1976). *The universe next door: A basic world-view.* Downers Grove, IL: Intervarsity Press.

Sue, D. W. (1978). Worldviews and counseling, *Personnel and Guidance Journal, 56,* 458-462.

Sue, D. W., & Sue, D. (1990). *Counseling the culturally different: Theory and practice.* New York, NY: Wiley.

Sue, D. W., & Sue, D. (2003). *Counseling the culturally different.* New York, NY: John Wiley & Sons.

Sue, D. W., & Sue, D. (1999) *Counseling the culturally different: Theory and practice* (3rd edition). New York, NY: Wiley.

Sue, D. W., & Sue, D. (2016). *Counseling the culturally diverse: Theory and Practice.* (7th ed). New York, NY: John Wiley & Sons, Inc.

Swim, J. K., Cohen, L. L., & Hyers, L. L. (1998). Experiencing everyday prejudice and discrimination. In J. K. Swim, & C. Strangor (Eds.), *Prejudice: The target's perspective* (pp. 37-60). San Diego, CA: Academic Press.

Terry, R. W. (1977). *For Whites only.* Grand Rapids, MI: William B. Eerdmans.

Vontress, C. E. (1971). Racial differences: Impediments to rapport. *Journal of Counseling Psychology, 18,* 7-13.

CHAPTER 3

Exploring Your Own Values and Biases

In order to become a culturally competent career professional, it is important to not only understand one's own culture, as discussed in the previous chapter, but also to understand one's culture as it relates to working with people from other cultures. When career professionals believe that their own cultural perspective is the only way to see and deal with the world, there is a problem. Wrenn (1962) described this phenomenon as cultural encapsulation. Cultural encapsulation is a symptom of racism and prejudice; it perpetuates oppression, because the belief in the superiority of one's own culture would mean that other cultures are inferior and deserve to be treated as such. One would hope that today the number of culturally encapsulated career professionals is small. The challenge, therefore, is not simply to increase career professional awareness of the dangers of cultural encapsulation but more specifically, to help them identify and eliminate cultural encapsulation in their practice.

The discussion of prejudice and biases involves some historical reflection. A review of the U.S. history is not intended here. Instead, our focus is to encourage career professionals and professionals-in-training to review their personal histories of prejudice, racism, and bias.

At the beginning stages of life, people have no biases and prejudices (Allport, 1979). During infancy, children have an endless curiosity, and rather than approaching strange people or things with the assumption that they are good or bad, they are just curious about them. Gradually, children learn about "others" (those who are different from them and their families). They also begin to understand how the significant people in their lives feel about the others and how others are treated by society and the media. Through these latter experiences, biases and prejudices begin. Although no one is born having biases or prejudices, everyone learns them. Children are typically praised, accepted, or encouraged when their opinions match those of significant adults. This reinforcement comes not only from the significant adults in their lives (parents, guardians, family members, teachers, neighbors), but also from the books they read, the television programs and movies they watch, and the impressions they gather watching interactions among strangers. When these factors contain negative undertones about "others," prejudices are born. The good news is that if biases and prejudices can be learned, they can also be unlearned. It is unlikely, however, that in changing their beliefs, people will receive even a fraction of the positive reinforcement they earned when they learned to be prejudiced. It is more likely that they will be rejected or ridiculed by peers for reducing their prejudices (D'Andrea & Daniels, 2001).

Because people learn biases and prejudices over their entire lifetimes, these prejudices are deeply embedded in their belief systems. Unlearning these biases is difficult and often painful. This chapter may challenge career professionals' beliefs, and it may even hurt their feelings. I encourage career professionals to assume that at least part of what they read about their prejudices and biases may be true. It is only in doing this kind of self-reflection that career professionals will be able to conquer their biases and prejudices and develop into culturally competent career professionals (National Career Development Association, 2015). Five manifestations of bias are discussed in detail: stereotyping, prejudice, racism and oppression, privilege and microaggressions.

Stereotyping

An innate cognitive process that is common to all humans is the propensity to categorize things and people into groups. This tendency for classification is useful in certain situations, such as scientific categorization of the natural world and organizing one's home or office. This innate propensity, however, can also lead to stereotyping, which is the root of biased beliefs and behaviors (McAuliffe, (2020). Everyone learns to stereotype to simplify complicated information, and so, unfortunately, the complexity of U.S. populations is ripe for stereotyping. If a few people in a group share certain traits, it is easier for people to simplify matters by generalizing the similar characteristics of those few persons to all members of the groups rather than understanding the differences among the group members. In conjunction with making stereotypical generalizations themselves, people may also learn about group stereotypes from others, which only reinforces their own generalizations. While stereotypical categorization is problematic in itself, the more compelling problem is that most stereotypes carry negative connotations, thus laying a foundation for prejudice. "A stereotype and a prejudice are similar only in that they both contain elements that are false or inaccurate, invite emotional feeling, and result from routinized habits of judgment and expectations" (Axelson, 1999, p. 49). Axelson has outlined some of the common characteristics of stereotypes:

- They are pervasive in that most people have their own "pet" personality theories about the characteristics of others.
- They tend to emphasize differences when applied to individuals or groups different from oneself but to emphasize similarities when applied to individuals or groups similar to oneself.
- They tend to be biased more by socioeconomic status roles than by ethnicity when applied to characteristics of individuals and groups

different from oneself or one's own group; and they tend to be negative if the stereotype serves as transmission for prejudice.
- They tend to become habitual and routinized unless challenged.
- First impressions are usually based on stereotypes.
- New stereotypes will supplement or supplant existent stereotypes as conditions and experiences in the culture change.
- Stereotyping and stereotypes impair the ability to assess others accurately and can readily lead to misinterpretations. (p. 50)

The following exercises are designed to help career professionals to assess the extent to which they stereotype individuals and groups and help break these habits.

Overcoming Stereotyping Exercise

It is extremely difficult to admit to stereotyping. Most people who hold stereotypical views have normalized their views as a perfectly natural response to complex data. To break free from this normalized perspective, try to view stereotypes in a different manner.

In this exercise, you are asked to use your own personal and cultural standards regarding work as an avenue for exploring your stereotypes toward others. Write your responses to the following prompts:
1. Your perceptions of success. How does a person become successful? How does a person know when he or she is successful?
2. Your work ethic. What makes a good worker? What is important about the work one does?
3. What personality characteristics are important for workers to possess?
4. After you have completed writing about your standards for work, write another paragraph expressing your thoughts about yourself and how well you live up the standards you have just written. What are your thoughts about family members who do not meet these standards?

Once you have taken a good look at your own standards, think about what you have heard about the standards of other groups (their standards of success, work ethic, and personality characteristics) and how those attributes measure up to your own standards. Knowing that no one, including you, is likely to meet all of your standards will give you permission to question stereotypes. This exercise is designed to help you to begin to understand how to turn around stereotypic and biased behaviors. There are more biases to discover and now that you are aware of them, they will be easier to recognize and work on overcoming.

Career Stereotypes Exercise

This exercise focuses on imagery.

List five high-status careers, five medium-level careers, and five low-status careers (you define which careers fit which categories). As you are listing each career, write down the first image that comes to mind regarding the person representing each career. What does that person look like? What is that person's gender, race or ethnicity, sexual orientation, ability status? For example, what image comes to mind when you think of college professors, funeral directors, housekeepers, designers, nurses? Next, write down someone in the same career who is completely different from your original image. Keep going with the imagery until you have covered all three lists.

What did you think and feel during the imagery exercises? What did you learn about your career stereotypes? Perhaps you found that some stereotypes were harder to imagine than others because some fields have become more diverse over time. The easier it is to imagine one type of person in a career, the stronger the stereotype.

Exploring Non-traditional Career Paths Exercise

Exploring stereotypes may involve examining the history of specific groups and identifying the jobs that were open to members of that group given the political and economic climate in the country at the time. For this exercise, do research on individuals who have entered career areas that are non-stereotypical for their specific group, such as African American scientists, Asian American clinical psychologists, gay police officers, and female engineers. Discovering the stories of these individuals and the obstacles they had to overcome will help you to understand how entrenched stereotypes can be. Write a brief summary of your research.

Stereotype Hunt Exercise

To reduce your tendency to stereotype, start practicing visualizing diverse people in the careers you routinely encounter, and notice when a stereotype causes you to do a double-take. For example, such a double-take occurred in the following scenario:

Marie recalls flying from New York to Florida a few years ago, and once the plane was at cruising altitude, a female voice came over the intercom, and Marie immediately stopped listening, thinking that it was probably the flight attendant informing passengers about the beverage service. When the voice went on for a while talking about the altitude and winds, she realized that it was the pilot speaking. Marie was really embarrassed because two of her occupational

> *stereotypes had been challenged—all flight attendants are women and all pilots are men.*

Career professionals need to learn to understand stereotyping and its characteristics by researching work stereotypes of various marginalized groups (see NCDA's Multicultural Resource List, 2020). This research will reveal the origins of the stereotypes and help career professionals to separate fact from fiction. Associating clients with careers because of race, ethnicity, gender, sexual orientation, ability status, or socioeconomic class is the first step to avoid in culturally sensitive career counseling. Because prejudice starts with stereotyping, an understanding of origins and harmful effects of stereotypes will help career professionals to begin to reduce their prejudices.

Prejudice

So much about prejudice and racism is intertwined that most people use the terms interchangeably; however, the terms are not one and the same. Allport (1979) defined prejudice as "thinking ill of others without sufficient warrant; or incorporating a bipolar (negative and positive) component as in 'a feeling,' favorable or unfavorable, toward a person or thing, prior to or based on actual experience" (p.6). Just as the word implies, prejudice involves making a judgment before having the fact—a pre-judgment. Ridley (1995) defines racism as "any behavior or pattern of behavior that tends to systematically deny access to opportunities or privileges to members of one racial group while perpetuating access to opportunities or privilege to members of another racial group" (p. 28). To expand Ridley's definition slightly, note that it may also be applied to groups oppressed in other ways not based on race, such as White women, persons with disabilities, LGBT persons, and so forth. Thus, Ridley's definition is also a definition of oppression in general. While prejudice is typically attitudinal, oppression involves behavior. Oppression "always involves harmful behavior, whereas... prejudice involves only negative attitudes, beliefs and intentions. Herein lies the major differences between these two phenomena. [Oppression] is behavioral and prejudice is dispositional" (Ridley, 1995, p. 18).

According to Dovidio, Kawakami, and Gaertner (2000), prejudice can also entail a passive behavioral component. In their view, prejudice consists of three components: cognitive, affective and behavioral. For example, an individual may think that people living in poverty people are too lazy to work hard (cognitive component); or an individual may feel discomfort when having to socialize with gays and lesbians (affective component); or an individual may seek out and move to a segregated part of town, one in which only members of that person's own race, sexual orientation, ethnicity, and so forth live (behavioral component). In the last instance, the behavior becomes racist if the individual in the segregated neighborhood works to keep "others" out or condones such behavior.

Some may insist that they have been brought up to believe that everyone is equal, therefore, they have no problem. Having this kind of upbringing does not insulate one from developing prejudices, especially if the lessons were purely cognitive. Prejudice can be passed from one generation to another without explicit lessons in prejudice. The old adage, "actions speak louder than words" is especially relevant when teaching children about prejudice. For example, if parents or guardians always told the child that "people are people and we always respect people no matter what color or religion they are," but those same parents or guardians nonetheless sent the child to segregated schools, lived in a segregated neighborhood, lacked friends from different cultural groups, never talked about race or failed to admonish racist behaviors of others, they have nevertheless communicated prejudice throughout the child's development (Ponterotto & Pedersen, 1993).

Likewise, even if a person's family and significant adults were vigilant about teaching acceptance of cultural differences through their words and deeds, education in prejudicial attitudes is still possible through mass communication. More than one might want to believe, the media (e.g., social media, television, magazines) constantly promotes prejudicial attitudes and perpetuates negative stereotypes of ethnic minorities and other marginalized groups (Ponterotto & Pedersen, 1993). For example, ethnic minorities and other marginalized group members consistently play stereotypic work roles on many television shows (such as African American janitors, Latina maids and housekeepers, Asian restaurant owners, gay hairdressers and designers). The few ethnic minorities who portray doctors, lawyers, police officers, and other high-level professionals on television are often seen as having sold out to the White culture or the storyline completely ignores the individual's differences. Even more distressing is the absence of people with disabilities in career roles on television. Not to single out television, the print media also does little to promote positive career images of marginalized groups. It is not likely that members of marginalized groups are sought after as experts for newspapers and magazines unless there is a special topic devoted to the particular group the expert belongs to. Instead, ethnic minorities are more prominent in daily papers for committing crimes than they are for any socially acceptable careers they may engage in. These negative representations reinforce prejudicial attitudes toward members of marginalized groups by the entire society. Speaking metaphorically, avoiding prejudice is like avoiding air pollution. Even if people and their families drive ecologically friendly automobiles, they will still breathe in the pollution from cars that are not ecologically friendly.

Despite all evidence to the contrary, there are, sadly, a number of people who truly believe that they are not prejudiced, even while they hold prejudicial attitudes toward ethnic marginalized groups (Dovido et al., 2000). This phenomenon has been labeled "aversive racism" (Dovido et al., 2000, p. 137). Dovido and colleagues (2000) noted, "Many people who consciously and sincerely support egalitarian principles and believe themselves to be nonprejudiced also unconsciously harbor negative feelings and beliefs about Blacks (as well as about other historically disadvantaged groups)" (p. 138). Aversive racists, however, while not overtly anti-Black or hostile to other racial and marginalized groups, are prejudiced in so far as they hold more positive beliefs about Whites than they hold negative beliefs about Blacks (Dovido et al., 2000). For example, a White high school career professional cannot understand why his academically brilliant African American student chooses to attend a historically Black college when she was accepted at one of the most prestigious White schools in the country. To this career professional, attending the White school would have been far better for this student's career aspirations than any of the historically Black college and universities in the country. He does not believe that Black schools are bad but that White schools are better. This belief system will be explained further in the section on racism and oppression.

Career professionals who want to be culturally competent might want to start by exploring their own prejudices. This historical self-review will help career professionals to restructure the cognitive component of their prejudices against marginalized groups. An understanding of affective and behavioral components of prejudice might be achieved by reducing or eliminating oppression and privilege, two further manifestations of bias that will be discussed next.

Racism and Oppression

When used in conversation in a culturally diverse group, the words racism and oppression are emotionally charged words that often have the effect of shutting down conversation. The definition of racism as it is used in this text states that "racism is a pervasive system of advantage and disadvantage based on the socially constructed category of race" (Adams, Bell, Goodman, & Joshi, 2016, p. 134). Similarly, oppression may be defined as the "nondominant groups systematically being subordinated, exploited, and marginalized by a dominant group's ideology" (Grothaus, McAuliffe, & Danner, 2020, p. 46).

The word racism, in particular, brings up images of angry mobs, confederate flags, guns, shouting obscenities, and spewing hate. Another likely image is that of ignorant, tobacco-spitting bigots, the historical stereotype of a racist. The word oppression, though more general and inclusive of all marginalized groups, conjures images of a construction worker catcalling a woman as she walks by the site, a drunken band of gay bashers, and the immaculately dressed upper-class person who places a handkerchief over his or her nose when encountering a homeless person.

Viewing the words racism and oppression in such starkly and stereotypically visual terms is a limited view that is detrimental for career professionals who wish to become culturally competent. The belief that racism and oppression are matters of the historical past or the belief that the stereotypical confederate-flag-waving image of a racist oppressor could hardly apply to anyone with sophistication and education such as a career professional is simply erroneous. Until career professionals are able to accept that they too can be oppressors, they will not be able to work effectively across cultures. There are probably as many definitions of racism and oppression as there are authors who write about them. In fact, the meanings have become so complex that the term "racism" has been broken down into several subcategories such as cultural racism, institutional racism, collective racism, individual racism, and internalized racism. Some understanding of each of these terms is necessary. Note that the terms, while created to define types of racism, can also be expanded to apply to oppression in general.

Institutional Racism

This type of racism occurs when the structure of society or an organization permits the creation and sanctioning of laws, policies, and customs that perpetuate the superior status of one group while denying or limiting access to goods, status, and economic opportunity to other groups (Axelson, 1999; Helms & Cook, 1999; Sue & Sue, 2016). Institutional racism is responsible for discrimination in the workplace and unfair practices within educations institutions and governments. For example, if an agency sends out important notices to clients or customers printed only in English when the agency is located in an area with a large Spanish-speaking population, that is institutional racism.

Collective Racism

"Collective racism is an informal type of institutional racism in that the policies are not written down but, there is a collective response by members of one cultural group to deny access to opportunities of another cultural group" (Utsey, Bolden & Brown, 2001, p. 318). For example, in 1996, the Texaco oil company policy of non-discrimination was clearly published and even though Texaco was engaged in multicultural education of its employees, Texaco executives were caught on audiotape making racist remarks about African American and Jewish people. The tapes lent support to a discrimination lawsuit levied by African American executives of the company. The company practice was to deny opportunities to specific groups even though its written policy stated otherwise.

Cultural Racism

This type of racism has been defined by a number of authors (Utsey, Bolden, & Brown, 2001; Jones 1972; Helms & Cook, 1999). In essence, cultural racism occurs when members of one cultural group believe in the superiority of their group and devalue the cultural practices, accomplishments, and creativity of other cultural groups. For example, a social media thread of a heterosexual woman that demeans and disparages a gay pride parade would be an example of cultural racism.

Internalized Racism

This occurs when an individual absorbs the stereotypes and attitudes held by those who discriminate against his or her group and internalizes them (Helms & Cook, 1999; Kohli, 2013). Internalized racism is characterized by individuals not believing in their own abilities and intrinsic worth or others who look like them. It involves accepting limitations to one's full humanity, including one's spectrum of dreams, right to self-determination, and range of allowable self-expression (Jones, 2000). Two examples of internalized racism include a three-year-old child who says to her Black/Hispanic parents that she does not want to be brown, she wants to be White, or the Chinese student who wants to be a career professional but dismisses it because she believes that she should probably go into a field that Chinese are good at like science.

Individual Racism

This refers to the discriminatory behaviors of a single individual. These behaviors are based on racial prejudice and a belief in the individual's own genetic superiority (Axelson, 1999; Ponterotto & Pedersen 1993). While institutional, cultural, and collective racism are of great concern in career counseling because they limit the career futures of clients, individual racism receives the greatest attention in career counseling literature and in training because it has the greatest impact on the one-on-one relationship between the career professional and the client. The multicultural competencies require career professionals to understand and overcome their own individual racism to protect the client's welfare.

Some definitions of racism or oppression suggest that behavior is not racist or oppressive unless the perpetrator has power and or is supported by a powerful institution. In this definition, if a person does not have the power to do harm to another person, that person may hold prejudicial attitudes but, is not considered racist or oppressive. Therefore, marginalized group members are typically not considered guilty of racism or oppression against the dominant group. The position taken in this text is that this distinction is moot when applied to the ethical behavior of career professionals. Career professionals are automatically in a position of power over their clients. Whether or not career professionals work for institutions that condone prejudicial attitudes and racist or oppressive behavior, and whether they belong to the dominant or marginalized group, if the result of a career professional's behavior toward a client is harmful, the career professional is considered to be racist or oppressive and therefore behaving unethically. For instance, if a gay Latino career professional intentionally or unintentionally supplies fewer referrals to his heterosexual male clients than to his gay clients, the career professional's actions will be considered unethical.

Ridley's (1981, 1995, 2005) work has helped career professionals to understand that even though they may not intend to hurt their clients, they can be guilty of racist behavior. Ridley (1995) contends that

> intentions should not be used as the criteria for determining whether or not a behavior is racist…racial prejudice does not always cause racism…A useful rule for determining racism is to look at behavior consequences first and motivation second. Regardless of a career professional's motivation, actual clinical behavior is what affects a client. (pp. 20-21)

In other words, if the end result of a behavior is that specific groups of clients are systematically denied access to opportunities, that behavior is racist. For example, consider the following scenario:

Joan is a White, female career professional in a high school. She is devoted to all of her students and believes that she does not harbor prejudices and biases. Joan is responsible for matching students with professionals they can shadow for one day to learn about the life in the real-world workplace. She is committed to matching marginalized students with professionals from their own backgrounds who can be role models. Two of her marginalized students are interested in careers for which Joan has only located White professionals as volunteer mentors. Joan is afraid that if she makes a cross-racial match, the students will get the idea that marginalized group members are not welcome in that profession. She decides to match the students with volunteer mentors from their own racial groups who work in closely related fields, not with the White volunteer mentors employed in the exact fields the students desire to enter.

Joan's plan in the above scenario would lead marginalized students to miss a learning opportunity they might not have missed if they had been White. Because Joan's behavior could result in harm to her marginalized clients, the behavior would be classified as racist or oppressive no matter how well intentioned it was.

Over past few years, the resurgence of traditional forms of overt racism and oppression is disturbing. The FBI reported that in 2017, hate crimes rose 17% over the previous year (Federal Bureau of Investigation [FBI], 2018). Specifically, 59.6% of the hate crimes related to race/ethnicity/ancestry, 20.6 percent related to religion, and 15% related to sexual orientation. In 2018, 11 Jewish worshipers were killed in their synagogue in Pittsburgh, PA. In 2017, three people died during a White Nationalists' rally in Charlottesville, VA and in 2015, nine African American people were killed in their church by a White nationalist sympathizer in Charleston, SC. There have been increased numbers of calls to police on African Americans for going about their normal lives in places where some White people did not think they belonged (Sacchetti, Jacobs & Hauslohner, 2020). Black Lives Matter is a movement created to bring awareness to the use of excessive force by the police on unarmed African Americans.

As opposed to the killing of unarmed individuals, most forms of racism in our society today are far more subtle and perhaps just as dangerous. An insidious form of racism identified early in this chapter is aversive racism. In this type of racism, core U.S. values like equality have been reinterpreted in such a way that the term "equality" becomes a weapon against the very group it was intended to help. For example, the word "equality" has been used to criticize Affirmative Action and other remedies for discrimination created to overcome hundreds of years of oppression. D'Andrea and Daniels (2001), and Dovidio and colleagues (2000) agree that this form of racism or oppression may be caused by a fear of the loss of privileges amongst dominant groups (such as Whites, men, heterosexuals, able-bodied people). Unfortunately, these attitudes have become more acceptable over time and, as a result, race privilege and privileges based on gender, sexual orientation, and so forth have been condoned under a reinterpreted definition of equality.

A second insidious form of racism has been labeled "color blind racial attitudes" (CoBRA; Neville, Worthington & Spanierman, 2001, p. 270). According to Neville and colleagues, CoBRA is different from individual racism because it lacks the element of the assumption of superiority. Neville and colleagues (2001) list several attributes of CoBRA including:

1. "forms of racial attitude expressions that are separate from, but related to racial prejudice…characterized by (a) persistent negative stereotyping (b) tendency to blame minorities…for racial disparities… and (c) resistance to ameliorate problematic social conditions" (p. 270).
2. "cognitive schema suggesting race is unimportant coupled with feelings of anxiety about race" (p. 272).
3. "multiple beliefs" in which individuals deny color or power differences (p. 273).

In short, CoBRA is a way of ignoring race while simultaneously allowing racial inequities to exist. A typical CoBRA attitude would be to fault people living in poverty (who just happen to be mostly single African American and Latina women) for having a number of children and living off welfare while denouncing a tax increase to cover the expense of adequate affordable day care through local governmental revenue since it favors people living in poverty over other types of families. Neville and colleagues (2001) point out that though the intent of CoBRA is to treat everyone equitably by a denial of differences, often the results will show inequities in counseling outcomes. In other words, ignoring differences does not make them disappear. When career professionals acknowledge and celebrate the differences between themselves and their clients, clients benefit from the relationship.

Racism and Marginalized or Culturally Diverse Career Professionals

In the multicultural literature, racism/oppression is a topic that has been well researched and discussed. Because White male heterosexuals have long been in a position of privilege in U.S. society, and because White male heterosexuals have been socialized and rewarded for oppressive behavior, most of the research attention has been given to overcoming oppressive behaviors in this population. Using Ridley's (1995) definition of racism (and by extension, oppression), career professionals who are members of marginalized groups also must understand how their prejudices against their own and other groups can result in racist or oppressive behavior. Sue and Sue (2016) devote an entire chapter to the issues of culturally diverse counselors (and by extension career professionals and career professionals-in-training). Often career professionals of color rate themselves as more culturally competent because of their own experience with oppression; however, "being in a helping profession or trainee of color does not automatically denote cultural competence in working with clients of color or with White clients (Sue & Sue, 2016, p. 76). In fact, Sue and Sue point out that many diverse groups harbor stereotypes about Whites and diverse groups other than their own. They also suggest that sometimes diverse career professionals may not have empathy for clients experiencing oppression because of a belief that their own experience of oppression is greater than other groups. Just as White career professionals need to do, culturally diverse career professionals should be vigilant about monitoring how they use the power of the counseling relationship. If they harbor biases against their own or other groups along with the power of the counseling relationship, their work with these clients may be harmful and, therefore, racist or oppressive.

Racism in the Form of Microaggressions

We have discussed the newer, more subtle forms of racism which are often manifested in behaviors described as microaggressions. Microaggressions are "brief and commonplace daily verbal or behavioral indignities whether intentional or unintentional, that communicate hostile, derogatory, or negative racial slights and insults that potentially have a harmful or unpleasant impact on the target person or group" (Sue, Bucceria, Lin, Nadal & Torino, 2007). When individuals have racist beliefs, they may intentionally or unintentionally make derogatory remarks. Sue and Sue (2016) say that these remarks can be sorted into three categories of microaggression: microassault, microinsult, or microinvalidation. A microassault is usually intended to hurt the targeted person(s). Before the backlash of multiculturalism took hold, individuals tended to refrain from this behavior unless (according to Sue & Sue, 2016) they could do so anonymously, they were among people they knew felt the same way or they lost control (e.g., drunk). Microinsults are more common and are usually unintended. They are defined as "behaviors or verbal comments that convey rudeness or insensitivity or demean a person's racial heritage/identity, gender identity, religion, ability, or sexual orientation identity. These acts or statements reveal someone's unconscious stereotyping and bias. Sue and Sue (2016) gave an example of a White male who refused to get on an elevator when a person of color was already in the elevator and telling Asian American or Latinos(as) "you speak good English."

Microinvalidation is "behaviors that exclude, negate, or dismiss the psychological thought, feelings, or experiential reality of the target group" (Sue & Sue, 2016, p. 189). One example is colorblindness (e.g., denying someone's race as not important or assuming a woman is a nurse and not a doctor).

Sue and Sue (2016) suggest that microaggressions that clients experience from their career professionals might be a main reason for premature termination. Owen, Tao, Imel, Wampold and Rodolfa (2014) state that half of the clients they studied experienced microaggression and that microaggressions "have a detrimental effect on the therapeutic working alliance" (Sue & Sue, 2016, p. 200). This finding is particularly concerning for career professionals because a failed working alliance could result in clients not getting the help they need.

The first step toward understanding one's own biases and prejudices is to understand how privilege affects behavior and beliefs, which will be discussed in the next section of this chapter. But before readers move on to the next topic, they should complete the following exercises (some designed for individuals and some collaborative) for overcoming prejudice and racism/oppression.

Exploring Your Own Values and Biases

Personal Reflection Exercise

Almost everyone has experienced being treated unfairly. Getting in touch with the feelings that accompany unfair treatment is a helpful way to understand racism or oppression and prejudice. Identify in your notebook an incident in which you were treated unfairly. Once you have identified the incident, write down all the details about it—especially your thoughts and feelings. Writing down your observations about this event will concretize the experience, and your notes will be a resource for you as your multicultural training continues.

What insights do your observations bring to mind about marginalized people? Some of you have experienced unfair treatment every day, but for others, reflect on being treated unfairly every day. How would you cope?

This exercise is designed to help you empathize with marginalized groups whether you are a member of a marginalized group or not. If you empathize with members of one group, it is difficult to mistreat members of other groups.

Cultural Exposure Exercise

Start increasing your exposure to a culturally different group you may have prejudices about. Begin with low risk-minimal contact activities (Fawcett & Evans, 2013; Parker, 1998) if you are at all timid about facing your own prejudices, racism or oppression. These low-risk activities do not require any person-to-person contact with a member of a marginalized group. Write down your impressions as you complete the following:

1. Read more about racism/oppression and prejudice from counseling texts (e.g., Jun, 2010; NCDA, 2015; Ponterotto, Casas, Suzuki & Alexander, 2010; Sue & Sue, 2016).
2. Read articles recommended on NCDA's Multicultural Career Resource List (NCDA, 2020).
3. Do research on discrimination lawsuits and affirmative action over the last ten years (See the U.S. Equal Employment Opportunity Commission [EEOC] statistics at https://www.eeoc.gov/statistics/enforcement-and-litigation-statistics).
4. Read biographies and autobiographies about those involved in the anti-racism struggle, the feminist movement, the gay rights movement, and the fight for people with disabilities (Adams et al., 2016).

Personal Assessment of Microaggressions Exercise

This exercise involves an assessment of your own microaggressions that could reveal your prejudices and oppressive behavior. It is much more likely that a person interested in counseling will need to combat aversive racism and CoBRA rather than overt, intentional racism, so assessing your own aversive racism and CoBRA is the focus here. Indicate in your notebook if you have ever thought about or spoken any of the following statements or similar statements. Then write down why these statements might be considered a microaggression (adapted from Ochs & Evans, 1993).

1. I don't see you as (Black, White, Asian, Latino/a, Indian, gay, lesbian, disabled, etc.). I see you as a person.
2. I don't know what's the matter with (insert name of marginalized group), after all, other people suffer oppression too.
3. Well, (insert name of marginalized group) are racists too.
4. I really don't know what to say when I'm around (insert name of a marginalized group).
5. Some of my best friends are (insert name of a marginalized group).
6. I'm afraid that I might be mugged, robbed, or terrorized by one of them.
7. I really cannot do anything about (racism, discrimination, oppression). It is not my problem. I have enough things of my own to worry about.
8. I don't have any prejudices against (insert name of a marginalized group); I've never even met any of them.
9. I just feel overwhelmed with how much I have to learn about other cultures.
10. My brother/aunt/cousin/friend/neighbor, etc. didn't get a job because of Affirmative Action.
11. I don't see why we have to put everything we write into two languages. Non-English speakers are going to have to learn to speak English anyway if they want to succeed in this country.
12. I'd really prefer to buy a house in a less integrated area. Not that I object to living in a neighborhood with people of color, I'm just afraid the property values may decline in the future.

If you have identified with even one of these statements, and you do not understand why that statement may be considered racist, consider discussing it with fellow career professionals and do more reading on microaggression and modern forms of racism and oppression.

Immersion Exercise

The most obvious strategy to work on racial issues is to spend more time with diverse populations. Throughout every week, you may have several interactions with people who are from a different culture than yours. To increase your cultural competence, your interactions need to be not only with people of your own culture and socioeconomic status level but, also with those whose cultures are different and whose socioeconomic statuses are lower and higher than your own. Also, if you simply spend more time with one person who is, for example, Japanese American, you learn some information about that person, but if you spend time with a number of Japanese Americans and other Asian Americans, you will be able to identify the inter-group differences in language, religion, and traditions among Asian Americans. After you have spent some time (3-4 months) with a group, write a short essay recounting your experiences and impressions.

Visual Exercise

Watch films that address prejudice and racism or oppression, such as *BlacKkKlansman, The Hate You Give, The Help, Crash, Grand Torino, Mi Familia, Color of Fear.* Such films stimulate an emotional awareness of oppression that is more poignant than reading alone (Arredondo et al., 1996). In fact, it is best to view those films with others and to debrief afterwards because the films are so powerful. Record your impressions in your notebook.

Privilege

A natural consequence of racism or oppression is that some people will be the beneficiaries of privileges while others are denied privilege. In U.S. society, there are the privileged groups and those who are oppressed. A general definition of privilege is that it is an advantage based solely on an accident of birth. For most people, that definition brings to mind the most privileged in our society—a White, wealthy, heterosexual, able-bodied, Protestant, male. Most people born to an advantageous station in life do not consider themselves to be privileged. They believe that because they are hard-working individuals, they have legitimately earned all that they possess and that they are deserving. Often, privilege is invisible to those who are on the receiving end, who simply believe that their privileged lifestyle is the way life should be. Jackson (1999) compares privilege to gaining permanent admission to an exclusive club the day one is born. In Jackson's analogy, membership to this club is neither desired nor requested, and it is almost impossible to resign. Privilege exists whether or not we condone it or seek it out. The invisibility of White privilege to so many people is understandable because in the United States citizens are socialized from childhood to believe that their achievements will be valued by others and that they will be rewarded for their efforts. In other words, most people believe that all achievements are based on merit and fairness. If this were true, then, it would be reasonable to assume that there is no such thing as race-based, gender-based, sexual orientation-based, and other forms of privilege (Crowfoot & Chesler, 1996; Haney & Hurtado, 1994; McIntosh, 1988).

In America, privileges are so ingrained in the fabric of the nation that they are apparent only to those who are not so privileged. In her article, "White Privilege and Male Privilege: A Personal Account of Coming to See Correspondence Through Work in Women's Studies," Peggy McIntosh (1988) could not understand how men in our society seemed oblivious to their privileges when it was so obvious to her. To help her understand this attitude, she decided to explore her own unearned privileges as a White person. In her landmark paper, McIntosh created a list of some of these privileges, which are listed below:

- I can turn on the television or open to the front page of the paper and see people of my race widely represented.
- When I am told about our national heritage or about "civilization," I am shown that people of my color made it what it is.
- I can arrange to protect my children most of the time from people who might not like them.
- I can speak in public to a powerful male group without putting my race on trial.
- I am never asked to speak for all the people of my race.
- I can remain oblivious of the language and customs of persons of color who constitute the world's majority without feeling in my culture any penalty for such oblivion.
- If a traffic cop pulls me over or if the IRS audits my tax return, I can be sure I have not been singled out because of my race.
- I can take a job with an affirmative action employer without having coworkers on the job suspect that I got it because of race (McIntosh, 1988, pp. 2-4).

As one of the authors of the book you are reading, I, Kathy Evans, have found that it helps people to explore their own privileges if I describe the ways that I, an African American woman, am privileged. A few examples are:

- I am able-bodied and can easily climb the stairs to any building without thinking about cut-out sidewalks, disabled parking, or ramps into the building.
- I am comfortably middle class and I can easily purchase most of the items that are advertised on television if I want to buy them. I can fill my refrigerator with food and I can buy the clothes I need.

- I am heterosexual, so I can openly display affection toward my partner without fear of disapproval or reprisal.
- I am a protestant so not only can I openly practice my religion but, I also know my religious holidays will be observed.

Then to underscore the presence of White privilege, I describe ways that I (a highly educated person) lack privilege in U.S. society due to my color. This includes:

- Though I can afford most items in my local grocery and drug stores, I cannot find stockings in my skin tone in these stores.
- I can rarely find a variety of greeting cards to send family and friends with people who look like me on the front.
- When my performance is criticized for some trivial reason, I often question whether the criticism was because of what I did or because of my race or gender.
- When I buy a house, I have to be careful that my realtor understands what I mean when I say I want to live in a comfortably integrated community, in which my racial and cultural heritage will be accepted and in which the neighbors who are not like me are not in a "flight or fight" mode.

Hays (1996) proposed a model that helps identify the privileged groups (which are typically the dominant group) as opposed to those who lack privilege (marginalized groups). The ADDRESSING model lists ten categories: Age, Disability, Religion, Ethnicity, Social Status, Sexual orientation, Indigenous heritage, National origin, and Gender. In the United States, the marginalized groups in these categories are: the elderly and the very young, people with disabilities, religions other than Protestant, ethnic minorities, sexual minorities, native people, immigrants and refugees, and women. Individuals who are part of the dominant groups are considered to have privilege. When presented with this information, most White people do not think of their "Whiteness" as a privilege (Vera, Feagin & Gordon, 1995)—especially those who have suffered discrimination based on their gender, religion, sexual orientation, physical ability status, or socioeconomic status. This leads us to back to the discussion of multiple identities and intersectionality in Chapter 2. It is likely that most people will find at least one of their identities will fall under the privileged umbrella.

Understanding privilege and its consequences is extremely important for the culturally competent career professional. To understand privilege is to understand oppression and to be able to guard against one's participation in either. Swigonski (1999) stated that oppression and privilege are two sides of the same coin. Oppression denies individuals access to resources and opportunities as a consequence of their membership in a particular group, typically as an accident of birth. Privilege provides special access to resources and opportunities—advantages—that accrue to individuals as a consequence of their membership in a particular group, typically as an accident of birth. (p. 128)

Admitting privilege means that one admits that discrimination exists, that one has benefitted from that discrimination, and that each individual must share responsibility for discrimination. The greater the number of White people who are oblivious to White privilege, the longer racism will continue (Neville et al., 2001). So, too, the greater number of men who are oblivious to gender privilege, the longer gender discrimination will continue; the great number of heterosexual people who are oblivious to sexual orientation privilege, the longer heterosexism will continue, and so forth.

Dismantling Privilege

Neville and colleagues (2001) point out that examining one's privileged status provides career professionals with a number of benefits. According to them, career professionals who are open to challenging and rejecting their own privileges are more likely to: (a) have a reduced tendency to stereotype, (b) apply systems and contextual approaches to working with clients of color, (c) reject culturally encapsulated counseling techniques, (d) accept individual client worldviews, and (e) discuss race, culture, gender, sexual orientation, and other marginalized clients.

As stated previously, privilege is typically invisible to those who benefit from their privileges and acutely apparent to those who do not benefit. McIntosh (1988) has assisted many people in determining which privileges they enjoy by exploring her own. After reading her article, McIntosh (2015) cautions readers not to use her observations as a questionnaire, checklist, or confessional. Instead, she encourages people to make observations about their own privileges, including privileges of gender, religion, vocation, class, language, and sexual orientation. More recently, McIntosh (2015) published a powerful group activity which helps career professionals explore not only their privileges but, also ways in which they experience oppression.

Here are some questions McIntosh (2015) suggests career professionals answer to increase their awareness of privilege:

1. What is one way you have had unearned disadvantage in your life? (p. 235)

Exploring Your Own Values and Biases

2. What is one way you have had unearned advantages in your life? (p. 236)
3. What is it like to [express your] unearned advantages or disadvantages? (p. 237)

The most important question for career professionals beginning to reject privilege is:

4. How can you "use unearned advantage to weaken systems of unearned advantages and why would [you] want to?" (p. 245)

In an effort to determine the level of awareness White counseling students possessed concerning their privileges, Ancis and Szymanski (2001) conducted a study in which White students were asked to react to Peggy McIntosh's 46 White privilege observations about herself. The students' reactions were categorized under three general themes:

1. "Lack of awareness and denial of White privilege," (p.554) - 10 students
2. "Demonstrated awareness of White privilege and discrimination" (p. 557) - 10 students;
3. "Higher order awareness and commitment to action," (p. 558) - 14 students.

More than a third of the students fell into the last category indicating "an awareness of the systemic nature of privilege...several students demonstrated an understanding of the parallels between multiple forms of oppression...and others took some type of action in the form of challenging their own or others' White privilege" (p. 558). Nearly another third of the students not only lacked awareness of their White privilege, but expressed anger and defensiveness regarding McIntosh's list. Seven out of ten students who stated that they possessed an introductory awareness of their White privilege "either accepted no responsibility for the position or clearly indicated that they were not willing to challenge or relinquish privilege" (p. 558).

Ancis and Szymanski (2001) expressed feeling shocked that students in a multicultural counseling class would voice such negative feelings and would be in denial of oppression. The authors were also surprised that there were so many students who were aware of the idea of "White privilege," which led the researchers to wonder whether or not the students were simply stating what they thought the instructor wanted to hear.

Overall, the study emphasizes the need for not only students but career professionals to explore White privilege as a key element in developing a non-racist identity (Ancis & Szmanski, 2001). McGrath and Axelson (1999) have devised an activity to help middle-class and able-bodied career professionals experience what it is like to live without some of their privileges. For example, they suggest spending a full day in a wheelchair or not using one of their hands for a day in order to understand their privilege as able-bodied individuals. Similarly, the following exercises will help career professionals begin to recognize and learn how to reject their middle-class privileges.

> **Exercise for understanding class privilege.** To simulate living in poverty, divide your living space in half and only use the one half of it for the simulation. Cut your weekly budget to the bare essentials. Use no vending machines, and do not buy any unnecessary items—no gifts, no movies, no eating out at restaurants. Only use cash (no checks or credit cards), put away your cell phone, give up your car, use only two or three sets of clothes and take your clothes out to a coin laundry for washing (McGrath and Axelson, 1999). Record your experiences living in simulated poverty in your notebook.
>
> **Understanding heterosexual privilege.** If you are heterosexual and in a partnership, (married or not), pay attention to how you and your partner behave in public when you are out on your next date or social event together. Ask yourself which of your normal behaviors together might be viewed as unacceptable for a same-sex couple. What would the others' reaction be to your public displays of affection (not just kissing but also holding hands, slow dancing together, gazing deeply into one another's eyes, sharing private looks in reaction to conversations, finishing each other's sentences, smiles and whispers, adjusting your partner's clothes or hair, making statements including your partner's role—my husband, my girlfriend).
>
> After doing these exercises, what were your reactions to the exercise? What impact (if any) did it have on your understanding of individuals who are marginalize? Are there things that you will do differently now that you have done these exercises?

Final Thoughts about Bias

U.S. society has been caught in a cycle of oppression that has lasted for generations. Those who have internalized myths and misinformation about others perpetuate this cycle when they do nothing to change the cycle and pass untruths on to the next generation. The cycle can be broken if more individuals take it upon themselves to research and reject stereotypes, do something to fight prejudice and promote non-racist or non-oppressive practices and laws, choose to be open about their prejudices and racist or oppressive beliefs, and decide to reject rather than tacitly accept the privileges they are born with.

Unfortunately, breaking the cycle of oppression is not easy, because doing so means going against deeply enculturated beliefs. This occurs all of the time. For instance, D'Andrea and Daniels (1999) found that the White career professionals, educators, graduate students, and practitioners they studied failed to act on their anti-racist beliefs to avoid negative reactions from other Whites. Similarly, Neville and colleagues (2001) explored the costs of suppressing privilege, which included being ostracized for an anti-racist position, losing friends, being isolated from other Whites, or being labeled a "race traitor." In addition, negative career consequences such as poor performance reviews and being refused promotions are also possible when one chooses to break the cycle of oppression. When most of a person's friends and family possess attitudes that reflect aversive racism and color-blindness, that person is unlikely to receive support or encouragement for his or her increased multicultural sensitivity.

Overcoming biases, prejudices, oppressive behavior, and privilege requires courage and perseverance. Those choosing to overcome these things will need to create coping strategies to stay on track. The following coping statements were submitted by several students as part of an exercise during a multicultural counseling course. It was at the end of the semester, and many of the students had found the class so supportive of their multicultural growth that the students wanted to create ways to maintain their awareness of cultural issues and continue to grow. Figure 3.1 constitutes a "mantra" the students created so that they would not be sidetracked and retreat back into color-blindness or aversive racism.

Figure 3.1
Students' Mantra: Multicultural Coping Statements

1. I will confront the racist behaviors of my friends and relatives because I love them. And because such behaviors hurt them as well as others.

2. Possessing biases and prejudices does not make me a bad person, nor does it mean that the people I learned these biases from are bad people.

3. Unlearning biases and prejudices is difficult. It took time for me to learn all these biases and prejudices and it will take time for me to unlearn them.

4. Before I categorically deny the truthfulness of a statement, I need to do my own research on both sides of the issue.

5. Before I categorically endorse a statement, I will do my own research on both sides of the issue.

6. If I feel angry, hurt, or sad about my beliefs and values, this is a sign that learning is beginning to occur and that I should not stop learning because it feels bad. The only way to feel better is to learn more.

Creating a mantra such as this is a valuable exercise. Using the mantra along with a personal plan to overcome any negative consequences from your participation in oppression reduction will help you to break the cycle of oppression within yourself, within your family, and with your clients.

REVIEW/REFLECTION QUESTIONS

1. Think of some positive and negative stereotypes about your own cultural group. How difficult or burdensome would living with these stereotypes be for you? What would you do to disprove the negative stereotypes or to prove the positive ones? How do you think these stereotypes affect a person's career choices?

2. CoBRA is considered the "new racism." The essence of the argument behind CoBRA is that all people are equal. How then would one reconcile one's own CoBRA beliefs with what we have discovered about privilege?

3. It is important for career professionals to learn to reject privilege to effectively work with their multicultural clients. How do you plan to reject privilege in your life to be more congruent as a multicultural career professional?

References

Adams, M. E., Bell, L. A. E., Goodman, D. J., & Joshi, K. Y. (2016). *Teaching for diversity and social justice*, 3rd Edition. New York, NY: Routledge/Taylor & Francis Group.

Allport, G. W. (1979). *The nature of prejudice*. Reading, MA: Addison-Wesley.

Ancis, J. R., & Szymanski, D. M. (2001). Awareness of White privilege among White counseling trainees. *Counseling Psychologist, 29,* 548-569.

Arredondo, P., Toporek, R., Brown, S. P., Jones, J., Locke, D. C., Sanchez, J., & Stadler, H. (1996). Operationalization of the multicultural counseling competencies. *Journal of Multicultural Counseling and Development, 24,* 42-89.

Axelson, J. A. (1999). *Counseling and development in a multicultural society*. Pacific Grove, CA: Brooks/Cole Publishing Company.

Crowfoot, J. E., & Chesler, M. A. (1996). White men's roles in a multicultural society. In B. J. Bowser & R. G. Hunt (Eds.), *Impacts of racism on White Americans* (2nd ed., pp. 202-229). Thousand Oaks, CA: Sage.

D'Andrea, M., & Daniels, J. (2001). Expanding our thinking about White racism: Facing the challenge of multicultural counseling in the 21st century. In J. G. Ponterotto, J. M. Casas, L. A. Suzuki & C. M. Alexander (Eds.) *Handbook of multicultural counseling.* (2nd ed., pp. 289-310). Thousand Oaks, CA: Sage.

Dovidio, J. F., Kawakami, K., & Gaertner, S. L. (2000). Breaking the prejudice habit: Progress and obstacles. In S. Oskamp (Ed.), *Reducing prejudice and discrimination* (pp. 185-208). Mahway, NJ: Lawrence Erlbaum Associates, Publishers.

Fawcett, M. L., & Evans, K. M. (2013). *Experiential approach for developing multicultural counseling competence*. Thousand Oaks, CA: Sage Publications, Inc.

Federal Bureau of Investigation. (2018). *FBI releases 2017 Hate Crime Statistics*. Retrieved from https://www.fbi.gov/news/pressrel/press-releases/fbi-releases-2017-hate-crime-statistics

Grothaus, T., McAuliffe, G. J., & Danner, M. (2020). Social justice and advocacy. In G. J. McAuliffe (Ed.), *Culturally alert counseling: A comprehensive introduction* (p. 46). Thousand Oaks, CA: Sage Publications.

Haney, C., & Hurtado, A. (1994). The jurisprudence of race and meritocracy: Standardized testing and "race-neutral" racism in the workplace. *Law and Human Behavior, 18*, 223-248.

Hays, P. A. (1996). Addressing the complexities of culture and gender in counseling. *Journal of Counseling and Development, 74*(4), 332-333.

Helms, J. E., & Cook, D. A. (1999). *Using race and culture in counseling and psychotherapy: Theory and practice*. Boston: Allyn and Bacon.

Jackson, R. (1999). White space, White privilege: Mapping discursive inquiry into the self. *Quarterly Journal of Speech, 85*, 35-54.

Jones, C. P. (2000). Levels of racism: A theoretic framework and a gardener's tale. *American Journal of Public Health, 90*, 1212-1215.

Jones, J. M. (1972). *Prejudice and racism*. New York, NY: Pergamon Press.

Jun, H. (2010). *Social justice, multicultural counseling, and practice: Beyond a conventional approach*. Thousand Oaks, CA: Sage Publications, Inc.

Kohli, R. (2013). *Race, ethnicity, and education*. London, UK: Rutledge.

McAuliffe, G. J. (2020). Culture and diversity defined. In G. J. McAuliffe and Associates (Eds.), *Culturally alert counseling: A comprehensive introduction* (3rd Edition, pp. 3-22). Thousand Oaks, CA: Sage Publications, Inc.

McGrath, P., & Axelson, J. A. (1999). *Accessing awareness and developing knowledge: Foundations for skill in a multicultural society*. Pacific Grove, CA: Brooks/Cole Publishing.

McIntosh, P. (1988). *White privilege and male privilege: A personal account of coming to see correspondences through work in women's studies* (Working Paper Series No. 189). Wellesley, MA: Wellesley College, Center for Research on Women.

McIntosh, P. (2015). Extending the knapsack: Using the White privilege analysis to examine conferred advantage and disadvantage. *Women and Therapy, 38*(3-4), 232-245.

National Career Development Association. (2020). *Multicultural career resource list*. Retrieved from https://www.ncda.org/aws/NCDA/pt/fli/38622/false

National Career Development Association. (2015). *Providing career services to multicultural populations*. Broken Arrow, OK: author.

Neville, H. A., Worthington, R. L., & Spanierman, L. B. (2001). Counselor roles in understanding and fighting oppression. In J. G. Ponterotto, J. M. Casas, L. A. Suzuki & C. M. Alexander (Eds.), *Handbook of multicultural counseling (2nd ed.,* pp. 257-288). Thousand Oaks, CA: Sage Publications.

Ochs, N. & Evans, K. M. (1993). How can White counselors help White clients with racial issues? In S. D. Johnson, Jr., R. Carter, E. I. Sicelides & T. R. Buckley (Eds.), *The 1993 Teachers College Winter Roundtable Conference Proceedings. Training for Competence in Cross-cultural Counseling and Psychotherapy.* New York, NY: Teachers College, Columbia University.

Owen, J., Tao, K., & Imel, Z. E., Wampold, B. E., & Rodolfa, E. (2014). Addressing racial and ethnic microaggressions in therapy. *Professional Psychology: Research and Practice, 45*(4), 283-290.

Parker, W. M. (1998). *Consciousness-raising: A primer for multicultural counseling* (2nd ed.). Springfield, IL: Charles C. Thomas.

Ponterotto, J. G., Casas, J. M., Suzuki, L.A. & Alexander, C. M. (2010). *Handbook of multicultural counseling* (3rd ed.). Thousand Oaks, CA: Sage Publications.

Ponterotto, J. G. & Pedersen, P. B. (1993). *Preventing prejudice: A guide for counselors and educators.* Newbury Park, CA: Sage Publications.

Ridley, C. R. (1981). Racism in counseling as an aversive behavioral process. In P. B. Pedersen, J. G. Draguns, W. J. Lonner & J. E. Trimble (Eds.), *Counseling across cultures* (3rd ed. pp. 55-77). Honolulu, HI: University Press of Hawaii.

Ridley, C. R. (1995). *Overcoming unintentional racism in counseling and therapy: A practitioner's guide to intentional intervention.* Thousand Oaks, CA: Sage Publications.

Ridley, C. R. (2005). *Overcoming unintentional racism in counseling and therapy: A practitioner's guide to intentional intervention* (Vol. 5). Thousand Oaks, CA: Sage Publications.

Sacchetti, M., Jacobs, S., & Hauslohner, A. (2020, May 27). Public outrage, legislation follow calls to police about black people. *The Washington Post.* Retrieved from https://www.washingtonpost.com/national/public-outrage-legislation-follow-white-womans-call-to-police-about-black-man-in-central-park/2020/05/27/94b219a6-a049-11ea-9590-1858a893bd59_story.html

Sue, D. W., Bucceria, J., Lin, A. I., Nadal, K. L., & Torino, G. C. (2007). Racial microaggressions and the Asian American experience. *Cultural Diversity and Ethnic Minority Psychology, 13,* 72-81.

Sue, D. W., & Sue, D. (2016). *Counseling the culturally diverse* (7th ed.). New York, NY: John Wiley & Sons, Inc.

Swigonski, M. (1999). Ways of knowing/oppression and privilege. In M. Kiselica (Ed.), *Confronting prejudice and racism during multicultural training* (pp. 123-136). Alexandria, VA: American Counseling Association.

Utsey, S. O., Bolden, M. A., & Brown, C. F. (2001). Assessing quality of life in the context of culture. In L. Suzuki & J. Ponterotto (Eds.), *Handbook of multicultural assessment: Clinical psychological, and educational applications* (2nd ed., pp 191-216). San Francisco, CA: Jossey-Bass.

Vera, H., Feagin, J. R., & Gordon, A. (1995). Superior intellect?: Sincere fictions of the White self. *Journal of Negro Education, 64*(3), 295-306.

Wrenn, C. G. (1962). The culturally encapsulated counselor. *Harvard Educational Review, 32*, 444-449.

CHAPTER 4

Awareness of the Client's Worldview

In addition to being aware of one's cultural history and personal biases, the next most important area of multicultural competency, according to Arredondo and colleagues (1996), is the counselor's awareness of the client's worldview. Arredondo et al. categorized each multicultural competency according to the awareness, knowledge, and skill counselors need to master. The awareness, knowledge, and skills needed for counselors to be attuned to their clients' worldview are covered in this chapter. Researchers have found that members of ethnic groups, gays and lesbians, individuals with disabilities, and other marginalized groups tend to gravitate toward occupations that are traditional for their groups. Reasons for this trend include an attraction by members of a group toward the historical legacy of their group's engagement in a particular occupation, an expectation of little or no discrimination in selected occupations, the avoidance of harassment or maltreatment by choosing particular professions, and family influence. A great deal of research has been conducted on the career issues facing ethnic minorities and women, especially with regard to demographic limitations placed on individuals from these groups. Less research has been done on the career issues (beyond the obvious discrimination issues) facing gay/lesbian/bisexual/transgendered persons, people with disabilities, and other non-ethnic marginalized groups, but research in these areas is ever-growing. Many of these issues will be addressed in later chapters. The primary focus of this chapter, however, will be on those factors that may influence and improve the relationship between client and counselor. The best place to start is to gain an understanding of the importance of history for ethnic minority and other marginalized clients, after which the chapter will focus on other ways in which career professionals can better gain an awareness of the needs of culturally diverse clients by understanding their worldview. In order to understand the client's worldview, career professionals are aware of client cultural mistrust, respect client cultural expectations and values, discern differences among members of the same cultural group (within group differences), consider the client's racial/cultural development identity status, comprehend client worldview as it relates to the world of work, and understand the current political climate for culturally different clients.

Understanding the Client's History

In 1964, Malcolm X stated, "History is a people's memory, and without a memory, man is demoted to the lower animals" (BlackPast, 2007). Too often counselors succumb to the temptation to disregard the cultural history of their clients. This may be done in a futile attempt to be color blind, or blind to the client's ethnicity, religion, sexual orientation, or other marginalized demographic. However, if ignoring history results in the dehumanization of a client, then a counselor cannot be called an effective multicultural career professional. Rather than ignore culture, an effective multicultural career professional respects a client's family and culture of origin. Read the following account of a client's experiences in therapy:

> Several weeks ago, I went to a White female counselor who was about my age. We were getting to know one another, and I told her about my childhood escapades. I mentioned some fond memories of visiting my many relatives in Georgia. She marveled at the closeness of my extended family and offhandedly asked me how my parents could leave family behind to go New York City. I was a little surprised by her question, but I thought I'd rather give her a gentle reminder. I said, "My parents left Georgia in 1957." Her reply amazed me, she asked again, "I know, but why did they leave?" I was quiet for a few moments hoping that the sheer stupidity of that question would finally dawn on her. Before I knew it, I got angry about her apparent ignorance and said, "My parents didn't want me to grow up in a place where I would be blatantly treated as a second-class citizen. They didn't want me to grow up in a place where I couldn't sit anywhere I wanted to sit on the bus or drink from any water fountain I saw. They didn't want me to grow up in a place where Whites would call my father and brother 'boy' no matter how old they got and if they protested in any way, they would risk being physically attacked or lynched.

It is not surprising that the counselor failed to connect the history of African American oppression in the South to the client's personal history, but the long-lasting effect of the client's experience with this lack of understanding is noteworthy. It is something the client has neither forgotten nor forgiven. Counselors can avoid mistakes like this by learning more about the history of oppression in the United States and keeping that information in mind as they work with their clients from marginalized groups.

No minority group in the United States has escaped oppression—in schools or in the workplace. Africans were enslaved in early U.S. history, and after the Civil War, African Americans were forced to live in segregation where civil rights, including job rights, were very few. Native Americans were murdered, uprooted, and denied access to employment. Chinese immigrants were exploited for their labor on America's railroads while being excluded from their new adopted home. Japanese Americans were taken from their homes and jobs and interned in War Relocation Camps on America's own soil during World War II. Hispanics have been exploited for their labor and kept from intermingling with the dominant population. White women were denied the right to vote and prevented from entering the American workforce in all but a few professions. People with disabilities were prevented access from most public buildings and workplaces. Gay, lesbian, and bisexual individuals live with the undesirable option of either being invisible and maintaining their rights or being visible while losing their civil rights, including the right to hold a job. It was not until the middle and late twentieth century that the United States made changes in its laws and policies, lessening the oppression of many of these groups.

Learning about the work histories of different marginalized groups lays the foundation for understanding their resentment and anger in a career counseling context. Such knowledge may also help counselors deepen their empathy towards their culturally different clients. In 2001, after the 9/11 terrorist attacks on the United States, this book's author fount it interesting that her White students were completely baffled by the attack, asking, "Why do they hate us so much?" Her ethnic minority students (who were equally fearful of their safety) did not seem as baffled at the hatred. Their own anger at many of the oppressive conditions they endure each day in the United States may have allowed for a greater understanding of foreign dislike of the United States. Career professionals who have not experienced oppression on a regular basis will need to expend a greater effort to better understand their marginalized clients.

It is beyond the scope of this work to provide a thorough history of the oppression of culturally different groups regarding work and career in the United States. However, the brief history above provides a head start. An enormous number of resources are available to inform counselors about the history, heritage, and values of specific populations as they pertain to the workplace. Volumes have been written about counseling every ethnic minority and other marginalized groups. Rather than attempt to duplicate the efforts of these many works, the focus of this section is on counselor acquisition of broad areas of knowledge applicable to all marginalized groups. Most important, the culturally-different client's perspective of work life in the United States, as a member of a marginalized group, is described in this section.

Reading history texts and biographies, and watching movies by and about members of specific marginalized groups are excellent strategies for gaining understanding and increasing empathy. Although the Internet provides a wide range of information, it is important, to verify the accuracy of Internet sources. There will be sites that paint a rosy picture of a particular group and blame all problems on the dominant culture, while other sites may post jokes and present negative images and stereotypes about different groups. All of this information is useful for the counselor—even the information found on the negative sites. What better way to gain an understanding of racists, sexists, and heterosexists than to view the open hostility, hatred, and cruelty on such web sites?

There is so much information available both in print sources and on the Internet that counselors may become overwhelmed by the sheer volume of information. One may be tempted to just throw up one's hands in frustration and think that there is no way to know it all. Knowing it all, however, is not the goal of multicultural training, and counselors are not expected to be experts on every group. Clients are the experts on how their own group memberships have impacted their lives. Career professionals can narrow the volume of information they need by focusing on the work histories of the culturally different groups served by their schools and agencies. Also, counselors can choose not to feel overwhelmed by looking upon the gathering of information as an exciting adventure into unknown territory. The end goal is that, while they may not be able to know everything about every culture, counselors need to be able to communicate to clients that they are not ignorant about cultural issues, they care about the effect of culture on clients' lives, and they are prepared to understand clients from the clients' own perspective.

Understanding Client Cultural Mistrust

Individuals who are targets of discrimination and oppression perceive events and people differently from their oppressors, which is why empathy is a critically important quality for counselors to possess. Using African Americans as the reference group, Parham and Brown (2003) noted that people who are oppressed "see and relate to life...[through lenses] colored by a set of experiences that contextualize their psychological growth and adaptation against a backdrop of socially oppressive phenomena" (p. 95). Most culturally different clients are constantly aware of how they differ from people from the dominant culture. They receive daily reminders of their differences while going about their routine tasks, and they rarely think of themselves outside the context of their own culture. It would not make sense, therefore, for counselors to decontextualize their clients' experiences by avoiding the discussion of race and culture. Equally as important as viewing the clients in the context of their culture is accepting clients' perceptions of discriminatory experiences. Truax, Cordova, Wood, Wright and Crosby (1998) stated that the targets of oppression are intimately familiar with discriminatory incidences, so it is essential for counselors to honor client assessments of oppressive incidents.

Human beings have learned to adapt to all kinds of environmental conditions, whether those conditions be geographical (for instance, adapting to harsh geographical climates), familial (such as living within a patriarchal or matriarchal family system), political (living under a dictatorship, for instance), or social. It is no wonder, then, that people would learn to deal with centuries of social oppression by developing coping strategies that, over time, become internalized by the cultural group. These coping strategies are passed from generation to generation, and even though the worst oppression is over for most of the groups in the United States, these coping strategies remain a part of the group culture as forms of self-protection and preservation. As a reaction to oppression, one self-protective coping strategy employed by people who are targets of discrimination is to distrust those who resemble the oppressor. Numerous studies have reported that clients generally prefer same race, same gender counselors. Coleman, Wampold, and Casali (1995) performed a meta-analysis of several studies and found that ethnic minorities prefer and rate ethnic minority counselors more highly than they rate European American counselors. "Given demographic information, potential clients will make inferences about the attitudes, values, and skills of the counselor" (p. 57). These findings seem to support the notion that clients inherently distrust cross-racial and cross-cultural counseling relationships. In other words, clients who expect to be discriminated against by European Americans are likely to distrust European American counselors because they are members of the dominant, discrimination groups (Swim, Cohen & Hyers, 1998; Baron, Burgess & Kao, 1991). Similarly, male counselors are more likely than not to be assumed to be sexist by women clients, and heterosexual counselors are more likely than not to be assumed heterosexist by gay/lesbian/bisexual/transgendered clients. Whaley (2001) called this phenomenon cultural mistrust. Counselors who encounter such mistrust, even hostility, from clients may be tempted to label this behavior as paranoid. Clients exhibiting such behavior may indeed be wary and suspicious, but rather than pathologize the behavior as paranoia, counselors need to be aware that the behavior would more appropriately be defined as cultural mistrust—a realistic suspicion and lack of trust (in other words, healthy paranoia) that is a result of ongoing, lifelong experiences with oppression (Whaley, 2001).

Further, counselors who are of the same race, culture, gender, sexual orientation, and so forth as their clients are not necessarily free from experiencing cultural mistrust from their clients. Those clients who tend to be highly mistrustful are even likely to suspect that such counselors are agents of the White or dominant institution (Whaley, 2001). When counselors, regardless of background, work as part of a perceived culturally dominant institution, they may be seen by clients as having sold out their identity. Such counselors are seen as essentially the same as or even worse than counselors from the dominant group. This cultural mistrust is of the system, not necessarily of the individual counselor. Counselors would do well to become familiar with cultural mistrust and work on their own trustworthiness as multicultural counselors. Parham and Brown (2003) warn, however, that counselors can try to do what they can to show trustworthiness, but trust is more internal than external. Clients have to decide for themselves if their counselors deserve to be trusted. Counselors who reach a point of empathy with their clients, who can truly put themselves in their clients' shoes and communicate this understanding to clients, are more likely to break through the barrier of cultural mistrust.

> **Exploring Cultural Mistrust Exercise**
>
> Think of someone whom you do not trust. It may be someone who has lied to you in the past, someone who has betrayed a confidence, someone who talks behind your back, or a spouse or significant other who has cheated on you. Using your own notebook, first, list the reaction you have when you find yourself having to interact with this individual. Include in the list your feelings and behaviors.
>
> - When I see the person I distrust I feel...
> - When I see the person I distrust I ... (list things you do)
>
> Next, generate a list of the things the above-mentioned person can do to regain your trust.
>
> Many people find that the second list is a lot smaller than the first. This exercise may help you get in touch with the mistrustful feelings your culturally different clients may have toward you. In addition, it gives a glimpse at how hard you may have to work to overcome this mistrust.

Respecting Client Cultural Expectations and Values

When you explored your own culture in Chapter 2, you identified cultural values and expectations for your own group. A different process may be needed to determine the values and expectations of groups other than your own. You may not have easy access to the people you need to interview. Rather than interviewing relatives and friends, you may need to interview representatives of culturally different groups, such as community leaders. Identifying the expectations and values within culturally different groups helps counselors pinpoint those expectations and values that may be in conflict with their own and to resist the temptation to impose their own expectations and values onto culturally different clients. More important, knowledge of culturally different expectations and values will increase counselor understanding of client issues and enhance the counselor-client relationship. If, for example, research has found that a particular cultural group rejects persons of different sexual orientations, a counselor can more easily understand the point of view of a client from that cultural group who is adamant about staying "in the closet" in relation to his or her family. The client from that cultural group may or may not have values that match those of the counselor, but culturally competent career professionals are knowledgeable about and respectful of those values nonetheless.

The expectation and value differences that seem to be particularly relevant to ethnic minority groups are those regarding family. Contrary to a collective or family focus, career counseling is often focused only on the individual following the dominant White Protestant middle class cultural norm of individuality rather than family. Nearly all ethnic minority groups, including White ethnic groups such as Italian Americans and Irish Americans, cherish the extended family. To be culturally competent, career professionals need to be especially familiar with the values their clients place on extended family before proceeding with career counseling. The following scenario, from a high school career counselor's experience, demonstrates what can happen when counselors fail to consider the importance of family expectations and values among ethnic minorities during the counseling process:

I counseled Jean, a young woman from Xingang (formerly Hong Kong), who entered counseling because she had to choose a college major and was having trouble coming up with one. She was witty, gentle, and very positive, and I enjoyed the time with her. In our third session, she confessed to me that she really wanted to become a counselor, and she said it almost apologetically. I explored with her what appealed to her about counseling, and her eyes lit up and she smiled all over. I suggested that she do some research on the counseling profession in Hong Kong—training, places of employment, and so forth. She came back the next week with a great deal of information and a lot of questions. She seemed to be a sponge—just soaking up everything she could find on the topic. I was very pleased with her progress, so it was a great surprise to me when Jean told me during our fifth session that she had changed her mind about counseling. When I asked why, she told me she had discussed the decision with her Chinese friends and her brother (who lived and worked in another state), and they told her that her English was not good enough for pursing counseling in the United States. They advised her to stick with something they (meaning her cultural group) do well, like math or science. I could hear sadness in her voice but saw acceptance in her face. I was unaware at the time that I had mishandled Jean's counseling and that I was completely culturally insensitive. If I had it to do all over again, of course, I would have assessed her level of acculturation before embarking on an information-gathering discussion. I would have asked about the opinions of her family and significant others in her culture, and I would have explored what it would mean for her to go against her family and friends' recommendations. I know now that I will not make that kind of mistake again.

Familiarity of a cultural group is necessary to deliver culturally effective assistance to clients. Of course every client's experience within a culture is going to be different but it is important for career professionals to understand the values and expectations of the culture and check in with the client to see how those values and expectations fit him or her.

Discerning Differences Within the Same Cultural Group

Learning about the values and expectations of various cultural groups comes with a very strong caveat: Do not use this information to stereotype clients. There is the temptation for counselors trained in cultural sensitivity to simply replace their uninformed stereotypes with "informed" stereotypes (Buchtel, 2014). This is typical behavior among Americans, who live in an information-heavy society and tend to convert complex ideas into simple shorthand, an example of which is the proliferation of acronyms in American speech (Ridley, 1995). Even in the multicultural counseling area, the tendency to use shorthand is apparent in the use of the generic "African American," "Asian American," "Latino," and "Native American." When viewed critically, these terms come dangerously close to stereotyping. For example, as long as Black people live in the United States, "African American" is the term that is used to describe them, whether they be U.S.-born Blacks or those born in the Caribbean, South America, or Africa. Though they share racial and cultural roots as well as a common ancestry, the people of these different regions differ in a number of significant ways. Several authors have recommended being specific when referring to particular ethnic groups (McAuliffe, Kim & Park, 2013). For example, they have recommended that Native Americans be referred to more specifically by tribal name, that Asian Americans of Japanese descent be called Japanese American, that Black Americans of Trinidadian descent be called Trinidadian Americans, and so forth.

The importance of being more specific when naming a client's ethnic group goes beyond correctness. Counselors need to be keenly aware of the unique within-group differences or within the culturally different groups they serve. An easy way for a counselor to lose credibility with a client is for the client to perceive that the counselor believes all African Americans are the same. The counselors whose clientele includes not only individuals of African descent whose ancestors were born in the United States, but also individuals who immigrated from Haiti, Jamaica, and Aruba, need to know the cultural variations among these groups. In addition, an understanding of the perceptions each group has of the other groups is needed. Few mistakes can be more damaging to a counseling relationship than a counselor mistaking a client's heritage for that of the groups his or her ethnic group despises. Further, not only do counselors need to be aware of these intragroup differences, but they also need to understand that some of their clients (especially immigrants) totally reject being classified as African American, Asian American, Latino, and so forth. Among the within-group differences that have the most profound effects on the counseling relationship are those related to racial and cultural identity. But note also that people from other marginalized groups are not all the same. For example, women differ (among other factors) in terms of race/ethnicity/culture, age, and marital status; people with disabilities differ in terms of types of disability—motor, visual, auditory, psychological; and though they tend to be identified as one group gay men differ from lesbians, and they both differ from bisexual and transgendered individuals. Counselors who take the time to learn about such differences are culturally competent, and can demonstrate an ability to see within-group differences.

Within-Group Differences Exercise

Using this list of the cultural groups that are the focus of this text, generate in your notebook as many subgroups that you can think of. For example, a few subgroups of African Americans have already been mentioned (African-born, Caribbean-born). Try not to limit your list to geography—think of all the areas of culture that may diversify a group (e.g., language or religion—such as Irish Catholics and Irish Protestants).

African Americans

American Indian/ Alaska Native

Asian American

Latinos and Latinas

People with Disabilities

Gay Men

Lesbians

Bisexual Individuals

Transgender Individuals

White Women

Some people find it hard to generate subgroups for one or more of the examples above. That usually means that they need to do more research on the group to understand the within-group differences.

Considering the Client's Racial/Cultural Identity Development Status

In Chapter 3, you became more aware of your own racial/cultural values, expectations, and traditions, and how you have internalized (or not internalized) those aspects of your identity. That is referred to as your racial/cultural identity development stage or status. Racial/cultural identity development stages/status is as relevant to clients as it is to counselors. An Asian American counselor at the Dissonance stage whose White client is at the Reintegration stage may have trouble with a client's disdain of other races and cultures. An Asian American client at the Conformity stage may resent and resist an Asian American counselor. For another example, consider the importance of being aware of the racial/cultural identity development stage in the following counseling scenario, in which the client is clearly in the Resistance stage of development:

Starr Adams is an African American high school counselor whose primary duties involve offering career counseling to the students. Star's first client as a nineteen-year-old Mexican American female, Patricia, who was openly hostile to Starr and requested that a Latina counselor work with her. Patricia stated further that the counseling center staff was racist because they "gave all the minority students to Starr no matter their race or ethnicity, and the White kids and Black kids got to work with counselors who look like them but the Latinos/as had to settle for whoever was in the office." She also voiced the opinion that the White counselors didn't want to be bothered with the Latinos or Blacks and didn't care what kind of service they got. Starr was devastated by Patricia's attitude and was clueless about what she should do. Starr didn't even get a chance to establish rapport, credibility, or trust.

As the above scenario demonstrates, counselors who rightfully approach the counseling situation with the notion that they must clearly demonstrate their own acceptance of racially and culturally different clients often fail to consider that due to the client's racial identity development stage, the client may reject the counselor simply because of the counselor's race or culture. Therefore, the counselor who is able to assess a client's racial identity development stage and work with the client from wherever the client may be on the continuum is more likely to be successful and culturally competent than the counselor who does not have such expertise. In the scenario, the hostile client in the Resistance stage might more effectively be referred to a European American counselor whose own racial/cultural identity development is of a higher status level. This is what Helms (1990) and Helms and Cook (1999) have suggested—that effective counselors must function at higher racial/cultural identity development stages/statuses than those of their clients. Starr may have been able to work well with Patricia if Starr was firmly in a position of positive racial identity. Helms and Cook (1999) presented a model, based on racial/cultural identity development stage/status, that illustrates the interactions between counselors and their supervisors and between group leaders and group members. Although the Helms and Cook model focused on a supervisor/worker relationship, a similar process occurs between client and counselor. In fact, Helms stated, "I originally proposed…and continue to believe that racial identity models will make it feasible to train therapists who can be responsive to intrapersonal as well as interpersonal racial dynamics both within and outside the therapy relationship" (p. 196). Helms described the interactions between two people (dyads) such as a counselor and a client (Helms, 1990) and devised four different relationship types based on the racial/cultural identity development stage/status of both the client and the counselor. Helms suggests that regardless of the number of people involved, the relationships are always progressive, parallel, regressive, or crossed.

The ideal counseling relationship is the progressive relationship. In a progressive counseling relationship, the counselor's racial identity status is at least one level higher than that of the client, and the counselor is therefore able to facilitate client growth. For example, the White counselor at the Pseudo-Independent status (the status wherein an intellectual understanding of racial/cultural differences has developed) can be a progressive counseling relationship if the client is in the Contact stage (the stage wherein the client is naïve about racism and other cultural groups). This relationship is productive and beneficial to the client (Helms, 1990).

The parallel relationship occurs when the client and counselor see the world in the same way. For example, a parallel relationship would be one in which a White counselor in the Contact status, who, as characteristic of this status, sees no need to change the status quo, works with an ethnic minority client who is in the Conformity stage and, as characteristic of that stage, thinks that racism does not exist and that the status quo is acceptable. There is little chance of conflict in a parallel relationship, because the goal for both the client and the counselor is to avoid conflict and tension (Helms, 1990). However, there is also little chance for growth on the part of the client or the counselor.

In regressive relationships, the client's racial/cultural identity development is at a higher stage than that of the counselor. Take for example an ethnic minority client who is at the Integrative stage of racial/cultural identity development (characterized by appreciating one's own group and other groups) meeting a counselor who is at the Immersion status (characterized as a White person intensively trying to understand why White people don't work hard enough correcting their racist attitudes). In the above relationship, there is little that the counselor can do to help the client grow and develop culturally, since the client has already worked through his or her issues with race/culture. In fact, the client, who is the one seeking help, is more sophisticated regarding race/culture than the counselor. This type of relationship is likely to be strained and unproductive (Helms, 1990).

The final relationship, the crossed relationship, is the most troublesome. These types of relationships are most likely to fail because the racial/cultural identity development stages/statuses of the client and the counselor are diametrically opposed. The client and counselor hold "opposing attitudes towards Blacks and

Whites" (p. 141). Helms states that these types of dyads are "antagonistic and short-lived" (p. 195). For example, if the ethnic minority counselor is in the Conformity stage while the White client is in the Autonomy stage, the relationship is considered crossed.

Whatever the relationship type, for both the client and the counselor, racial identity reflects the individual's way of coping with racism in U.S. society and contributes significantly to his or her worldviews—worldviews that include how the world of work is perceived.

> **Counseling Relationship Dyads Exercise.**
>
> In your notebook, identify the following counseling dyads as either Parallel, Progressive, Regressive, or Crossed: (a) Counselor – Client, (b) Conformity – Pseudo-Independent, (c) Disintegration – Dissonance, (d) Autonomy – Introspection, (e) Resistance – Reintegration.

Comprehending Client Worldview as it Relates to the World of Work

As noted in Chapter 2, Sue and Sue (2003) describe worldview using the locus of control and locus of responsibility paradigms. As you may recall, the locus of control pertains to whether or not people believe they have control over factors in their lives and the locus of responsibility pertains to whether or not people believe they are responsible for the things that happen in their lives. Refer back to Figure 2.1 in Chapter 2 for an illustration of these concepts. As you can see, Sue and Sue placed the locus of control and locus of responsibility perpendicularly on a continuum, resulting in four quadrants. Career professionals who comprehend where their clients fall within these four quadrants will be better able to help their clients.

Quadrant I—Internal Locus of Control and Internal Locus of Responsibility

The first quadrant is most descriptive of European American middle-class culture. Individuals with an internal locus of control and an internal locus of responsibility believe that they are responsible for whatever success they achieve and failures they experience. They also believe that they have the ability to attain success on their own merits and that no one has greater control over their lives than they do. The other three quadrants explain the various worldviews of ethnic minority and marginalized group members.

Quadrant II—External Locus of Control and Internal Locus of Responsibility

Quadrant II represents the first minority worldview. Individuals who perceive the world from this perspective tend to resemble those whose racial/cultural identity development is in the Conformity stage. Individuals in this quadrant hold a negative view of those in their own racial/cultural group and believe that the problems of the group, such as difficulties locating and/or sustaining employment, are due to their own shortcoming, rather than blaming oppression. In counseling, these clients tend to give full credibility to their counselor only if the counselor is a member of the dominant cultural group. Culturally competent career professionals from the dominant group, therefore, are careful to properly manage the power clients hand over to them. Ethnic minority counselors, on the other hand, need to work harder at credibility and building trust.

Quadrant III—External Locus of Control and an External Locus of Responsibility

Clients in this category can prove to be a challenge to counseling professionals because these clients take no responsibility for their actions and believe that they have no control over their own lives. Clients with this worldview suffer from what has been coined learned helplessness—they have tried and failed so many times that they stop trying. These clients sincerely believe that no matter what they do, nothing changes and that someone or some institution will make all of the major decisions in their lives. Such clients are difficult to motivate into the world of work or into a career change because they do not believe that they have any power over their own lives.

Quadrant IV—Internal Locus of Control with an External Locus of Responsibility

This quadrant represents the healthiest of the minority worldviews. Individuals with this type of worldview believe that there are marginalized groups who are discriminated against and who are treated unfairly. But these individuals also believe that they can succeed on their own merits when discrimination is taken out of the equation (Sue & Sue, 2003). These clients are likely to be distrustful of counselors from the dominant culture. As a result, counselors from the dominant culture will be required to provide their competence. If dominant culture career professionals expect the Quadrant IV clients to take all the responsibility for changes in their work lives, the counseling relationship will be strained or, perhaps, prematurely terminated. These clients believe that it is the system that is broken and needs changing, not themselves. The counselor who is able to empathize with these clients and see the world from their eyes will be more successful than the counselor who does not comprehend what "the system" means.

Understanding the Current Political Climate for Marginalized Groups

Multiculturally competent career development professionals are aware of the social and political influences affecting ethnic minority and other marginalized clients. Racism, sexism, ableism, heterosexism, and other "isms" oppress groups to the point that they become victims. Ridley (1995) explains that victims suffer from feelings of shame, self-blame, rage, vulnerability, and violation. What is worse, as Ridley contends, "many victims, because their feelings are unresolved, continue to play the victim role...[and] when victimization is selective and repeated, it is not just victimization...[Targets are] singled out for who they are to inflict harm on them" (p. 5). In other words, when a person is subjected to oppression on a continuous basis, significant psychological harm often results—harm that the mental health system can sometimes contribute to as well; even in counseling and psychotherapy, clients are victimized (Sue & Sue, 2016). They are frequently misdiagnosed, their symptoms are often ignored or minimized, and they are regularly patronized (Ridley, 1995). Clients who have experienced any or all of these situations may enter counseling with negative expectations and will likely be suspicious of and uncooperative with their counselors.

The sociopolitical reality for marginalized groups is that there are systems in place that limit their potential, erect barriers for them, and deny them privileges. These discriminatory institution policies exist at the local, state, federal, and private levels. All effective counselors need to stay current about the policies, procedures, and laws that affect their clients. Multiculturally competent counselors go a step further and are watchful for the political realities that are especially relevant to their clients from marginalized groups. Still further, knowledge is not enough. Effective multiculturally competent counselors are also advocates for their clients. Social injustices are often as responsible for client issues as the client's behavior. It would be rather short-sighted for counselors to assume that changing the client's behavior alone will rectify the injustices he or she has experienced.

Some federal laws are particularly relevant to multicultural career counseling, such as the Civil Rights Act of 1964 and 1991, Americans with Disabilities Act of 1990, Welfare Reform Bill of 1996, Equal Pay Act of 1963, and the Lilly Ledbetter Fair Pay Act of 2009, which will be described in detail in this chapter. Most of these measures have proved to be beneficial for many marginalized populations. Although none of them have eliminated oppression altogether, these laws have provided some relief and can be considered moves in the right direction. From a counseling perspective, the existence of these laws may not be felt in the everyday lives of clients. Counselors may be able to use their knowledge of the laws to empower their clients and support the notion that client problems are not all of their own making. These laws represent the fact that there really are powerful forces working against people but that sometimes people can fight against those in power and effect positive change. For example, the Defense of Marriage Act (DOMA) prohibited married people of the same sex to be eligible for federal benefits. The fight against that law resulted in the Supreme Court striking it down in 2013, indicating that the denial of same-sex marriage was unconstitutional (Peralta, 2013). This ruling not only made same-sex marriage legal across the country but also opened up a number of work benefits that did not exist for same-sex couples in some states.

The Civil Rights Act

The law with the most sweeping changes, of course, was the Civil Rights Act of 1964, which was designed to eliminate discrimination. Ethnic minority group members and White women were able to enter professions they never believed they could enter. However, during the 1980s, the Supreme Court handed down some decisions that effectively wiped out advances already gained through the Civil Right Act. For example, the court's ruling made it difficult for plaintiffs to receive monetary compensation for discrimination, because the burden of proof was placed upon them to prove employer discrimination. Under the 1991 Civil Rights Act, the plaintiff is entitled to monetary damages for pain and suffering and economic loss resulting from the discriminatory acts of the defendant, which was previously not allowed even if the defendant was determined to have discriminated against the plaintiff.

Affirmative Action

The original Civil Rights Act in 1964 led to the development of Affirmative Action, a policy that sought to redress past discrimination through active equal opportunity measures. Under Affirmative Action, for instance, companies actively began recruiting women into jobs traditionally only held by men, such as jobs in engineering. Today, however, Affirmative Action faces the same uphill battle once faced by the Civil Rights Act. The objections to Affirmative Action range from the accusation that it is reverse discrimination to the claim that Affirmative Action is psychologically harmful. While claims of reverse discrimination may come from traditionally privileged populations, the psychological harm theory is focused on the beneficiaries of Affirmative Action. The claim posits that these beneficiaries may believe that others will "question their competence...which would then lower self-esteem" (Truax et al., 1998, p.171). Steele (1991) assumed that an individual's hiring into a job via Affirmative Action would result in that individual feeling stigmatized. This assumption has not held up under research. Several studies (Ayers, 1992; Taylor, 1994; Truax et al., 1998) found that Affirmative Action hiring created "positive rather than negative effects for one minority group" (Truax et al., 1998, p. 178) and that any stigma was not related specifically to Affirmative Action but public opinion of Affirmative Action hires. In fact, Gallup (1995) reported that fewer than 30 percent of the ethnic minority respondents polled seemed to be worried about any perceived negative consequences of being hired through Affirmative Action. Therefore, it seems that shame and embarrassment are not the emotions attached to being hired through Affirmative Action.

However helpful Affirmative Action has been, its effects have not reached all marginalized groups. Research shows that the population that has benefitted most from Affirmative Action is White women (Crenshaw, 2006; Hall, 2015). Few poor ethnic minorities have been able to cross the cultural divide of race and poverty. White women are most likely to be acculturated to the middle-class societal structure, and as such they are more readily accepted by institutions of higher education, business, and industry. In addition, middle-class White women have at their disposal more resources that contribute positively to their career aspirations and educational advances. Additional remedies are needed to cover the other marginalized groups more effectively.

The Americans with Disabilities Act

Affirmative Action also has not been as helpful as it might have been for individuals with disabilities, which is why the Americans with Disabilities Act (ADA) was created. The ADA was a major political feat for people with disabilities. It was passed in 1990 and took effect in 1992. The goal of the act was to eliminate hiring discrimination against people with disabilities in both private companies and government. It is important to note that while a person seeking treatment for drug and alcohol use is covered under the ADA, active drug use is not. In addition, the ADA prohibits discrimination in all other areas of employment, such as insurance coverage and other benefits. Finally, the ADA requires not only employers but also state and local governments to make accessible transportation available.

Gay, Lesbian, Bisexual, and Transgender Rights

The Civil Rights Acts of 1964 and 1991 and Affirmative Action at first did not protect gays, lesbians, bisexual or transgendered individuals from discrimination of any sort. However, during the Clinton administration, the President issued an Executive Order regarding the treatment of federal employees, which stated that they would no longer be discriminated based on sexual orientation. While this was not a law and offered no new expressed civil rights to gays and lesbians, the order set a precedent for considering sexual orientation in future antidiscrimination policies. In a ground-breaking decision on June 15, 2020, the Supreme Court of the United States, in a decision on *Bostock v. Clayton County, GA*, found that the civil rights acts do indeed apply to sexual orientation and transgender status (Totenberg, 2020).

In 1994, however, an official United States policy on military service by gays, bisexuals, and lesbians, instituted by the Clinton Administration known as "Don't Ask, Don't Tell" (DADT) was implemented and lasted until September 20, 2011. Though the intent was to make a safer workplace for members of the LGBT community by prohibiting harassment or discrimination based on sexual orientation, it barred openly gay, lesbian, or bisexual individuals from joining the military. Reversing the practice of discharging military members of this already marginalized community, "Don't Ask, Don't Tell" was later repealed in 2010 (Alford & Lee, 2016). In 2017, President Trump noted his desire to ban transgendered individuals from serving in the Armed Forces (Coon, Neira, & Lau, 2018). In 2019, the Supreme Court of the United States allowed President Trump to restrict transgender people from joining the military. This means that under the Trump Administration, individuals who are transgendered are being barred from military service or receiving scholarships on college campuses to join the military. In January 2021, President Biden reversed this policy by issuing an executive order that allowed transgender individuals to join and stay in the military.

Interestingly, gay White males enjoy the highest incomes of any of the marginalized groups, but because of the limits on discrimination laws, their incomes may come at the price of being closeted to their colleagues and superiors in the workplace. Discrimination against gay, lesbian, bisexual, and transgender populations is now illegal in many cases. In September of 1996, the United States federal law known as the Defense of Marriage Act (DOMA) was enacted. This law viewed marriage as between a man and a woman, allowing states to refuse to recognize same-sex marriage. Later, in June 2015, this law was struck down and amended, citing it unconstitutional, by the Supreme Court of the United States, to make same-sex marriage legal (Crumlish, 2015).

Women's Rights

Women of all races were slotted to benefit from the Equal Pay Act of 1963. It provided that individuals doing the same job for the same company would earn the same amount of money. Under this legislation, employers are not allowed to reduce the pay of men in order to comply with the law. Even with this law in place, however, women are still earning less than men for the same work (Herlihy & Watson, 2006). A direct response to this type of discrimination and "to the 2007 U.S. Supreme Court's infamous decision to side with Goodyear over Lilly Ledbetter in her claim of gender pay discrimination" (p. 80) is what prompted the Lilly Ledbetter Fair Pay Act of 2009 to be enacted (Gring-Pemble & Chen, 2018). Apparently some employers seem to have circumvented this legislation since wage disparities between men and women still exist.

Another law that has benefitted working women was Title VII of the Civil Rights Act of 1964, which stated in one of its provisions that sexual harassment is a form of discrimination, and that an employer cannot fire or demote an employee who sues due to the violation of this law. This allowance of discrimination to occur against women among some employers led to the #MeToo Movement, which spread virally on social media in October 2017 as a hashtag to demonstrate the prevalence of sexual harassment, particularly in the workplace.

Additionally, positive legislative acts that have benefitted both female and male workers are the Pregnancy Discrimination Act of 1978 (PDA) and the Family and Medical Leave Act of 1993 (FMLA). The PDA amended the Civil Rights Act of 1964 to prohibit sex discrimination on the basis of pregnancy. The Pregnancy Discrimination Act of 1978 prohibits employment discrimination against female workers who intend to become pregnant, including discrimination in hiring, failure to promote, and wrongful termination. FMLA made it possible for individuals to take time off from work to provide for their families without losing their jobs. The act does not require that employees be paid for the time off, but there is a guarantee that the employee may return to his or her job after taking the leave. These pieces of legislation are especially helpful for single parents (overwhelmingly female, and overrepresented in ethnic minority groups). Both the Pregnancy Discrimination Act and Family Medical Leave Act are first steps toward a better lifestyle for workers.

The Welfare Reform Bill

On the negative side of the coin, the Welfare Reform Bill of 1996 made sweeping changes to the welfare system and impacted immigrants negatively. Not only did it cut off assistance for illegal immigrants, but it also eliminated benefits for legal immigrants. Those who have legally immigrated to the United States can no longer receive food stamps, nor do they receive supplemental social security benefits if they are disabled. It is legislation that seems to put undue hardship on the poor immigrants of this country. So far, Congress has not renewed the Welfare Reform bill, but neither has it terminated the bill's practices. The renewal is, at this writing, still being delayed in Congress.

Poverty

Along with legislation affecting ethnic minorities and other groups who are oppressed, multiculturally responsible career professionals are aware of another major political issue in American society today: poverty.

In 1999, 12.4 percent of the U.S. population lived at or below the poverty line. Ethnic minority groups have continued to be overrepresented among the poor. The tendency in the past was for writers and researchers to combine race/ethnicity and poverty in their findings. Unfortunately, by collapsing these categories precious data has been lost at best, and the worst-case scenario is that inaccurate assumptions have been made based on the results of this flawed methodology. Even though the majority of ethnic minority families are not classified as poor, their numbers among the poor, in general, are far greater than the 7.3 percent of Whites living in poverty in 2019 (Semega, Kollar, Shrider, & Creamer, 2020). Almost 25.7 percent of Native Americans/Alaska Natives live at or below the poverty line as well as 18.8 percent of African Americans, 15.7 percent of Latinos and Latinas, and 7.3 percent of Asian Americans.

Many people who are poor have jobs and this has become such a prevalent phenomenon that a term has been coined to describe these individuals—the working poor (Rank, 2000). People who are poor, regardless of race, present a dilemma for the career professional. Individuals living in poverty often do not see the relevance of career counseling, because their focus is on making enough money to pay for food, clothing, and shelter. Making career choices also becomes irrelevant to those who have limited education and limited prospects for increasing their educational level. Clients who come from generations of people living in poverty may be particularly wary of counselors, who they believe may look down on them and their lifestyle. It is unlikely that poor workers would seek career counseling on their own. They are more likely to become clients if they have lost their jobs, become part of the welfare to work initiative, or experienced some other time-sensitive program. If a working poor client is also struggling to survive, dealing with an employer's discriminatory policies, completing demeaning job duties, or facing problems either of intolerance or invisibility from co-workers, the counseling problems are magnified.

Similarly, clients who are unemployed encounter multiple problems. While unemployment affects all socioeconomic levels, it is more likely to result in homelessness when it occurs to those who are already poor. In 2019, although unemployment among African Americans was a record low of 5.5%, it was still higher than that of Latinos/as at 4.2% and higher still from the overall average of 3.5% (Bureau of Labor Statistics, 2020). Besides needing to find a job, clients who are unemployed are more likely angry, grieving, ashamed, and doubtful of their own abilities (Evans, 2006).

Poor and unemployed clients may view counseling with desperation (a last chance) or as too little too late. It is also likely that after a long relationship with the bureaucracy, they will have little faith in their employment counselor's ability to help them with their problems. The client may take one look at his or her middle-class counselor and determine that the counselor would have no earthly idea how to help. The counselor may be resented if change does not happen quickly or if the counselor does not take time to establish credibility and trustworthiness. Therefore, counselors need to be aware not only of the existence of and ramifications of poverty, but also of community resources and information.

Final Thoughts about Client Worldview

Because career professionals serve as a gateway to a client's livelihood and lifestyle, awareness of the client's worldview is imperative because awareness can increase the length of time a client stays in counseling, drawing greater benefit from the process. Oppression has had a detrimental effect on ethnic minorities, White women, gays, lesbians, bisexuals, transgendered persons, and people with disabilities. Because of oppression, counselors who may simply desire to help others, may be resented and treated as the enemy. It is really important for counselors to be prepared for any negative reactions that their clients may have. Rather than taking these reactions personally, culturally competent career professionals cope with such responses. Knowledge of the client's cultural history can go a long way in understanding client reactions to the dominant culture and may also increase the counselor's empathy toward the client's cultural group. Client racial/cultural identity status helps the counselor understand more about how to manage the counseling relationship as does the client's view of his or her locus of control and locus of responsibility. Finally, knowledge of the effects of poverty and socio-political oppression helps the career counselor encourage proactive measures in the client and commit to doing more herself or himself.

All the above factors translate into a counselor's genuine interest in the client's success and well-being. When a counselor is genuinely interested in his or her clients, the clients will know and they are likely to respond positively to the counselor and the counseling process.

REVIEW/REFLECTION QUESTIONS

1. A client who is culturally different from you is being openly hostile when you try to help her define her particular career problem. Record your reactions to the following in your notebook:
   a. your feelings regarding the treatment the client is giving you
   b. strategies you can use to depersonalize the client's attack
   c. how you would respond to such a client.

2. Affirmative Action, the ADA, and the Pay Equity legislation affect career counseling more than any other field of counseling. Write a brief reaction paper that reflects your attitudes and beliefs about these laws and policies. Also, discuss how your attitudes may affect your work with clients protected by these practices.

3. The knowledge of the career development history of culturally diverse clients is stressed in the chapter. It is a step that many counselors like to skip. How should you go about motivating yourself to explore the work histories of the client populations you serve or will serve.

4. The dominant middle-class perspective on work and getting ahead can be a detriment when working with clients who have only known poverty. It may one of the most difficult differences for career professionals to understand. What five strategies could be helpful in understanding a life of poverty?

References

Alford, B., & Lee, S. J. (2016). Toward complete inclusion: Lesbian, gay, bisexual, and transgender military service members after repeal of don't ask, don't tell. *Social Work, 61*(3), 257. https://doi.org/10.1093/sw/sww033

Arredondo, P., Toporek, R., Brown, S. P., Jones, J., Locke, D.C., Sanchez, J., & Stadler, H. (1996). Operationalization of the multicultural counseling competencies. *Journal of Multicultural Counseling and Development, 24*, 42-78.

Ayers, L. (1992). Perceptions of affirmative action among its beneficiaries. *Social Justice Research, 5*, 223-238.

Baron, R. S., Burgess, M. L., & Kao, C. F. (1991). Detecting and labeling prejudice: Do female perpetrators go undetected? *Personality and Social Psychology Bulletin, 17*, 115-123.

BlackPast. (2007, October 15). *(1964) Malcolm X's Speech at the Founding Rally of the Organization of Afro-American Unity.* Retrieved from https://www.blackpast.org/african-american-history/speeches-african-american-history/1964-malcolm-x-s-speech-founding-rally-organization-afro-american-unity/

Buchtel, E. E. (2014). Cultural sensitivity or cultural stereotyping? Positive and negative effects of a cultural psychology class. *International Journal of Intercultural Relations, 39*(3), 40-52.

Bureau of Labor Statistics. (2020). TEC: The economic daily. Retrieved from https://www.bls.gov/opub/ted/2020/unemployment-rates-in-15-states-were-lower-than-the-3-point-5-percent-u-s-rate-in-december-2019.htm

Coleman, H. L. K., Wampold, B. E., & Casali, S. L. (1995). Ethnic minorities' ratings of ethnically similar and European American counselors: A meta-analysis. *Journal of Counseling Psychology, 42*, 55-64.

Coon, D., Neira, P. M., & Lau, B. D. (2018). Threats to United States fully reviewed and strategic plan for integration of transgender military members into the armed forces. *American Journal of Public Health, 108*(7), 892.

Crenshaw, K. W. (2006). Framing affirmative action. *Michigan Law Review First Impressions, 105,* 123-133. Retrieved from http://repository.law.umich.edu/mlr_fi/vol105/iss1/4

Crumlish, J. P. (2015, January/February). The end of the defense of marriage act: The tax status of legally married same-sex couples. *Value Examiner,* 6–10.

Evans, K. M. (2006). Career counseling with couples and families. In D. Capuzzi & M. Staufer (Eds.), *Career and Life Style Planning Theory and Application* (pp. 336-359). Boston: Pearson Education, Inc.

Gallup. (July, 1995). *Gallup Poll Monthly, 358,* 34-61.

Gring-Pemble, L., & Chen, C. W. (2018). Patriarchy prevails: A feminist rhetorical analysis of equal pay discourses. *Women and Language, 41*(2), 79–103.

Hall, P. D. (2015). White fragility and affirmative action. *The Journal of Race and Policy, 12*(2), 7.

Helms, J. E. (1990). *Black and White racial identity: Theory, research, and practice.* New York: Greenwood Press.

Helms, J. E., & Cook, D. A. (1999). *Using race and culture in counseling and psychotherapy: Theory and process.* Boston: Allyn and Bacon.

Herlihy, B. R., & Watson, Z. P. (2006). Gender issues in career counseling. In D. Capuzzi & M. Staufer (Eds.), *Career and Life Style Planning Theory and Application* (pp. 363-385). Boston: Pearson Education, Inc.

McAuliffe, G., Kim, B. S. K., & Park, Y. S. (2013). Ethnicity. In G. McAuliffe (Ed.), *Culturally alert counseling: A comprehensive introduction* (2nd ed., pp. 75-88). Thousand Oaks, CA: Sage Publications.

Parham, T. A., & Brown, S. (2003). Therapeutic approaches with African American populations. In F. D. Harper, & J. McFadden (Eds.), *Culture and Counseling: New Approaches* (pp. 81-98). Needham Heights, MA: Allyn & Bacon.

Peralta, E. (2013, June, 26). Court overturns DOMA, sidesteps broad gay marriage ruling. *NPR News.* https://www.npr.org/sections/thetwo-way/2013/06/26/195857796/supreme-court-strikes-down-defense-of-marriage-act

Rank, M. R. (2000). Poverty and hardship in families. In D. H. Demo, K. R. Allen & M.A. Fine (Eds.), *Handbook of family diversity* (pp. 293-315). New York: Oxford University Press.

Ridley, C. R. (1995). *Overcoming unintentional racism in counseling and therapy: A practitioner's guide to intentional intervention.* Thousand Oaks, CA: Sage Publications.

Semega, J., Kollar, M., Shrider, E.A., & Creamer, J. F. (2020). *U.S. Census Bureau, Current Population Reports, P60-270, Income and Poverty in the United States: 2019,* Washington, DC: U.S. Government Publishing Office.

Steele, S. (1991). *The content of our character.* New York: St. Martin's Press.

Sue, D. W., & Sue, D. (2003). *Counseling the culturally different.* New York: John Wiley & Sons, Inc.

Swim, J. K., Cohen, L. L., & Hyers, L. L. (1998). Experiencing everyday prejudice and discrimination. In J. K. Swim & C. Stangor (Eds.), *Prejudice: The target's perspective* (pp. 38-61). San Diego: Academic Press.

Taylor, M. E. (1994). Affirmative action: Insights from social psychological and organizational research. *Basic and Applied Social Psychology, 15,* 1-21.

Totenberg, N. (2020, June 15). Supreme court delivers major victory to LGBTQ employees. *NPR.* https://www.npr.org/2020/06/15/863498848/supreme-court-delivers-major-victory-to-lgbtq-employees

Truax, K., Cordova, D. I., Wood, A., Wright, E., & Crosby, F. (1998). Undermined? Affirmative action from the target's point of view. In J. K. Swim, & C. Stangor (Eds.), *Prejudice: The target's perspective* (pp. 172-188). San Diego, CA: Academic Press.

Whaley, A. L. (2001). Cultural mistrust and mental health services for African Americans: A review and meta-analysis. *Counseling Psychologist, 29,* 513-521.

Awareness of Your Client's Worldview

CHAPTER 5

Using Career Development Theories

Theories provide career professionals with a guide to follow when they assist clients; however, to be useful in the real world, a theory has to pass certain tests. One of the tests of the effectiveness of a counseling theory is whether the theory is comprehensive. That is, effective theories have the capability of being applied to diverse clients regardless of their racial/cultural background, ability status, sexuality, or religion. The modernist or traditional career theories based on the scientific method tend to fall short of comprehensiveness, because they describe the behaviors of a specific group of people (typically White males) rather than a broad range of people. As Gottfredson (1986) and Leong and Brown (1995) have both said, "there is yet to appear a detailed description and explanation of how political, social, economic, and cultural conditions affect individuals and their career choice behavior" (Leong & Brown, 1995, p.143). Picking up from where Gottfredson, Leong and Brown left off, Neville, Gysbers, Heppner, and Johnston (1998) identified five main problems with the modernist career development theories.

1. They place great significance on the individual without mention of others involved in the career decision-making process;
2. They assume that clients are at least at a middle-class socioeconomic level and can therefore afford to take advantage of training opportunities;
3. They assume that work is freely available for those who want it;
4. They assume that work is of equal importance in everyone's life;
5. They depend on linear and objective reasoning.

As alluded to above, the most troubling shortcoming of the modernist career development theories is that despite extensive research on career development that has accompanied these theories, little evidence exists that supports the appropriateness of these theories for all groups of people (Leong, 1995). In some studies, the research has supported the cross-cultural nature of the theory, while in other studies the results have been either contradictory or inconclusive. In fact, career development texts commonly mention that modernist career development theories are suspect when applied to ethnic minority populations and other marginalized groups. Career development theorists themselves acknowledge the importance of considering matters not under the control of clients, such as oppression and socioeconomic factors, and more recent theories tend to allow for the strong impact societal restrictions may have on the career choices and advancement of many individuals.

In this chapter, several modernist career theories still widely used today are presented, followed by some suggestions for adapting these theories to multicultural populations. Also covered are more multiculturally inclusive theories. The chapter will conclude with two career counseling models that were designed to provide guidelines for practice with diverse populations.

Modernist Career Development Theories

Most of the modernist career development theories fall short of taking into consideration political, social, economic, and cultural factors that affect clients from diverse, marginalized populations. The modernist theories covered in this chapter include Parsons' trait and factory theory, Super's career development theory, and Holland's personality types and environments theory.

Frank Parsons' Trait and Factor Theory

No discussion of career development theory would be complete without reference to trait and factor theory. It was founded on the propositions of Frank Parsons in 1909. The essence of the theory is that it posits that individuals possess measurable traits and abilities that can be matched with occupational requirements. When the match is appropriate, the result is a life of occupational satisfaction and productivity for an individual (Brown, 1984; Herr, Cramer, & Niles, 2004).

In its early days, traditional trait and factor counseling extensively utilized paper and pencil inventories to assess client interests, values, personality, aptitudes, and abilities (Sharf, 2002). Upon completion of the inventories, clients would have objective information about their traits, which they could compare with job specifications.

As simple and useful as trait and factor inventories sound, multicultural theorists have criticized trait and factor theory's overdependence on measurement methods that do not take into consideration norms (standard patterns of behavior) for culturally different groups. Rather, only the norms of the dominant White, middle-class, male, heterosexual group are taken into consideration (Fouad, 1993). Because of the lack of norms for diverse groups in trait and factor theory, the theory forces a career professional to compare a culturally different client to a set of norms that may not apply. Fouad therefore suggests that until norms for culturally different clients are developed, it is important for career professionals to use caution. Some career test publishers are becoming more responsive to this problem. For example, the 1994 revision of the Strong Interest Inventory considered race and ethnicity for the first time by reporting the race and ethnicity of the comparison groups (Harmon, Hansen, Borgen, & Hammer, 1994).

Fouad (1993) has pointed out another problem with trait and factor theory as it relates to culturally different populations. The problem is the use of language in trait and factor testing. Career professionals need to always ask, "Is the test written in a language most appropriate for the testee?" If not, then career professionals are advised to seriously consider whether the test should be administered.

In addition, Prince, Uemura, Chao, and Gonzalez (1991) have suggested that some cultural groups do not benefit from the introspective behaviors required in trait and factor inventories, and therefore it would be inappropriate to administer these tests to these clients.

Finally, Leong and Serafica (2001) have questioned whether the traits that have been determined by trait and factor testing to fit certain occupations are the same for all racial groups. Leong and Serafica suggest that the traits that are considered important for European American men to perform a particular job well might be considered inappropriate for Latinos and Latinas or White women. For example, competitiveness in women in the same occupation that men are competitive in is still looked upon negatively. Or there may be separate criteria to enter an occupation for ethnic minorities and other marginalized groups—criteria that cannot be determined through objective testing. Because of discrimination and oppression, even if clients have the stated traits needed for the job, they may not be satisfied and happy in the career because of unspoken criteria.

In trait and factor counseling, clients are the ones who must find information about careers, not career professionals, which means clients must not only understand how the job-finding process works, but also understand the specific abilities they possess, and the specific responsibilities various jobs entail. The creation of the O*NET database has made this process much easier than it used to be. Clients can enter O*NET from the Department of Labor's website and access the worker attributes and job characteristics by clicking a link (http://online.onetcenter.org). After clients receive information about their traits, they need to match their traits with the occupations that require those traits. Matching (that is helping individuals find fitting careers) is the ultimate goal of all career counseling. Therefore, trait and factor theory must take into consideration culturally different clients, if career professionals are to be able to use trait and factor theory to help clients locate work.

Trait and factor theory has, of course, evolved since 1909. Today, trait and factor career professionals are less likely to rely only on test scores to predict career choices, and they are more likely to consider other factors that contribute to client decision making. Trait and factor approaches such as the Person/Environment Fit is an example of this type of evolution. Other adaptations of trait and factor theory will be discussed next.

Adapting trait and factor theory for diverse clients. In 2001, Leong and

Serafica devised a list of "cultural accommodations" that are important to implement to extend trait and factor theory to help ethnic minority and other marginalized clients. These cultural accommodations consist of a three-step process:

1. Identifying the cultural gaps or cultural blind spots of the theory
2. Selecting current culturally specific concepts and models from cross-cultural and ethnic minority psychology to fill in the gaps and adapt the theory for racial/cultural minorities
3. Testing the culturally adapted theory to determine whether or not it has incremental validity above and beyond the culturally unadapted theory. (Leong & Serafica, 2001, p. 185)

As stated previously, what is missing in the trait and factor theory is both an understanding that certain traits desirable for one group may not be as desirable for other groups, and a realization that there is no way to determine test bias if test publishers do not include normative samples for ethnic minority and other marginalized groups in their reports.

In adapting trait and factor theory to work more appropriately for ethnic minority and other marginalized groups, the concept of cultural encapsulation should be kept in mind. The assumption that what is good for one group is good for all groups is cultural encapsulation. Therefore, career professionals need to forewarn their clients that information on traits that particular occupations require may in fact differ from one racial group to another. In addition, career professionals and clients need to do the research to find out the cultural biases that exist toward the client's group within a particular profession.

Career professionals themselves will demonstrate that they are culturally encapsulated if they use tests that are based on norms for one group without regard to the possibility that the norms of the tests may not be applicable to other groups. Culturally competent career professionals, therefore, always determine if the tests they use are culturally appropriate. In summary, the trait and factor theory may be useful as it exists if career professionals are extremely cautious about using tests that do not report norms for culturally different groups or that do not have a representative sample of those groups. Failing that, career professionals need to be willing and able to collect and use their own data to create local norms for tests that are culturally encapsulated.

Theory adaptation exercise. In this section we have mentioned the shortcomings of the trait and factor theory as it applies to culturally different clients. Using Leong and Serafica's guidelines, choose a culturally different group and outline in your notebook how you would adapt the trait and factor theory to work with individuals from that particular group.

Donald Super's Career Development Theory

Perhaps the most comprehensive, well-researched career counseling theory continues to be the career development theory of Donald Super (Herr, Cramer & Niles, 2004). In his theory, Super (1957) describes the process individuals employ to learn about, gain, maintain, and leave their careers. Super explains that the primary purpose for choosing a career is fulfillment of one's self-concept. Factors that influence the fulfillment of self-concept are life span and life space, which will be discussed in more detail next.

Fulfillment of self-concept. Super (1957) originally proposed that each occupation defines a unique role for its occupants. That occupation is chosen on the basis of perceived compatibility of that role with the individual's self-concept. The self-concept may be defined as the perception individuals have of themselves combined with how others perceive them. Unfortunately, evidence that Super's theory is applicable to diverse groups has been elusive. The fulfillment of self-concept theory has been questioned in regard to ethnic minorities and other marginalized groups because discrimination and poverty may prohibit individuals from fulfilling their self-concepts through work. Except for the fact that work provides the income for life's necessities, work is not a salient aspect of many marginalized individuals' lives (Murray et al., 2002).

Life span. The "life span" segment of the theory involves career maturity, or an individual's readiness to move through the stages of career development based on his or her age. Super's (1957) Career Pattern Study pinpointed these stages of career development as growth, exploration, establishment, maintenance, and disengagement. In the growth stage, a person develops a sense of self and identity and gains an understanding of the world of work. During the exploration stage, an individual crystallizes and implements a career choice. In the establishment stage, an individual stabilizes, consolidates, and moves up the career ladder. During the maintenance stage, the individual holds on to his or her place in the organization by updating skills or reinventing the career to fit his or her life better. Finally, in the disengagement stage, the individual plan for retirement, reduces pace and/or workload, and eventually engages in full-time leisure activities.

Originally, Super (1957) presented these stages as age-specific, with growth ending at age fourteen and maintenance ending at age sixty-four. In subsequent discussions of his theory, Super (1990) responded to one of the major changes that had occurred in society since he originally mapped out the theory—that individuals no longer stay in the same careers their entire lives, as was once common. Super came to recognize that when changing careers, individuals go through much the same process as they did when they chose their first career, and that the career development process continues in cycles throughout a person's lifetime. To adjust his theory accordingly, he called the initial career choice a maxi-cycle and subsequent career changes mini-cycles.

The multicultural criticisms of Super's concept of career maturity are based on findings that career maturity correlates with socioeconomic status (Smith, 1983). Because career maturity depends on career information and because those in poverty have limited access to career information, the concept of career maturity does not easily translate to this population. Further, the overrepresentation of ethnic minority group members among the poor indicates that career maturity is not applicable to many members of marginalized cultures either. Research will need to be conducted to determine just what the career development stages are for ethnic minorities and those living in poverty. The best approach to such research would be a longitudinal (over time) approach.

Life space. The life space segment of Super's theory involves the various roles people play in their own lives (for instance the roles of parent, child, student, worker, citizen, homemaker, leisure, and so forth). The importance or salience an individual places on each of these roles constitutes the individual's life structure (Super, Savickas, & Super, 1996). As opposed to the life span segment of Super's theory, the life space segment of the theory is readily adaptable to ethnic minority and other marginalized groups, because it takes into account the individual's perception of his or her world, and it allows for the differential application of the importance of roles according to the individual's cultural background.

Adapting Super's career development theory for diverse clients. As well-known and popular as Super's (1957; 1990) theory is, he was always open to new research and constructive criticism. Super was able to adapt a great many facets of his theory to incorporate the lifestyles of groups who were not as privileged as those representing his original research subject pool. Late in his career, Super (1990) added what he termed the "archway model" to his theory, where he integrated socioeconomic, environmental, and individual factors, which interact and continue the career development process. (Murray et al., 2002; Super, 1990, 1994). Super also added the notion that all people may not fulfill their self-concepts through their work. Unfortunately, Super stopped short of incorporating the developmental influences of gender, race, sexuality, and ability status on occupational behavior (Leong & Brown, 1995; Leong & Serfica, 2001).

Adapting Super's self-concept segment. Since Super revised the self-concept theory, it more closely fits with marginalized groups, however, this revision needs to be emphasized when working with them. Career professionals can facilitate this process by helping clients explore their self-concept without reference to their work. Questions that might be asked of a client include "What do you think are your best qualities?"; "What are your strongest skills?"; "What are the things you have done that you are most proud of?"; and "Where are you most likely to use these qualities and skills?" If "work" is not among the responses, then explore with the client how important it is to use these qualities in their work.

Adapting Super's life span segment. While culture, socioeconomic status, discrimination, and social policies make it difficult to apply the life span concept to marginalized populations, Sharf (2006) suggests a way of understanding how it may work by cross referencing life span to cultural identity. Cultural identity was covered in Chapter 2 of this text. In his model, Sharf discusses how clients' cultural identity attitudes (e.g., conformity attitudes are self-depreciating and group depreciating) make exploration difficult. It may be difficult to find a career that clients feel they are qualified for. By combining the two concepts (life span and cultural identity), career professionals will have a greater appreciation of the challenges they may face when taking clients through the career development stages.

Occtalk and Psychtalk Exercise. In early discussions of Super's theory, Starishevsky and Matlin (1963) coined phrases to understand how self-concept and career choice were connected. They suggested that people use psychological terms to convey their self-concepts. For example, they will say that they are smart, athletic, brave, artistic. They called this "psychtalk." "Occtalk" was used when people want to convey these same attributes about themselves but using occupations to do so. Rather than say, "I am smart," they may choose an occupation that they believe requires a great deal of intelligence, for example, "I want to be an astrophysicist." Explore your own self-concept using psychtalk and occtalk in the following activity as if you were the career client.

Take a sheet of paper and fold it in half for two vertical columns. In the first column, list five careers that you are considering, leave the second column blank for now. Turn the paper over and in the first column list five careers that tend to be traditional for a cultural group of your choice. These occupations in the first columns are the "occtalk" in this exercise. Turn the paper over to your own list of careers and in the second column, next to the first career you listed, think of, and then record, the psychtalk that goes with that field. For example, 'counselor' might be the occtalk and 'empathic' might be the psychtalk. Complete a psychtalk term for each of the careers you listed on both sides of the page.

This exercise was designed to help you look at careers in terms of your own self-concept and to get an understanding about why certain cultural groups choose the careers they enter. It also might help you, or your culturally different clients answer the question, "what does my choice of a career say about who I am?"

John Holland's Career Theory of Personality Types and Environments

Holland (1966, 1985, 1992, 1997) developed one of the most popular career theories in use today that employs personality types and environments. Compared to the complexity of Super's model, Holland's theory is clear and parsimonious. Essentially, Holland outlines six personality types and six work environments. The six environments are

1. *The Realistic Environment*: requires physical strength and agility, and includes many outdoor types of careers
2. *The Investigative Environment*: requires dealing with ideas and research
3. *The Artistic Environment*: requires creativity and independence
4. *The Social Environment*: involves helping people with their problems
5. *The Enterprising Environment*: involves influencing people
6. *The Conventional Environment*: requires attention to detail and organization.

The six personality types parallel the environments, and so in Holland's theory, people's personalities can be broken into six types: those who are realistic, investigative, artistic, social, enterprising, and conventional (RIASEC). Holland theorizes that individuals are most drawn to the work environments that best match their personalities. For example, people who are drawn to careers in the enterprising environment enjoy using skills of persuasion to influence others in their personal lives.

To support this theory, Holland (1985, 1992) has developed two popular career assessment instruments, the Vocational Preference Inventory (VPI) and the Self-Directed Search (SDS). Each of these generates an occupational code, which is a combination of the six personality/environments. Individuals use the code to search for occupations with the same code. For example, the results of the SDS may yield an occupational code of Social, Artistic, and Enterprising (SAE). The client would then search for occupations that fall under SAE and learn more about those occupations. Holland codes are also used for the Strong Interest Inventory, which is one of the most widely used career assessment instruments to date.

Two major problems with using Holland's theory with groups who are oppressed by society are (1) the occupations reflect career stereotypes in terms of gender and ethnicity and (2) the theory fails to address the impact of race, gender, socioeconomic status, sexual orientation, and ability status. The theory assumes that matching personality with environment is sufficient for clients to locate appropriate jobs (Betz & Fitzgerald, 1987; Carter & Swanson, 1990; Fouad & Kantamneni, 2010).

Research has shown that diverse groups tend to score higher on occupations that are traditional or stereotypic for their groups. These are occupations where members of marginalized groups can be found in large numbers and where discrimination against them is minimized. Most of these occupations are lower in prestige and income than occupations populated by White men. For example, women typically score higher on the Social and Conventional codes, and less acculturated Asian Americans score high on Realistic and Investigative codes. Career professionals attempt to assist clients by broadening their ideas about suitable careers. With Holland's theory, rather than generating fresh career ideas for clients to consider, the same traditional fields emerge as possibilities.

In response to the criticism that his theory neglects cultural issues such as race, gender, socioeconomic status, sexual orientation, and ability status, Holland (1997) states that he does not need to address these issues because they are reflected in people's personalities, which are determined by taking the VPI or SDS. Recent studies that have employed Holland's interest inventories, as well as studies that investigate the validity of his theory, have revealed that the theory does, in fact, represent the interests of African Americans, Mexican Americans, Asian Americans, Native Americans, and European Americans (Day, Rounds & Swaney, 1998; Sharf, 2002). However, more study is needed before conclusions can be reached. The problem for multicultural clients is not whether Holland's inventories measure diverse populations correctly. Rather, the problem is whether the messages this theory's applied results send to the client are appropriate. Even though a theory represents the reality of the society, it does not mean that reality is what is desired. The failure of Holland's theory to recognize the impact that continued oppression may have upon one's ability to pursue a career is a major flaw in the theory and one that will need to be addressed to use his theory with diverse populations (Leong, 1995).

Adapting Holland's theory for diverse clients. Although Holland's theory seems to adequately predict career choice for ethnic minority groups, it fails to offer a sufficiently wide range of career opportunities for people from marginalized groups because it primarily focuses on stereotypic careers (Fouad, 2002). The multicultural competencies recommend that counselors consider how sociopolitical influences and pervasive institutional oppression impact individuals. In addition, the NCDA Code of Ethics in Section A speaks to the need for adapting theories by stating that career professionals (a) advocate for their clients in regard to barriers and obstacles to their clients' wellbeing (b) explain the nature of career services and, most important, (c) avoid harming the client (NCDA, 2015). With these guidelines in mind, Holland's theory could be adapted to explore how the socialization process discourages women, ethnic minorities, gays, lesbians, bisexuals, and people with disabilities to pursue certain careers. Strategies are also needed to separate the skills involved in certain careers from the stereotypical images of these careers. For example, hand/eye coordination is needed for several fields but when those skills are used by a car mechanic, they are often viewed as a man's job. Helping children develop these abilities regardless of gender will pave the way for plenty of skilled workers to enter the workforce for whatever career they want to enter. If we continue to think of such skills as "male" skills, as Holland admitted was true of his theory (Holland, 1997) because it reflects our society's sex-based career values, we have already lost half the potential workers in those fields. The following story from an elementary school counselor, illustrates the importance of overcoming occupational stereotyping.

I was taking a course in techniques of career counseling, and one evening we discussed different strategies to overcome occupational stereotypes. I decided to do something different with my career day in the elementary school where I work. I contacted different professional organizations and told them I wanted a speaker who would be considered nontraditional for the field. For example, I called the fire fighters union and told them that I needed a female speaker. I got some really positive reactions from most of the people I contacted. I was able to find several people who were working in nontraditional fields (a male nurse, a woman carpenter, a male secretary, a female pilot). We played a game with the children on career day. Each child had a set of cards with the career names written on them, and the children put their own names on the backs of the cards. Our visitors introduced themselves and only gave brief clues as to what their professions were. The children then went to the tables where the visitors sat and would give each visitor the career card, they thought represented that person's career. The child who got the most careers correct won a prize. After the prize was given, we talked as a class a little about why the children placed the cards where they did. It was a very enlightening experience in debunking occupational stereotypes.

The Holland code exercise using card sort. In this exercise you may use a commercial card sort kit or you can create the cards yourself. If you choose to do it yourself, print just the title of the occupation on one side of the card and a brief description of the occupation on the other side. You will also need cards with the following printed on one side: Strong Interest, Moderate Interest, Neither Interested or Not Interested, Moderately Disinterested, and Strong Disinterest.

Once you have the cards ready, you will need to get a volunteer to act as the client. Have the client sort the occupational cards into the five categories. After explaining the Holland codes to the client, pick the Moderately Disinterested cards first (address the Strong Disinterest cards after you finish with moderate cards). Ask the client:

- Where in the Holland code do you think this career would fall? Why?

- What about this career don't you like?
- Do you know anyone in this field? If so, does this person resemble you or anyone in your cultural group (gender, ability status, sexuality, religion)?
- Depending on the client's answer to the question above--Do you know why people like you go into this field (or do not go into this field)?
- What do you think the work would be like in this field? If the client does not know what the work will be like, then it is a good field for the client to investigate.

This activity is an informal way to assess the client's interest in careers, get his or her understanding of the Holland codes, and determine any biases the client may have about certain careers. It also will address some of the client's thoughts about cultural barriers when you explore the reasons for rejecting a particular field. Most important, however, exploration of these rejected occupations may help the client discover careers he or she never thought of before. If there is a glimmer of interest in a non-traditional career, those are the careers that you would encourage the client to explore by finding more information and finding mentors if interest is piqued.

More Inclusive Theories

Each of the modernist career counseling theories has its own shortcomings regarding multicultural inclusiveness. The theories discussed below manage to avoid most of those shortcomings.

John Krumboltz's Social Learning Theory of Career Development

The social learning theory of career development is typically associated with the work of John Krumboltz (1979). Following the lead of Albert Bandura (1986), Krumboltz developed a theory based on how learning experiences influence career decision making and development. Krumboltz's social learning theory of career counseling purports that people tend to choose careers based on their personal and vicarious learning experiences. According to Krumboltz, one way that learning occurs is through instrumental (reward and punishment) learning. For instance, when individuals are rewarded for a particular behavior, they are inclined to repeat that behavior. If individuals are punished for a particular behavior, they will most likely stop that behavior. Another way that learning occurs is through associative learning by observation or conditioning. For example, a girl may observe a woman pediatrician and decided that being a pediatrician is an acceptable occupation for a woman, or a boy who is repeatedly encouraged to build model airplanes may be conditioned to believe that aeronautics is an acceptable occupation for a man. Instrumental learning and associative learning can also have consequences related to race or culture. For instance, if an individual from an ethnic minority group is punished as a child for asking too many questions about a "White" career option, or if the child observes or is repeatedly reminded that a particular profession discriminates against people from his or her cultural group, that individual will likely not pursue a career in that profession.

In 1996, Mitchell and Krumboltz outlined four factors influencing career paths:

1. Genetic endowment: one's physical self and one's innate abilities and talents
2. Environmental conditions and events: factors beyond one's control, such as societal changes, acts of nature, and technological advances
3. Learning experiences: instrumental learning and associative learning
4. Task approach skills: literally, how the individual approaches performing tasks.

When an individual's genetic endowment, environmental conditions, and learning experiences interact, the result is the individual's task approach skills. People approach tasks such as career decision making by using their natural abilities, their ability to cope with the world around them, and their observations about themselves and the world.

Putting the above concepts into a career counseling context, Krumboltz (1996) describes how people make their career decisions and provides strategies for helping them with these career choices. According to Krumboltz, people choose occupations that either

- entail tasks they have succeeded in doing in the past,
- are valued by significant people in their lives, or
- they have observed in practice via a role model.

In their most recent writings (Krumboltz & Levin, 2004; Mitchell, Levin, & Krumboltz, 1999), Krumboltz has added "planned happenstance" to his theory, encouraging clients to prepare for the unexpected (such as encountering discrimination), which may require them to regroup. Mitchell et al., suggested a four-step process for using the happenstance approach as follows:

Step 1. Normalize planned happenstance in the client's history

Step 2. Assist clients to transform curiosity into opportunities for learning and exploration

Step 3. Teach clients to produce desirable chance events

Step 4. Teach clients to overcome blocks to action. (Sharf, 2006, p. 321)

Step 4 is one that would assist career professionals in addressing marginalization with their clients. It can get clients talking about discrimination, harassment and how to handle those experiences. Counselors would also be able to help clients explore their own beliefs about discrimination that might present roadblocks to their success.

There is not much multicultural criticism of Krumboltz's learning theory of career counseling. In fact, most research appears to support the theory (Jackson & Nutini, 2002; Tyson, 2007). This acceptance is most likely due to the fact that the theory allows for the influence not only of culture, but also of environmental factors outside the control of the client.

In addition, there is support for Krumboltz's theory regarding the use of career role models with ethnic minority children (Raposa et al, 2019). Role models also help women to choose non-traditional or male-dominated careers (Williams et al., 1998). In fact, their research showed that even when women were showed videotapes of women being reinforced for choosing non-traditional careers, they tended to choose more non-traditional careers than those who had not seen the video.

Linda Gottfredson's Developmental Model for Counseling

Linda Gottfredson (1981) proposed a developmental model for career counseling that helped fill some of the gaps left by Super's theory. Specifically, Gottfredson speaks to gender issues, social class, and motivation that apply across cultures. Expanding upon Super's stages of career development model, Gottfredson's model points out that during early childhood, children learn about gender differences; in late childhood, children develop an understanding of social class and prestige; in adolescence, children gain self-awareness and develop perceptions of others. All of these factors impact the career development stages outlined by Super.

Gottfredson (1981) speaks to women and ethnic minorities via her concepts of circumscription and compromise. According to Gottfredson, circumscription involves the narrowing of career choices based on gender in early childhood, and based on prestige in middle childhood and early adolescence. Children start to eliminate careers they believe are inappropriate for their gender when they are under the age of nine, and they start to eliminate those without prestige after the age of nine. This thinking can be extended to ethnic minority and other marginalized groups. They tend to eliminate careers that seem inappropriate for their cultural group fairly early in their lives.

Compromise involves children changing their career choices as they become more realistic about attaining their careers. They will let go of choices that seem to be beyond their reach (people like them do not do that kind of work) or that take more effort than they are willing to expend. Gottfredson (2005) states, "compromise is the process by which they [children] begin to relinquish their most preferred alternatives for less compatible but more accessible ones" (p. 82). When compromising, children will sacrifice prestige before they sacrifice a "gender appropriate" career.

As far as women are concerned, Gottfredson's circumscription and compromise theories both clearly demonstrate how career choices are influenced by gender. As far as ethnic minority groups are concerned, Gottfredson's compromise theory also explains how social class and ethnicity influence career decision making. The idea that people choose careers based on their social accessibility is especially relevant for ethnic minority groups. If one chooses a career that is foreign and unacceptable to the community, one runs the risk of alienating everyone in the community, perhaps making it a career that will take more effort than it is worth.

While there has been research to support the circumscription concept (Cochran, Wang, Stevenson, Johnson & Crews, 2011; Henderson, Hesketh, & Tuffin, 1988; Helwig, 1998, 2001), Ivers, Milsom, & Newsome (2012) also suggested the usefulness of Gottredson's aspirational concept with Latinx college students. There has not been similar support for the compromise concept. In fact, researchers have found that individuals will sacrifice gender-appropriateness for prestige (Hesketh, Durant & Pryor, 1990; Hesketh, Elmslie & Kaldor, 1990), a finding that unfortunately calls the usefulness of this segment of Gottfredson's theory for women and ethnic minorities into question. However, Lapan, Loehr-Lapan, and Tupper (1993) have designed a workbook for middle schoolers focused on the compromise concept, "Mapping Vocational Challenges," which has been supported by research (Gottfredson & Lapan, 1997; Scharf, 2002).

Social Cognitive Career Theory

A career theory conducive to multicultural career counseling is Social Cognitive Career Theory (SCCT; Brown & Lent, 1996; Lent, Brown & Hackett, 1994, 1996, 1999). Philosophically, it combines the theories of Bandura (1986), Krumboltz (1979), and Hackett and Betz (1981). Although SCCT is similar to Krumboltz's social learning career theory, Lent and colleagues (1996) make a distinction between the theories, stating that SCCT focuses more on cognitive processes than social learning career theory's focus on behavior and the interrelationships between personal characteristics, environment, and behavior. Lent's (2005) description of the theory is

> SCCT highlights people's capacity to direct their own vocational behavior (human agency) …yet it also acknowledges the many personal and

environmental influences (such as sociostructural barriers and supports, culture, disability status) that serve to strengthen, weaken, or, in some cases, even override human agency in career development. (p. 102)

The factors that drive the SCCT model include: self-efficacy, outcome expectations, and personal goals.

Self-efficacy is a term originated by Bandura (1986) and refers to a person's belief in his or her own ability to perform a particular task. For example, when asked how confident she would feel about performing an oil change on her car, Ann replies, "extremely confident." This indicates that Ann has a strong belief in her ability to do that task or high self-efficacy regarding the task.

Outcome expectations occur when an individual predicts the outcome of an event or interaction; for example, "If I don't graduate in May, then I'll never get a job" or "If I pass the Bar exam, I will have my pick of law firms to work for."

Goals refer to the individual's plans to accomplish certain tasks within a given amount of time, for example, "I will finish my doctorate in three years."

In SCCT, race/ethnicity, gender, and contextual variables (such as culture and family), as well as learning experience, influence self-efficacy and outcome expectations. For instance, view the case of CJ:

CJ is a nineteen-year-old, third generation, Cuban American, middle-class male who has been playing baseball since he was four-years-old. He has made his college baseball team but has dreams of playing for the major leagues. CJ's parents are proud of his athletic accomplishments and that he is following a family tradition of excellent baseball players—he has an uncle who played in the minor league for ten years (Familial and Cultural Support). His high batting average and his ability to steal bases (Experience) have contributed to his confidence (Self-Efficacy). CJ practices longer and harder than others on the team and believes that if he does so, when the major league scouts come to watch his team he will be noticed (Outcome Expectation).

A criticism of SCCT comes from those who doubt the usefulness of the concept of self-efficacy with ethnic minority populations. Brown and Lent (1996) point out that self-efficacy for ethnic minorities is influenced by both positive and negative feedback. While an individual may receive positive feedback regarding his or her achievements from European Americans, those same accomplishments may be disparaged by family and friends. These contradictions can lower the individual's self-efficacy and reduce the individual's willingness to pursue careers related to that activity.

SCCT is a complex theory which has been supported for use by culturally different populations (Ali & Menke, 2014; Lee, Flores, Navarro, & Kanagui-Muñoz, 2015; Lent et al., 2018; Inda, Rodriguez, & Peña 2013). Swanson and

Fouad (1999) point out that the strengths of using this model with multicultural groups are

- the model includes provisions that help career professionals identify whether or not clients have made prematurely limited or foreclosed career decisions because of erroneous perceptions of their abilities (e.g., girls cannot do math, African Americans cannot do science, Asian Americans do not have people skills);
- the model provides an avenue for exploring the barriers clients perceive, barriers that make them eliminate career choices prematurely; and
- the model allows for restructuring the client's erroneous beliefs.

Hackett and Byars (1996) point out specific strategies for using SCCT with African American women, particularly with regard to self-efficacy. These ideas are most likely applicable to other marginalized groups. For example, Hackett and Byars recommend that for vicarious learning experience, role models should not only be similar to the client in race and cultural background, but also in age and social background. Career professionals can help clients recognize when the feedback they are given is racially motivated and develop "strong efficacy for coping with racism" (p. 7).

Theory Blending Exercise

Often career professionals will use theories in combination to meet their clients' needs. In this exercise you will blend two of the theories presented above (Krumboltz's Social Learning Theory, Gottfredson's Developmental Theory, Social Cognitive Career Theory). Use your notebook to describe how you would apply your newly combined theory to a client. In the previous chapter, there was a brief discussion about intersectionality—when individuals identify with more than one marginalized groups (e.g., an Asian American woman with a disability; a White male who lives in poverty and is gay; a Muslim female who is an undocumented immigrant). Describe the elements you would include from each theory in your new model and why. How will you discuss the possible barriers the clients may come across in their career search? Finally, discuss how difficult or easy combining the two theories was for you and how the exercise helped you learn.

Postmodern Approaches

The postmodern approaches to career counseling began to emerge as the world of work was changing and the modernist theories did not fit the kinds of work experiences people were living. The security of work and lifelong employment that was the norm from the 1950's until almost the end of the 20th century began disappearing in the 21st century. Full-time employment with benefits changed to part-time and temporary. More people became self-employed as they began working as independent contractors and consultants (Gysbers, Heppner & Johnston, 2009). With this type of employment, job security is non-existent. As workers would likely have at least ten jobs/contracts/assignments in their lifetimes, the theories that involved finding a life-long career would not apply (Savickas, 2012). Postmodern approaches to career development began to emerge as more relevant.

Postmodern approaches differ quite significantly from modernist theories. Instead of focusing on the one truth of the modernist approaches, postmodern approaches focus on each individual's personal truth. In other words, in postmodernism, there are multiple truths unique to each individual. Also, rather than being determined by objective and measurable concepts of the scientific method that is the foundation of modernism, postmodern approaches are based on the subjective meaning that individuals make of their social interactions and the social context of their lives. Because of the philosophical nature of the models, (focused on the individual's personal experiences) the client's lived experiences are assumed to be included. It is believed that this approach allows career professionals and clients to explore how clients perceive their marginalized status. Postmodernist approaches, by design, are more culturally friendly because there is no standard to be measured against, no comparison between the individual and anyone else, no norms, no below average or above average.

Reading about postmodern career theories and models can be confusing because of the similarity of terms and how they are used in the literature. Gysbers et al. (2009) point out that the terms "constructivism, constructivist, social constructionism, contextualist, and narrative" (p. 39) are all used when writers refer to postmodern approaches to career development. However, according to Gysbers et al., the terms that seemed to be used most often are constructivism and social constructionism. McAuliffe and Emmet (2017) distinguished between the two terms as follows:

> Social constructionism: emphasizes the inevitably social, or communal context of human meaning making. Another way to describe social construction is to say that all meaning is saturated in culture, history, place, and time in the form of discourses such as social class, gender, ethnicity, race, disability, and religion.
>
> Constructivism: an umbrella term that refers to locating the meaning of all experience in a person's subjective world...Constructivists seek to understand the lenses that people use to make meanings of experience. (p. 39)

There are multiple postmodern approaches to career development but Busacca & Rehfuss (2017) suggest it would be beneficial for career professionals use these approaches to complement traditional theories. An example of such a combination is the theory of career construction created by Mark Savickas (2002). In 2005, Savickas stated that his career construction theory

> updates and advances Super's (1957) seminal theory of vocational development for use in a multicultural society and global economy. It incorporates Super's innovative ideas into a contemporary vision of careers by using social constructionism as a metatheory with which to reconceptualize central concepts of vocational development theory. (p. 42)

Transforming Super's theory in a social constructionist manner, Savickas (2005) takes three perspectives: vocational personality types, career adaptability, and life themes. In vocational personality Savickas addresses individual differences especially as they represent how people implement their vocational self-concepts. In terms of career adaptability, Savickas explains that because people and environments change over time, they make career adjustments with a goal of the career being able to validate the individual's self-concept. The third perspective, life themes, refers to the stories clients tell about their lives and through those stories discovering the meaning behind the choices people make.

There is a caveat to using the postmodern approaches that may or may not require some adaptation by career professionals. Just because these approaches may be culturally friendly, they do not absolve the career professional from becoming culturally competent. If a client is reluctant to share stories about his or her marginalization and cultural socialization, which may happen, especially when there are cultural differences between the client and career professional, then it is important that questions are raised to bring those aspects of the client's life forward.

Narrative Exercise

Go to www.vocopher.com/CSI/CCI_workbook.pdf and complete the exercises. When you are finished, write a brief summary in your notebook about the career themes you found from your own stories.

Career Counseling Process Models for Multicultural Groups

Two models that are specifically applicable to career counseling with ethnic minority and other marginalized populations are discussed here. Both of these models are process models, not philosophically based theories. In other words, contrary to the theories described throughout this chapter, these models focus directly on the counseling process. The two multiculturally focused career models are Leong and Hartung's Integrative Sequential Conceptual Framework for Career Counseling (1995) and Fouad and Bingham's (1995) Culturally Appropriate Career Counseling Model (CACCM).

Leong and Hartung's Integrative Sequential Conceptual Framework for Career Counseling

Leong and Hartung's (1997) model describes five stages of the career counseling process. During stage one, which occurs prior to the client entering counseling, the client recognizes that she or he has career problems and realizes that seeing a career counseling professional would be beneficial. In stage two, the client seeks help for the problem (Leong & Hartung, 1997). To accommodate this stage, it is important that the career agency has staff who are receptive to diverse clienteles, which entails among other things providing bilingual career professionals. In stage three, the client's counseling issues are assessed in five dimensions: cultural identity, cultural view of the problem, cultural environmental influences, cultural barriers to counseling, and cultural planning (Swanson & Fouad, 1999). In stage four, the career professional implements the intervention, which may include career assessment. Lastly, in the fifth stage, the client implements his or her career plan. This model assumes that culture will be woven into the counseling throughout the counseling process.

Fouad and Bingham's Culturally Appropriate Career Counseling Model (CACCM)

The CACCM model involves seven steps, beginning with step one, relationship building that is sensitive to the client's culture and counseling expectations. The second step is to assess the client's problem and decide whether the problem is cognitive, social/emotional, behavioral, environmental, and/or external. Step three determines the cultural factors affecting the career problem, using a concentric circle diagram with the client's unique individual qualities at the core of the diagram and circles for gender, family, racial ethnic group, and the dominant majority emanating from the core. Each of these circles impacts clients differently, depending on clients' career issues or life circumstances (Swanson & Fouad, 1999). Also, these factors may interact and affect career choices. In step four, the career professional and client set culturally appropriate goals and culturally sensitive interventions. Steps five and six involve assisting the client in decision making. Finally, in step seven the client executes the plan, and the career professional follows up on client progress.

Final Thoughts about Career Counseling Theories

Most of the modernist theories can be used with diverse populations as long as career professionals are aware that race, ethnicity, gender, sexual orientation, disability, and socioeconomic class must be accounted for. Career professionals need to challenge those theories that perpetuate occupational stereotypes by assigning activities that will promote appropriate career alternatives in non-stereotypic occupations. Finally, career professionals may want to explore the more inclusive theories or those that are intentionally designed for culturally diverse groups.

Career theories are the maps we use to help clients find their preferred lifestyle. Just as all good map makers know, maps must be updated and changed to reflect population growth and diverse travel needs of map users. Using culturally appropriate applications of career theories, career professionals can help all their clients to map out a road in life where they can make decisions effectively, adapt smoothly to a new career or position, and enjoy a fuller, more satisfying lifestyle. Until a more comprehensive theory is developed, we are able to identify the weaknesses of existing theories and adjust them.

REVIEW/REFLECTION QUESTIONS

Brandi is a twenty-five-year old European American lesbian who has recently graduated from college and is at a stage in her identity development where she is immersed in the lesbian community. She came out at work and makes frequent references to her sexual orientation during casual conversations with colleagues and during professional meetings. It seems to Brandi that since she has come out, her relationships with her boss and colleagues have been strained. Everyone seems to have isolated her. Brandi has become very disenchanted with her job and comes to you for help finding a new job.

1. What theory seems to be the best fit for Brandi and her career counseling needs?
2. Which theory seems to be the least appropriate and explain why?
3. Using one of the theories above, outline the steps you would take regarding Brandi's career issue.

References

Ali, S. R., & Menke, K. A. (2014). Rural Latino youth career development: An application of social cognitive career theory. *The Career Development Quarterly, 62*(2), 175-186.

Bandura, A. (1986). *Social foundations of thought and action: A social-cognitive theory.* Upper Saddle River, NJ: Prentice Hall.

Betz, N. E., & Fitzgerald, L. E. (1987). *The career psychology of women.* Orlando, FL: Academic Press.

Brown, D. (1984). Trait and factor theory. In D. Brown & L. Brooks (Eds.), *Career choice and development, applying contemporary theories to practice* (pp. 8-30). San Francisco, CA: Jossey-Bass.

Brown, S. D., & Lent, R. W. (1996). A social cognitive framework for career choice counseling. *The Career Development Quarterly, 44*, 211-223.

Busacca, L. A., & Rehfuss, M. C. (2017). *Postmodern career counseling: A handbook of culture, context, and cases.* Alexandria, VA: American Counseling Association.

Carter, R. T., & Swanson, J. L. (1990). *Minorities in higher education: Tenth annual status report.* Washington, D.C.: American Council on Education.

Cochran, D. B., Wang, E. W., Stevenson, S. J., Johnson, L. E., & Crews, C. (2011). Adolescent occupational aspirations: Test of Gottfredson's theory of circumscription and compromise. *The Career Development Quarterly, 59*(5), 412-427.

Day, S. X, Rounds, J., & Swaney, K. (1998). The structure of vocational interest for diverse racial-ethnic groups. *Psychological Science, 9*, 40-44.

Fouad, N. A. (1993). Cross-cultural vocational assessment. *The Career Development Quarterly 42*, 4-13.

Fouad, N. A. (2002). Cross-cultural differences in vocational interests: Between-group differences on the Strong Interest Inventory. *Journal of Counseling Psychology 49*(3), 283-289.

Fouad, N. A., & Bingham, R. (1995). Career counseling with racial/ethnic minorities. In W. B. Walsh, & S. H. Osipow (Eds.), *Handbook of vocational psychology* (2nd ed., pp. 331-366). Hillsdale, NJ: Lawrence Erlbaum.

Fouad, N. A., & Kantamneni, N. (2010). Cultural validity of Holland's theory. In J. G. Ponterotto, J. M. Casas, L. A. Suzuki, & C. M. Alexander (Eds.), *Handbook of Multicultural Counseling (p. 703–714).* Thousand Oaks, CA: Sage Publications, Inc.

Gottfredson, L. (2005). Applying Gottfredson's theory of circumscription and compromise in career guidance and counseling. In S. D. Brown & R. W. Lent (Eds.), *Career development and counseling: Putting theory and research to work* (pp. 71-100). Hoboken, NJ: John Wiley & Sons, Inc.

Gottfredson, L. S. (1981). Circumscription and compromise: A developmental theory of occupational aspirations. *Journal of Counseling Psychology, 28*, 545-579.

Gottfredson, L. S. (1986). Special groups and the beneficial use of vocational interest inventories. In W. B. Walsh & S. H. Osipow (Eds.), *Advances in vocational psychology, Vol 1: The assessment of interests* (pp. 127-198). Hillsdale, NJ: Lawrence Erlbaum Associates, Inc.

Gottfredson, L. S., & Lapan, R. T. (1997). Assessing gender-based circumscription of occupational aspirations. *Journal of Career Assessment, 5*, 419-441.

Gysbers, N. C., Heppner, M. J., & Johnston, J. A. (2009). *Career counseling: Contexts, processes, and techniques*. Alexandria, VA: American Counseling Association.

Hackett, G., & Betz, N. E. (1981). A self-efficacy approach to the career development of women. *Journal of Vocational Behavior, 18*, 326-339.

Hackett, G., & Byars, A. (1996). Social cognitive theory and the career development of African American women. *The Career Development Quarterly, 44*, 322-340.

Harmon, L., Hansen, J. I., Borgen, F., & Hammer, A. (1994). *Strong Interest Inventory: Applications and technical manual*. Palo Alto, CA: Consulting Psychologists Press.

Helwig, A. A. (1998). Gender-role stereotyping: Testing theory with a longitudinal sample. *Sex Roles, 38*, 403-423.

Helwig, A. A. (2001). A test of Gottfredson's theory using a ten-year longitudinal study, *Journal of Career Development, 28*, 77-95.

Henderson, S., Hesketh, B., & Tuffin, A. (1988). A test of Gottfredson's theory of circumscription. *Journal of Vocational Behavior, 32*, 37-48.

Herr, E. L., Cramer, S. H., & Niles, S. G. (2004). *Career guidance and counseling through the lifespan: Systematic approaches*. Boston, MA: Pearson Education, Inc.

Hesketh, B., Durant, C., & Pryor, R. (1990). Career compromise: A test of Gottfredson's (1981) theory using a policy-capturing procedure. *Journal of Vocational Behavior, 36*, 97-108.

Hesketh, B., Elmslie, S., & Kaldor, W. (1990). Career compromise: An alternative account to Gottfredson's theory. *Journal of Counseling Psychology, 37*, 40-56.

Holland, J. L. (1966). *The psychology of vocational choice*. Waltham, MA: Blaisdell.

Holland, J. L. (1985). *Making vocational choices: A theory of vocational personalities and work environments* (2nd ed.). Upper Saddle River, NJ: Prentice Hall.

Holland, J. L. (1992). *Making vocational choices* (2nd ed.). Odessa, FL: Psychological Assessment Resources.

Holland, J. L. (1997). *Making vocational choices: A theory of vocational personalities and work environments* (3rd ed.). Odessa, FL: Psychological Assessment Resources.

Inda, M., Rodríguez, C., & Peña, J. V. (2013). Gender differences in applying social cognitive career theory in engineering students. *Journal of Vocational Behavior, 83*(3), 346-355.

Ivers, N. N., Milsom, A., & Newsome, D. W. (2012). Using Gottfredson's theory of circumscription and compromise to improve Latino students' school success. *The Career Development Quarterly, 60*(3), 231-242.

Jackson, M. A., & Nutini, C. D. (2002). Hidden resources and barriers in career learning assessment with adolescents vulnerable to discrimination. *The Career Development Quarterly, 51*(1), 56-77.

Krumboltz, J. D. (1979). A social learning theory of career decision-making. In M. L. Savickas & W. B. Walsh (Eds.), *Social learning and career decision making* (pp. 19-49). Cranston, RI: Carroll Press.

Krumboltz, J. D. (1996). A learning theory of career counseling. In M. L. Savickas & W. B. Walsh (Eds.), *Handbook of career counseling theory and practice* (pp. 55-80). Palo Alto, CA: Davies-Black.

Krumboltz, J. D., & Levin, A. S. (2004). *Luck is no accident: Making the most of happenstance in your life and career.* Atascadero, CA: Impact Publishers.

Lapan, R. T., Loehr-Lapan, S. J., & Tupper, T. W. (1993). *Tech-prep careers workbook: Counselor's manual.* Columbia Department of Educational and Counseling Psychology, University of Missouri-Columbia.

Lee, H. S., Flores, L. Y., Navarro, R. L., & Kanagui-Muñoz, M. (2015). A longitudinal test of social cognitive career theory's academic persistence model among Latino/a and White men and women engineering students. *Journal of Vocational Behavior, 88,* 95-103.

Lent, R. W. (2005). A social cognitive view of career development and counseling. In S. D. Brown & R. W. Lent (Eds.), *Career development and counseling: Putting theory and research to work* (pp. 101-127). Hoboken, NJ: John Wiley & Sons, Inc.

Lent, R. W., Brown, S. D., & Hackett, G. (1994). Toward a unifying social cognitive theory of career and academic interest, choice, and performance. *Journal of Vocational Behavior, 45,* 79-122.

Lent, R. W., Brown, S. D., & Hackett, G. (1996). Career development from a social cognitive perspective. In D. Brown, L. Brooks & Associates (Eds.). *Career choice and development* (4th ed., pp. 255-311). San Francisco, CA: Jossey-Bass.

Lent, R. W., Hackett, G., & Brown, S. D. (1999). A social cognitive view of school-to-work transition. *The Career Development Quarterly, 47,* 297-311.

Lent, R. W., Sheu, H. B., Miller, M. J., Cusick, M. E., Penn, L. T., & Truong, N. N. (2018). Predictors of science, technology, engineering, and mathematics choice options: A meta-analytic path analysis of the social–cognitive choice model by gender and race/ethnicity. *Journal of Counseling Psychology, 65*(1), 17.

Leong, F. T. L. (1995). *Career development and vocational behavior of racial and ethnic minorities.* Hillsdale, NJ: Lawrence Erlbaum Associates, Inc.

Leong, F. T. L., & Brown, M. T. (1995). Theoretical issues in cross-cultural career development: Cultural validity and cultural specificity. In W. B. Walsh & S. H. Osipow (Eds.), *Handbook of vocational psychology: Theory, research, and practice* 2nd ed., pp. 143-180. Hillsdale, NJ: Lawrence Erlbaum Associates, Inc.

Leong, F. T. L., & Hartung, P. J. (1997). Career assessment with culturally different clients: Proposing an integrative-sequential conceptual framework for cross-cultural career counseling research and practice. *Journal of Career Assessment, 5,* 183-201.

Leong, F. T. L., & Serafica, F. C. (2001). Cross-cultural perspective on Super's career development theory: Career maturity and cultural accommodation. In F. T. Leong & A. Barak, *Contemporary models in vocational psychology: A volume in honor of Samuel H. Osipow* (pp. 167-205). Mahwah, NJ: Lawrence Erlbaum Associates, Publishers.

McAuliffe, G. J., & Emmett, J. (2017). The postmodern impulse and career counselor preparation. In L. A. Busacca & M. C. Rehfuss (Eds.), *Postmodern career counseling: A handbook of culture, context and cases* (pp. 37-50). Alexandria, VA: American Counseling Association.

Mitchell, L. K., & Krumboltz, J. D. (1996). Krumboltz's theory of career choice and counseling. In D. Brown, L. Brooks & Associates (Eds.), *Career choice development* (3rd ed., pp. 233-380). San Francisco, CA: Jossey-Bass.

Mitchell, L. K., Levin, A. S., & Krumboltz, J. D. (1999). Planned happenstance: Constructing unexpected career opportunities. *Journal of Counseling and Development, 77,* 115-124.

Murray, P., Williamson, L., Boudrot, K., Reents, E., Roberts, T., & Evans, K. M. (2002). Synthesizing career and family theories: Relevant issues. In K. M. Evans, J. C. Rotter, & J. G. Gold (Eds.), *Synthesizing family, career, and culture: A model for counseling in the twenty-first century* (pp. 35-60). Alexandria, VA: American Counseling Association.

National Career Development Association. (2015). *2015 NCDA code of ethics.* Retrieved from https://www.ncda.org/aws/NCDA/asset_manager/get_file/3395

Neville, H. A., Gysbers, N. C., Heppner, M. J., & Johnston, J. (1998). Empowering life choices: Career counseling in cultural contexts. In N. C. Gysbers, M. J. Heppner, & J. Johnson, *Career counseling: Process, issues, and techniques.* Boston, MA: Allyn & Bacon.

Parsons, F. (1909). *Choosing a vocation.* Garrett Park, MD: Garrett Park Press.

Prince, J. P., Uemura, A. K., Chao, C. S., & Gonzalez, G. M. (1991). Using career interest inventories with multicultural clients. *Career Planning and Adults Development Journal, 7*(1), 45-50.

Raposa, E. B., Rhodes, J., Stams, G. J. J., Card, N., Burton, S., Schwartz, S., Sykes, L. A., Kanchewa, S., Kupersmidt, J., & Hussain, S. (2019). The effects of youth mentoring programs: A meta-analysis of outcome studies. *Journal of Youth and Adolescence, 48*(3), 423-443.

Savickas, M. L. (2002). Career construction: A developmental theory of vocational behavior. In D. Brown (Ed.), *Career choice and development* (4th ed., pp.149-205). San Francisco: Jossey-Bass.

Savickas, M. L. (2005). The theory and practice of career construction. In S. D. Brown & R. W. Lent (Eds.), *Career development and counseling: Putting theory and research to work* (pp. 42-70). Hoboken, NJ: Wiley.

Savickas, M. L. (2012). Life design: A paradigm for career intervention in the 21st century. *Journal of Counseling and Development, 90*(1), 13-19.

Sharf, R. S. (2002). *Applying career development theory to counseling*. Pacific Grove, CA: Thomson Learning.

Sharf, R. S. (2006). *Applying career development theory to counseling*. Belmont, CA: Thomson/Brooks/Cole.

Smith, E. J. (1983). Issues in racial minorities career behavior. In W. B. Walsh & S. H. Osipow (Eds.), *Handbook of vocational psychology, Volume 1, Foundations*. Hillsdale, NJ: Lawrence Erlbaum.

Starishevsky, R., & Matlin, N. (1963). A model for the translation of self-concepts into vocational terms. In D. E. Super, R. Starishevsky, N. Matlin, & J. P. Jordaan (Eds.), *Career development: Self-concept theory* (Research Monograph No. 4; pp. 33-41). New York, NY: College Entrance Examination Board.

Super, D. E. (1957). *The psychology of careers*. New York, NY: Harper & Row.

Super, D. E. (1990). A life-span, life-space approach to career development. In D. Brown, L. Brooks & Associates (Eds.), *Career choice and development: Applying contemporary theories to practice* (2nd ed., pp. 197-261). San Francisco, CA: Jossey-Bass.

Super, D. E. (1994). A life-span, life-space perspective on convergence. In M. L. Savickas & R. W. Lent (Eds.), *Convergence in career development theories* (pp. 63-74). Palo Alto, CA: Consulting Psychologists Press.

Super, D. E., Savickas, M. L. & Super, C. M. (1996). The life-span, life-space approach to careers. In D. Brown, L. Brooks, & Associates (Eds.), *Career choice and development* (3rd ed., pp. 121-178). San Francisco: Jossey-Bass.

Swanson, J. L., & Fouad, N. A. (1999). *Career theory and practice: Learning through case studies*. Thousand Oaks, CA: Sage Publications, Inc.

Tyson, C. T. (2007). *Social learning theory and the career aspirations of adolescent African American males* (Unpublished doctoral dissertation). University of South Carolina, Columbia, SC.

Williams, E. N., Soeprapto, E., Like, K., Tourandji, P., Hess, S., Hill, C. E. (1998). Perceptions of serendipity: Career paths of prominent women in counseling psychology. *Journal of Counseling Psychology, 45*, 379-389.

CHAPTER 6

Multiculturally Competent Career Counseling Skills

Career professionals have the expertise to access and communicate to clients the seemingly endless amount of information available about careers and the career decision-making process. However, career professionals who are unable to work effectively with all people, including people from diverse backgrounds, will have clients who will not be able to effectively process all of the information they have been given. To work effectively, career professionals need three types of skills—general counseling skills, multicultural counseling skills, and career counseling skills. In this chapter, the merging of these skills are discussed. Posted in Appendices A and B are the National Career Development Association's Minimum Competencies for Multicultural Career Counseling and Development (NCDA, 2020), and the relevant Association for Multicultural Counseling and Development (AMCD) competencies (Arredondo et al., 1996; Roysircar, Arredondo, Fuertes, Ponterotto, & Toporek, 2003), both of which were discussed in Chapter 1 of this book.

Integrating Personal Counseling and Career Counseling

Even among counseling professionals, there is a great deal of confusion as to what career counselors actually do. Consider the following scenario.

Skye is starting her third week as a career counselor in a college counseling center. She loves her job so far and thinks that career counseling seems to be her ideal counseling focus. To see clients who come in voluntarily and to focus on positive, happy things like the future is definitely the right way to go in her eyes. Skye is relieved to find that she doesn't have to use all that depressing information about mental disorders that she studied in her psychopathology class in graduate school. She thinks, "This job is going to be fun and not hard at all."

However, when Skye returns from lunch, on the first day of her fourth week, a client responds to her question "How can I help you today?" by bursting into tears. The client says, "I don't really think anyone can help me. I just want to die."

Contrary to what some people believe, career counseling is counseling, not simply the relaying of information to clients. In fact, individual and group counseling skills are the first competency areas listed in the NCDA Minimum Competencies for Multicultural Career Counseling and Development (NCDA,

2020). As the Skye scenario above indicates, competency in individual counseling is needed to effectively help clients. It is difficult to do personal counseling without doing some career counseling and just as difficult to do career counseling without also doing personal counseling. (Blustein, 2008; Gallagher, 2012, Herr, 1989; Lenz, Peterson, Reardon, & Saunders, 2010). There are few people who are able to separate their careers from the rest of their lives. People who place little importance on the work they do outside of the home still find that work and personal issues become intertwined. For example, when a client is delayed getting to a part-time job on time because of a day care problem or a client is called out of town by a supervisor at the last minute and must miss an important family function, personal and professional issues become intermingled. The more complicated one's personal and/or career roles happen to be, the more the issues become intermingled, and the harder it is for clients and career professionals to sort out personal and career issues from one another. Because of this dilemma, a number of authors have advocated that career professionals need to acquire mental health counseling skills, including an understanding of psychopathology and the effects of psychotropic drugs (Niles & Pate, 1989) and that those who practice personal counseling need to increase their career counseling skills (Evans, 1997; Evans & Larrabee, 2002; Lenz et al., 2010; Zunker, 2008).

The importance of integrating career counseling and personal counseling is especially significant when one considers cultural variables. As has been discussed throughout this book, counseling clients outside their reference groups leaves wide gaps in treatment. Multiculturally competent career professionals do not separate career counseling from personal counseling. In fact, the opposite is necessary; culturally competent career professionals consider the personal contexts of culturally different clients in order for the career counseling process to fully succeed. The next section of this chapter will address the integration of career counseling skills with personal and multicultural counseling skills by integrating the NCDA and AMCD competencies.

Stages of Career Counseling

When career professionals master the integration of career and multicultural competencies, career counseling becomes much more effective and relevant for clients from culturally different groups. All counseling proceeds through various stages, and counselors-in-training need to become familiar with these stages to assure that their clients make steady progress through each stage. For example, Yost and Corbishley (1987) divided career counseling into eight different stages: Stage 1 (Initial Assessment), Stage 2 (Self-Understanding), Stage 3 (Making Sense of Self-Understanding Data), Stage 4 (Generating Alternatives), Stage 5 (Obtaining Occupational Information), Stage 6 (Making Choices), Stage 7 (Making Plans), and Stage 8 (Implementing Plans).

In this section, the eight stages of the Yost and Corbishley model are outlined in more detail. The NCDA and AMCD multicultural career competencies are integrated within this framework utilizing an ongoing case study. The case study begins with some background on the client, Luis Alverez, and his career professional, Ivy:

Luis Alverez is a twenty-six-year-old Puerto Rican man living in an openly gay lifestyle in a large city in the Southeast. He is tall, attractive, outgoing, and energetic. Luis is appropriately dressed for his interview and appears physically and intellectually strong. While Luis is openly gay in the city where he lives, he has yet to come out to his family, who live in New York City. Luis is a high school graduate who grew up in poverty. After graduating from high school, he accompanied a couple of friends on a road trip to Florida and never went back to New York. Currently, he is employed as an Assistant Manager at a national chain of fast food restaurants where he has worked for the past five years. It is a job he has come to despise. Luis is undecided between becoming a chef or an interior designer. He jokingly states that interior design is just too cliche for a gay man; however, he wants to decide now, because he believes that his life is going nowhere fast.

Luis has strong ties to the gay community but, also has strong familial ties and deep appreciation of his Puerto Rican heritage. Unfortunately, he says, he has suffered discrimination and lack of tolerance under both identities.

When Luis sought career help at a nearby center, he was assigned to Ivy, who is a 42-year-old career professional with seventeen years of counseling experience. Ivy is African American (born and raised in the southeastern United States) and heterosexual. Therefore, her work with Luis will involve a number of cross-cultural dimensions—gender, race, ethnicity, geography, age, sexual orientation, and socioeconomic status.

Stage 1: Initial Assessment—Part 1: Establishing the Counseling Relationship

In this initial stage of the Yost and Corbishley model, the career professional prepares for the counseling relationship, meets and greets the client, establishes rapport and starts to build a relationship with the client, and creates a structure for the career counseling process. This beginning stage is always important, but it is even more essential to establish the counseling relationship effectively in the case of cross-cultural counselor/client dyads than it is with same-culture dyads. When considering the basic counseling competencies as stated by Ivey, Ivey and Zalaquett (2018), this falls under stage one of the five stages of the counseling session, when a career professional would develop an empathic relationship with the client. Because stereotypes, discrimination, and bias are commonplace in U.S. society, it is not uncommon for diverse clients to mistrust and harbor suspicions about counseling and career professionals. These attitudes can easily sabotage the career professional-client relationship if it is not established effectively from the start (Whaley, 2001).

Career professional preparation. The first step in establishing the counseling relationship in a multicultural career counseling situation is career professional preparation, especially career professional introspection, in which career professionals assess their own biases and stereotypes (Gold, Rotter, & Evans, 2002; Ridley, Li, & Hill, 1998). ACA has made it clear in its code of ethics and in position statements that career professionals may not use lack of multicultural training as an excuse to turn away (or refer) clients whose cultures and values differ from theirs. Instead, they are to receive the training they need to be able to effectively serve all clients. More important, while effective career professionals know themselves better than anyone else, they may have blinders on regarding certain issues and be guilty of microaggressions. It is always good practice for career professionals to engage in ongoing supervision with someone who may offer an objective opinion of their work.

In Chapter 4, we discussed cultural mistrust on the part of clients from culturally different groups, client views of career professionals from the dominant European American cultural group, and client reactions to institutional racism. When preparing for the first contact, it is helpful for the career professional to understand the possibility that the client may have negative perceptions not only of the counseling process, but also of the career professional (Helms & Cook, 1999; Ridley, 1995; Sue & Sue, 2016; Whaley, 2001). Career professionals need to plan to be as open and honest with the client as possible and understand the origins of client feelings of anger and distrust. Sue and Sue (2016) also warn that career professionals need to know that "tests of *credibility* may occur frequently in the therapy session, and the onus of responsibility for proving expertness and trustworthiness lies with the therapist" (p. 174). While career professionals cannot predict specific client reactions, they need to employ strategies to facilitate growth of good client-career professional working relationships. Regardless of cultural background, some clients are easier to relate to than others, but it is the responsibility of career professionals to establish strong working alliances. Such an alliance can transcend racial, cultural, gender, sexual orientation, and other differences, as the continuing case study demonstrates:

Ivy explores the values she holds as an African American woman, careful to consider the ones that may interfere with her acceptance of her client, Luis. Ivy's experiences with gay males have been limited to friends, who were treated as "mascots" among her circle of female friends. They were never full members of the group. Ivy realizes now how patronizing that behavior was and decides that she must monitor any maternal or protective feelings she may have toward Luis. She will make sure to solicit her supervisor's help on this.

Ivy has also been taught by family to be suspicious of Puerto Ricans and other Latinos or Latinas. In the past, the reasons for this suspicion were never clear, but today she believes it comes from the fact that Latinas and Latinos now outnumber African Americans as the largest ethnic minority group in the United States. Ivy thinks that her family and friends are fearful that African Americans may lose their privileged status among oppressed groups. Ivy has also never knowingly resented Latinos or Latinas, but she is aware that it is difficult to dismiss what has been learned over a long period of time. She will inform her supervisor of this issue as well.

Ivy has counseled her share of male clients, but she believes that this client will expect to explore his masculinity in more depth than other clients have, since he brings up that issue in relation to his sexual orientation. Her familiarity with gender socialization among Latinas and Latinos will be helpful here.

Although her middle-class upbringing may have dictated certain values about school and career, Ivy has not had problems accepting people from all socioeconomic backgrounds. She has been successful with very poor and very affluent clients, and she does not foresee a problem with Luis in this regard.

Meeting and greeting. Meeting anyone for the first time can be awkward. The awkwardness of meeting a new client may be slight for the career professional, but it may be nerve-wracking for the client. Although career counseling may seem less stigmatizing than other kinds of counseling, clients may feel just as vulnerable. Members of some cultures frown upon seeking help outside of the family, even if it is career help rather than psychological help. Therefore, some clients will be reluctant and nervous about entering into any kind of counseling. The career professional's job is to help the client feel as comfortable as possible the first time the client walks into the counseling agency.

To facilitate client comfort, the physical environment of the counseling agency needs to be as welcoming as the agency can afford. For example, if certain cultural groups are especially likely to be clients at the agency, the agency needs to provide waiting room magazines representative of those cultural groups. If subscriptions are not in the budget, career professionals may be able to obtain copies of magazines from other sources, including fellow career professionals at the agency. When clients see familiar magazines and books, the message to clients is that they belong there. Also, if possible, pictures of community members and the staff taken at specific community events (festivals, block parties, holiday celebrations, and so forth) need to be hung on the walls, because this reinforces the image that the agency is part of the community and further helps clients feel welcome.

The employment of individuals from underrepresented groups in the front office also signals that the agency is an accepting and welcoming environment for all. Ideally, bilingual staff members will be available to accommodate clients who are more comfortable speaking in their first language. It is important that notices and printed materials are available in more than one language, and any pictures of people should illustrate a diverse population. These cosmetic details increase the possibility that career professionals will establish rapport with culturally different clients and that the clients will return to the agency after their initial meetings.

Greeting clients for the first time can also affect rapport. Recent research has found that first impressions of unfamiliar people are made within 100 milliseconds of being exposed to that new person (Willis & Tolorov, 2006). This is true with job interviews and career professional-client relationships as well. In the 1980s and 1990s, much was written about the appropriate ways to address a culturally different client. For instance, some authors suggested that African American clients felt inferior and disrespected when White career professionals called them by their first names (reminiscent of slavery and service jobs) (Sue & Sue, 2003). Perhaps the best advice to consider when addressing all clients is to address them by their title and last name (e.g., Mr. Alverez) and to wait until clients give permission to use their first names. It is better that career professionals refrain from asking for that permission because it would still seem to come from a place of privilege. Once clients get to know their career professionals better, they may invite their career professionals to call them by the name their friends and family use.

Similarly, many clients may believe that using the career professional's first name diminishes the career professional's credibility (Sue & Sue, 2003). The hierarchical nature of many cultures demands that the career professional (someone with knowledge and wisdom) be treated with respect. For example, early in the first author's counseling career, an African American woman client discovered after the second session that the career professional (also an African American woman) had a Ph.D. The client was embarrassed for calling her Miss Evans and apologized profusely. Even though the career professional told her it did not matter to her, it mattered to the client that she was disrespectful of the career professional's position and the career professional herself. During their time together, their relationship grew stronger, and the client accomplished a great deal in therapy. They never were on a first-name basis, however. The career professional was always Dr. Evans to her client and her client was always Mrs. Jones.

The culturally competent career professional appears competent, confident, and in control (but not controlling or arrogant) during these first minutes. Herr, Cramer, and Niles (2004) also point out that self-disclosure, an attitude of no condemnation, and an aura of wisdom and stability on the part of the career professional are important qualities to bring across during the first meeting with the client. However clients are greeted, career professionals need to exude warmth and understanding.

Rapport and relationship building. The foundation of counseling is the career professional-client relationship, and there is no relationship if there is no rapport. The relationship between culturally different clients and career professionals is especially important (Bingham & Ward, 1994; Constantine, 1998; Flores, Spanierman, & Obasi, 2003). The skills important for rapport building with culturally different clients are taught to every beginning-level career professional, and include such skills as reflection of feelings, open rather than yes or no questions, paraphrasing, and summarizing (Niles & Harris-Bowlsbey, 2005; Brammer, 1993). More important, genuineness, respect, and empathy create an environment of warmth and caring for all clients, including those from different cultural backgrounds (Patterson, 1996; Pedersen, 1996).

Career professionals of clients who differ from them are faced with a greater challenge of establishing credibility than career professionals working with clients of the same background as themselves, but overcoming the challenges is essential for a good working relationship (Ridley et al., 1998; Sue & Sue, 2003). Credibility is enhanced not only by career professionals discussing their credentials, but also by their apparent genuine interest and openness to client questions. Sue & Sue (2016) warn that displaying one's degrees may have the opposite effect on some clients in that they may perceive education as being part of an oppressive system which may even reduce career professional credibility. Also, while some career professional self-disclosure helps establish trustworthiness and genuineness (Ivy, D'Andrea, Ivy & Simek-Morgan, 2002), Sue and Sue suggest that clients will test trustworthiness again and again and that it is important to avoid being defensive when tested by clients.

Career counseling research reports that many ethnic minority clients prefer direct answers to their direct questions (Sue & Sue, 2003). This type of communication is not uncommon in career counseling, and it may be essential in building rapport with ethnic minority clients; however, it is important not to use research data to stereotype individual clients. Every client is unique no matter his or her cultural or racial background. While it is important to be knowledgeable about cultural influences on career development, it is equally important to realize that a client is an individual within the context of his or her culture. Along those same lines, the culture of counseling promotes skills such as genuineness and empathy to build rapport and establish relationships with clients; however, it is important that career professionals adapt those skills to the needs of the individual client. As such, Pedersen (1996) warns that, "respect for client, genuineness, and empathic understanding are themselves products of a cultural context, and they will need to be interpreted differently in each complex and dynamic cultural situation" (p. 236).

To reduce time spent gathering data in the initial session, some agencies ask clients to fill out an intake form, which can be simple or as complicated as the agency desires. The form should be available in the predominant languages of clients served by the agency. While many intake forms collect only basic client demographic data and a brief description of the client's problem, some intake forms are a great deal more in-depth and may include such information as work history, family work history, history of mental and physical health problems, illegal drug history, current family situation, and so forth (Yost & Corbishley, 1987). If the client fills out an intake form, the career professional may want to take the liberty of following up on some of the client's answers during the rapport building stage, for example saying to the client, "I see that you play soccer. Tell me a little more about this activity." Or the career professional may highlight items that the career professional may have in common with the client, for instance, "My very first job in high school was with your fast food chain. Tell me how you got started there." Connecting in this way with the client enables the client to relax; however, career professionals also need to balance connecting with the client and overemphasizing similarities. Highlighting one or two similarities to get the client talking is advisable, but career professionals need to be aware that an overemphasis on similarities may appear to the client as if the career professional is trying too hard to find common ground where none really exists (Brown & Brooks, 1991). Many oppressed groups (ethnic minorities as well as LGBT persons, and people with disabilities) value their uniqueness and emphasizing similarities tends to minimize that uniqueness.

Another rapport-building strategy is to mention racial and cultural dissimilarities with the client early in the first session (Brown & Brooks, 1991). Dealing with racial and cultural differences early in the relationship rather than waiting until it is obvious that the client is having difficulty with these differences is advisable. Such an approach clears the air and may prevent culturally different clients from prematurely terminating counseling. The career professional might introduce the topic by saying something like this:

"Mr. Alverez (notice that the career professional addresses the client by his last name), we have clients from many different backgrounds come to our center. Sometimes clients and career professionals with differences such as race, like us, are paired up in the initial interview. There may be other differences between the client and the career professional that may not be as obvious as race. These pairings have worked out very well; however, we want our clients to feel comfortable with their career professionals. Because counseling is so personal, we believe you should be matched with someone who is most likely to meet your needs. Often clients prefer to work with career professionals of their own racial/cultural group, with similar sexual orientation, religion, age, or disability. We try our best to accommodate those

requests. If you would like to be paired with a career professional who is more like you, please let the office know and I am sure they will do everything they can to make it happen. Today, though, I would like for us to talk about our differences a little bit before you make that decision. I want you to be comfortable with whomever you choose to be your career professional. If you do decide to stay with me, I feel confident that I will be able to help you with your problem, and we can discuss any racial/sexual orientation issues that might arise as we go along."

Introducing cultural differences in this manner gives the client options and it brings race and cultural issues to the forefront; however, keep in mind that the opposite may be true in the case of European American clients working with a career professional of color. For example, an African American career professional stated in a workshop she attended that when she brought up race with her White clients, the subject seemed to make them uncomfortable, nervous, or defensive. She decided that in the future, if a client reacted in this way, she would quickly add, "You don't have to make up your mind today. If you want, you can go home and think about it. Even if you decide to stay with me, if at any time you feel uncomfortable about working with me because of racial or cultural differences, you are welcome to ask to be transferred to another career professional and you won't have to clear it through me first." A statement such as this may lower client discomfort and may enhance relationship building. In addition, some agencies include a question about career professional preferences on the intake form. In fact, it is usually easier on both the client and the career professional if such preferences are handled through the intake form in order to avoid uncomfortable face-to-face situations. Then, if no career professionals are available who match the client's preferred list of background characteristics, the assigned career professional is able to address this issue in session. Depending on the client's racial identity status, it may be necessary in some cases to refer the client to another counseling agency if the client is adamant about career professional preference.

Relationship building may also be enhanced when career professionals make clients aware that they are familiar with their culture (Brown & Brooks, 1991). One caveat applies here: It is better to be modest about cultural knowledge than to show off. Instead of going on at length about their cultural knowledge, career professionals need to let the clients do most of the talking about their culture. Career professionals need to gain knowledge about culture to educate themselves to be better prepared to assist with the cultural issues clients bring to counseling, not to impress their clients. The on-going case study illustrates how the career professional can introduce her knowledge of the client's culture into the discussion in order to build rapport:

Ivy says, "Mr. Alverez, I have visited Puerto Rico a couple of times and have enjoyed my visits. I have tried to learn as much as I can about Puerto Rico and about the culture through these visits and through my friends. My spoken Spanish is awful, but I understand more than I can speak. I'm hoping that what I know of your culture will be helpful in our work together. I hope, too, that you will let me know when I've got it all wrong."

Creating structure. Some career professionals tend to overlook the essential relationship-building task of providing a structure to the counseling process. The more the career professional can tell the client about what will happen during the counseling process, the more comfortable clients will feel about that process, and the more receptive they will be toward counseling. In addition to easing client worries about the counseling process, structuring helps build credibility by demonstrating the career professional's professionalism (Sue & Sue, 2016). Structuring includes informing clients of the procedures that will be followed, explaining the rules of confidentiality, defining the limitations of the counseling process, discussing any limitations on the issues that can be addressed and the possible outcomes, and relating rules about attendance, tardiness, and fees. Career professionals need to also explain to clients how counseling session work without using jargon or complicated terms (Niles & Harris-Bowlsbey, 2005), as illustrated in the ongoing case study. Ivy introduces structure to the session by saying:

"Mr. Alverez, what I thought we'd do first is spend a little bit of our time getting to know one another and then we'll talk some about counseling—what it is, how it's done, what your role is, and what my role is. Then if everything sounds okay to you, we'll go on and talk about what brought you in to see me—what the problem seems to be. How does that sound to you?"

After roles are discussed, Ivy discloses her career counseling theory as illustrated here. Whichever way the career professional chooses to explain the counseling process, the outcome should be that the client feels both informed and comfortable about what is to come.

I believe that it is important that all clients find careers that are compatible with their personalities. Through counseling, I can help them take a good look at their own personalities to see whether or not the career they are interested in gives them an opportunity to use their greatest personality strengths. I believe that clients are unhappy and dissatisfied with their work when they haven't found careers that match their personalities.

For some clients, confidentiality is one of the most important features of the structuring process. For instance, many ethnic minority populations frown upon sharing family problems outside the family and so confidentiality helps these clients feel more secure about engaging in the counseling process. Gay, lesbian, and bisexual clients may need to be assured that if they have chosen not to be out of the closet with coworkers, family, and friends, then the counseling process will not result in their being outed. Reassurances about confidentiality may also curb clients' feelings of cultural distrust of the career professional (Brown & Brooks, 1991; Helms & Cook, 1999; Whaley, 2001).

A structuring method known as role induction also helps to reduce client anxiety, and it has been effective with ethnic minority clients whose familiarity with counseling may be limited (Galassi, Crace, & Martin, 1992; Niles & Bowlsbey, 2005). Essentially, role induction involves informing clients of what is expected of them during the counseling process. The career professional's role is also presented. Spokane (1991) recommends that career professionals create handouts that describe both the career professional's and client's responsibilities and give these handouts to clients. Some agencies provide handouts that describe what the career professional will not do, explaining not only the limitations of the counseling agency but also the limitations of the counseling process itself.

Once a structure is in place, the relationship-building stage should continue until the career professional perceives that the client is comfortable enough to discuss his or her problem. Career professionals may find that when working with clients from oppressed groups, rapport and relationship building may go on for several sessions. Continued rapport and relationship building is time well spent, because the career professional is able to use the additional time to regroup and approach the client more slowly to strengthen the relationship when resistance is encountered.

Whatever the case, the primary goal at the beginning of counseling is to make a connection with the client via preparation, successful meeting and greeting, rapport building and structuring. If the client is comfortable with the process, better results can be achieved. Career professionals who continue to have problems establishing relationships with culturally different clients need to seek consultation or supervision from someone with a specialty in multicultural counseling. The career professional may be unconsciously communicating negative verbal and/or nonverbal messages and microaggressions toward the client, which can be seen in a videotape or via live supervision.

Stage 1 Initial Assessment—Part 2: Identifying the Counseling Issues

Once a career professional-client relationship has been firmly established, the career counseling process enters Part 2 of Stage 1, identifying the counseling issues. In Part 2, the questions that need to be answered are: (1) Is there a career problem here? (2) If there is a career problem, what kind of problem is it? Assessment of career issues begins with the first session, usually via an intake interview. Often the client's presenting career problems are not the real counseling issues. Sometimes clients think they want to change their careers, when in reality they want to see a change in the organization for which they work. Or sometimes the real issue is not specific to career development, for example, in the case of a woman who wants to change careers because she has been sexually harassed on the job, but has not yet addressed the effect the harassment has had on her. An assessment of the real counseling issue is imperative for counseling to proceed. Part of the career professional's job is to determine if career counseling is appropriate, or if the client needs to deal with psychological or emotional issues first (Walker & Petersen, 2012). Crites (1981), among others, has recommended that career counseling follow personal counseling. The rationale is that if an individual has emotional or psychological challenges, informed career decisions are not possible. Career professionals have an open mind and are able to assist clients whatever the issues.

Determining a client's emotional and psychological state is particularly delicate with ethnic or other minority clients who may be hesitant, nervous, or cautious about the counseling process in general (Highlen & Sudarsky-Gleiser, 1994). The culturally competent career professional is able to determine the severity of the emotional status of the client through psychological training and knowledge of the client's culture. It is important for career professionals to be careful not to use European American standards of mental health to evaluate people of color (Ridley, 1995; Sue & Sue, 2016). Similarly, care needs to be taken not to apply sexist or heterosexist standards to women or to LGBT individuals. The combination of knowledge of psychiatric disorders and cultural manifestations of those disorders is paramount when serving diverse populations appropriately. If a career professional discovers that the client's emotional and mental health issues may interfere with career decision-making processes, this determination needs to be discussed with the client before proceeding.

If there are no intervening psychological issues, the next decision is to determine the type of career counseling needed. Campbell and Cellini (1981) have identified over thirty-seven different career problems in their diagnostic taxonomy. These problems are divided into four categories: (1) problems in decision making, (2) problems in implementing career plans, (3) problems in organization/institutional performance, and (4) problems in organizational/institutional adaptation. Some specific client issues that would fall under these categories include performance anxiety, depression over failures, and role confusion (Lowman, 1993). Each of the problems listed by Campbell and Cellini (1981) can be exacerbated by discrimination and bias. For example, in a situation where a client is seen as deficient by a supervisor who holds culturally different supervisees to a higher standard, the client's problems may be the result of racism, sexism, or heterosexism. There is a need for career professionals to discuss client issues with clients in enough detail to ascertain exactly what the career problems are, while keeping in mind that these problems may be negatively influenced by larger social/cultural barriers.

Stage 2: Self-Understanding

Once particular career counseling issues are identified, career professionals need to assist clients in becoming more aware of their personal interests, abilities, values, and personalities (Krumboltz & Coon, 1995). To expedite this process, interests, abilities, values, and personality are typically measured through standardized assessment; however, with diverse clients, culture and ethnicity heavily influence these personal factors, and therefore both Ridley and colleagues (1998) and Highlen and Sudarsky-Gleiser (1994) recommend non-standardized assessment for culturally different clients. As will be discussed in Chapter 7, standardized assessment has come under great criticism for its bias against ethnic minorities, therefore, it is best to be very careful and knowledgeable when using standardized assessment with culturally different clients. In addition to qualitative assessments, qualitative interviewing allows career professionals to obtain more information on clients' cultural characteristics. Assisting clients to develop an awareness of their culture and to internalize this information is essential in multicultural career counseling. For example, an African American sixth grade boy decides to stop studying because his peers tell him he is trying to be White. Through cultural self-awareness exploration during the counseling process, he may learn about his cultural identity and the importance of education in the history of African Americans. In another example, an Asian woman works with a group of strong European women and is uncomfortable with her job setting because the women disrespect their elders and their spouses. She may discover through exploration of her own culture during the career counseling process how to become tolerant to different world views. Similarly, the friends and family of a twenty-two-year-old Latina have teased her about her interest in becoming a veterinarian, to the point that she has chosen a sociology major. Through cultural self-awareness exploration during counseling, she may learn to broaden her concept of *familismo* to include seeking their support to pursue a career they may not have chosen for her. And as a final example, a gay male child who has become a moody, withdrawn adolescent due to homophobic behavior of his classmates may learn how to cope with discrimination and become empowered to advocate on his own behalf through self-awareness exploration during counseling.

Expanding on the above examples, the following three sections will explore in further detail how cultural issues, sociopolitical influences, and client attitudes and biases toward work and other workers affect client self-awareness and understanding. Career professionals who understand these factors in depth will be able to help clients obtain the self-awareness and understanding they need to attain during the third stage of the career counseling process, and move on to subsequent stages of the process.

Cultural issues. Arredondo and colleagues (1996) state that knowledge of a group's cultural heritage, including its history, religion, language and family structures, is important information for the culturally skilled career professional. However, simply being knowledgeable about this information is not enough. Career professionals still need to understand how all of these factors influence their clients. To gain the fuller understanding, culturally competent career professionals collect not just the cultural facts from the client, but also ascertain their clients' perception of their cultures, unearth their clients' cultural and racial identity statuses, and then explore the socio-political barriers their clients have experienced (personally or vicariously through experiences of others within their cultures). Career professionals may assess this information by interviewing the client using the Career-in-Culture Interview protocol, which includes getting the client's career story, having the client appraise his or her skills, and an exploration into the client's cultural background, values, and family expectations, the client's view of his or her own community, and experiences with or beliefs about oppression and barriers (Ponterotto, Rivera, & Sueyoshi, 2000). Highlen and Sudarsky-Gleiser (1994) suggest obtaining this information via storytelling, art, discussion, meditation, and dream analysis. These methods all provide the career professional with an opportunity to open a discussion of cultural issues with a client. Highlen and Sudarsky-Gleiser (1994) also advocate asking qualitative questions in order to assess the career characteristics of clients. For example, they suggest asking, "What activities do you participate in where you lose track of time?" (p. 323) in order to ascertain a client's vocational calling. In fact, if career professionals wish to forgo formal testing, they can access a great deal of information by just asking the client qualitative questions such as:

- I learn more about people when I know more about their stories. Tell me the story of your life as a(n) _____ (fills in client's cultural/racial group).

- Have you ever been discriminated against? If so, what were the circumstances? How do you think _____ (racism, sexism, classism, heterosexism, ableism) affects you now? How do you think it will affect you in the future?

- Tell me a little about how you are the same or different from people in your culture or your family.

- How would the head of your family describe you?

The culturally competent career professional is sensitive to any information learned that may prove detrimental to a client's career development, such as acculturative stress, conflicts clients may have with their family and cultural group regarding differences in acculturation, feelings of not fitting into any cultural group, and racial identity problems. These may be issues that need to be worked out in advance to best facilitate moving into more action-oriented stages of the career counseling process. Depending on the client's cultural group and level of acculturation within that cultural group, the career professional may suggest individual or group counseling to approach these issues.

Several studies have found that while ethnic minorities have encountered and identified barriers to entering their chosen professions, they have been able to succeed because of support from family and friends (McWhirter, McWhirter, McWhirter, & McWhirter, 2016). The implication is that with support from the right people, barriers are easier to overcome. Lee (1984) has found in a comparative study of adolescents that parental impact on career decisions is greater for minority children than it is for White children. Therefore, it is important for career professionals to assess family influences on their clients. In fact, when counseling people from collectivist cultures (Latinos and Latinas, American Indian) career professionals may find it helpful to invite their clients' families into the counseling process when possible to give input into counseling, since clients from these cultures may be unwilling to make career decisions without family input (Fernandez, 1988; Perry & Calhoun-Butts, 2012). This may prove difficult, however, in some situations, as it is in the case of Luis, who though a member of a collectivist culture, is also gay in a culture whose members of the group often disapprove of his sexual orientation:

Luis' beliefs about his cultural group and his perceptions of what is expected of him are the focus of many of his early career counseling sessions with Ivy. There are legitimate reasons why gay, lesbian, bisexual, and transgendered individuals do not disclose their sexual orientation to certain groups, and it may be that Luis will decide against such a disclosure, but first he and the career professional need to explore why he is in conflict and whether or not coming out to his family will ease that conflict. Luis may decide that there are specific members of his family that he wants to come out to because of the guilty feelings he has about lying to them. The fact that he is reluctant to choose a career that he believes will be a red flag to his sexual orientation indicates that there are members of his family that he does not ever want to know about his sexuality. Luis and Ivy discuss and explore the possible reactions of his family members and how his disclosure may affect his relationships with them. Ivy encourages Luis to read the biographies of other gay Latinos (for example, Michael Nava's chapter, "Abuelo: My Grandfather, Raymond Acuna," in A Member of the Family: Gay Men Write About Their Families *to get some idea of how they successfully handled family reactions.*

Socio-political influences. In addition to looking at personal cultural influences that may affect self-awareness and understanding in ethnic minority and other marginalized clients during the career counseling process, career professionals also have to look at and integrate socio-political variables, such as racism, sexism, heterosexism, discrimination, and internalized oppression. This has been discussed in much of the career counseling literature. For instance,

Hawks and Muha (1991) believe that career professionals need to make sure their clients know that they are knowledgeable about racism and that they are aware that it still exists. Additionally, Helms and Piper (1994) suggest that career professionals need to become aware that a person's race or culture may be a limiting factor in obtaining and/or maintaining a career because of discrimination and other institutional barriers (such as the proverbial glass ceiling). Similarly, Krumboltz and Coon (1995) state that career professionals should recognize the limitations faced by women, who typically must juggle several roles at one time. To help counter the socio-political factors diverse clients are faced with, career professionals should assist clients in developing coping skills, understanding societal stereotyping of certain careers, and finding role models who defy stereotypes and who will encourage clients to broaden their career search options.

It is essential for career professionals to be aware of how sexual and racial discrimination can manifest itself as workplace harassment. Harassment can be either overt or covert. In the latter case, the subtle behaviors of individuals in the workplace may not seem to be overt sexual or racial harassment, but clients feel uncomfortable around such persons nonetheless. A client's perceptions of harassing behaviors are a legitimate concern and should be addressed during the counseling process in order to explore client self-awareness and understanding. The career professional needs to not minimize these perceptions but explore how they are helping or hurting the client. If these perceptions are disturbing or hurtful, the career professional needs to outline strategies for both coping with the present situation and changing the situation through client action.

Much of what clients need to do to cope with discrimination and harassment is covered in Chapter 9 of this book. An example of a strategy that may empower the client is to encourage the client to collect data documenting discrimination. If the client is unable to substantiate the claim, he or she may alternatively wish to learn how to cope with oppressive policies and individuals. Coping strategies that have been said to be effective include diplomatic confrontation, learning to control one's anger toward the situation through anger management, learning to come to some peace with the situation via spirituality and prayer, proving one's worth to oneself and others by excelling at one's job, garnering support by joining supportive organizations, ignoring, or avoiding the perpetrator, or if all else fails, finding a new job (Evans, 1997). Luis's career issues are certainly impacted by socio-political factors, as the continuing case study illustrates:

Although Luis does not feel much discrimination from fellow co-workers where he is currently employed, he worries that to sustain a career as a chef he may need to hide his sexual orientation. It is one of the concerns he has about changing to this new career—how will he be accepted as a gay Latino? Luis is less worried about his sexual orientation regarding interior design but, is concerned about whether or not he will be able to get a job in the city where he now lives—where there are few Latinos and Latinas and some very narrow-minded people regarding race and culture.

Clients from culturally different groups not only experience discrimination, but they often internalize the negative stereotypes that are part and parcel of discrimination. These internalized negative stereotypes limit clients' career development because they lower self-esteem and increase doubt in their own abilities. These kinds of beliefs are evident when girls (and boys) use their gender to explain their inability to perform certain career duties. For example, a seventh-grade girl (who was a straight A math student during elementary school) justifies her C in pre-algebra by saying, "Everybody knows girls can't do math." Career professionals need to assess the impact of stereotyping on clients to help them reach a state of more positive self-awareness and understanding, from which they may evaluate their worth more realistically.

Client attitudes and biases toward work and other workers. In addition to cultural and socio-political influences, reaching self-awareness and understanding in this stage of the career counseling process is also impacted by clients' own attitudes toward work and toward other workers.

Attitudes toward work may have a cultural origin. In some ethnic minority cultures, competition is discouraged, whereas competition is valued by the dominant White culture in the United States. Further, sometimes competition creates tension among individuals from culturally different groups. Career professionals need to work with clients so that clients do not perceive competition as cultural warfare and therefore do not take personally any defeats or wins in the competitive arena. If the competitors are, in fact, using cultural dominance as a means to suppress the competition, then career professionals need to help clients decide what is in the client's best interest in terms of dealing with the situation.

Competition is not the only factor that impacts attitudes toward work among culturally different clients. Helms and Cook (1999) point out that the policies and expectations in many places of employment reflect dominant White European American values, which may be in direct conflict with cultural experiences of some groups. Helms and Cook (1999) suggest that many ethnic minority clients' careers may be limited, because the work culture may be foreign to them. Such a client does not know what to do to fit in (Thomas & Alderfer, 1989). Additionally, women clients, those with disabilities, as well as gay, lesbian, bisexual, and transgendered clients may feel at odds with the prevailing old boy network of many workplaces, in which there exists an underlying assumption by management that able-bodied, heterosexual men are in control and women, sexual minorities, and people with disabilities are subordinate. Such attitudes may cause these clients to feel powerless and discouraged, believing that there is no chance that they will have real success in their careers. Perceptions of work, therefore, may be influenced by this perception of difference. Stereotypes about ethnic minority workers prevail. Some groups are perceived as lazy, and those stereotypes can color an employer's perceptions of that group's work styles. In fact, stereotypes such as this may lead to a self-fulfilling prophecy because the client knows that co-workers or supervisors expect laziness and may decide to cut corners, since he or she will be blamed for slacking off anyway.

Although clients may have negative attitudes toward work for the reasons described above, sometimes clients' own issues impact self-awareness. Clients themselves may harbor biases and prejudices against other groups. For instance, they may complain that certain groups are taking over, unclean, lazy, or stupid. Sometimes animosity is aimed toward the supervisor, whom the client may correctly or incorrectly think is prejudiced or biased. Career professionals must work with clients to discover these biases, which may result in problems within the workplace and lack of success in interpersonal relationships. Again, familiarity with the racial/cultural identity models and the client's cultural history will help prepare the career professional to challenge clients on their beliefs and help them to grow into self-awareness and understanding.

Stage 3: Making Sense of Self-Understanding Data

After clients have explored with their career professionals the factors described above and reached a point of career self-awareness and understanding, the career professional's job is to help clients synthesize self-awareness with career objectives. Clients have to make decisions about the skills they want to use, pinpoint the activities that they are interested in, make up their minds about what values are most important to them, and reach conclusions about how well their cultural and personality traits will fit in certain occupations. Yost and Corbishley (1987) have outlined a set of factors to help career professionals and clients approach this sorting out process. Through the intake interview and/or the initial assessment, as well as through appropriate standardized assessments, clients discover their work preference factors, such as work tasks (routine, physical), working conditions (environment, teamwork, autonomy), location (indoor/outdoor, geographical area), and benefits (prestige, salary, challenge). Other factors outlined by Yost and Corbishley include information about clients' parents and other significant adults, and their work and attitudes about work, and their early experiences with work. Cultural influences will have been assessed so that clients are aware of these factors as well as environmental factors such as discrimination and socioeconomic status.

To put all this information together in the Yost and Corbishley system, clients are asked to prioritize the factors, using any prioritizing system that seems to work for them. The goal is for clients to come up with only five top factors important in the work they choose. Yost and Corbishley also suggest that clients list three to five factors they would want to avoid at all costs. Clients will now have generated a list of their work-related preferences, taking into account influences of culture and ethnicity. Career professionals may question clients about any inconsistencies in these top five factors, such as wanting a high prestige, high paying job but only wanting to complete high school to get it. Sometimes a resolution to the inconsistencies is not apparent until after clients have explored some of the alternatives available to them.

Stage 4: Generating Alternatives

The next two stages of the career counseling process call for the client to generate some career choices (alternatives) based on preferences determined by the client during the previous stage and to conduct research on those career choices. This idea aligns with Ivey, Ivey, and Zalaquett (2018), as it helps enable clients to think differently about concerns, issues, and challenges they may face in regards to satisfying employment.

Stage 5: Obtaining Occupational Information

Clients will need to do their own research, with motivation from the career professional. Motivating clients to do the work of gathering information may involve including family and friends in the process. The client may have friends and family with computer access the client may not have. The client's parents or spouse may be interested in some of the careers the client needs to research and may be happy to help with the research. In this way, the search for information becomes a group project and clients—especially those from collective cultures—may be more inclined to participate in data collection. Some clients will abhor library research, so the career professional will need to find alternative approaches to information gathering that will meet that client's learning styles:

Luis is motivated to research the two areas he is interested in, but to sustain his motivation, Ivy encourages him to get Harry, Luis' Anglo partner of five years, involved. Harry is an attorney and is well established in his current firm. He is concerned about the possibility of moving on Luis' behalf because he feels very accepted as a professional gay man by his own co-workers. Therefore, Harry is most interested in knowing where the jobs are located for the careers Luis is considering. He is also concerned about the annual salaries of Luis' potential jobs, and about the time it will take for Luis to be trained. Luis is interested in learning more about Latinos in these fields—how they got started, how successful they are, and so forth. Luis and Harry meet with Ivy to share the information they have gathered.

Stage 6: Making Choices

The time comes in most career counseling situations when the client must make a career decision. Decision-making styles are typically individual, but to help clients discover their own decision-making styles, most career professionals try to teach their clients decision-making skills. Sue and Sue (2016) have stated that because career professionals operate from a linear model, their approaches to problem solving may be in conflict with those of people from other cultures. Some cultures entail problem-solving styles that are more holistic and harmonious than linear, such as Native American cultures. In fact, Sue and Sue (2003) state, "When American Indians undergo therapy, the analytic approach may violate their basic philosophy of life" (p. 112).

Some individuals may believe that there is so much discrimination in a particular field they would not have a chance of prospering there (Arbona, 1990; Herring, 1990). More recently, Grossman and Porche (2014) found that although marginalized adolescents experienced microaggressions and believed that they would experience discrimination in their careers, they also believed they would be able to overcome such obstacles. Herr, Cramer, and Niles (2004) suggest that it is the career professional's job to assure culturally different clients that they do indeed have choices and they can overcome discrimination. A good strategy is to try to connect clients with role models from their own cultural groups who have succeeded despite the barriers.

Ivy and Luis do not discuss career decision-making until his work with her has resulted in some resolution about how he will handle his family and cultural situation. Luis' decision-making style is rather impulsive. He has given Ivy several examples of how his decision-making style has been somewhat successful but, most of the time, he has ended up regretting his decision. Ivy points out that the decision he made to come out to his family is anything but impulsive. Luis, therefore, can and has employed different styles to a greater success than his impulsive preference for decision making would indicate.

Luis has enjoyed collaborating on his decisions and wants to include his partner, Harry, in the career decision-making process, since Harry will be other person most affected by his career choice. Harry is invited to the sessions involving the gathering and evaluating of career information and provides feedback on his perceptions of Luis' abilities, values, and desires. Both he and Luis agree that the ultimate decision is Luis' but that it is important that they both be able to live with it.

Stage 7: Making Plans

One of the final steps in the career counseling process is the job search, which is undertaken with the assumption that the client already possesses the skills necessary to actually perform the duties of the desired position. For ethnic minority clients, the job search can be very stressful. Unfortunately, one of the by-products of affirmative action is that there is a pervasive assumption among both employers and prospective ethnic minority employees that ethnic minority applicants are not qualified for certain jobs. This bias handicaps the chances of ethnic minorities getting hired, and if hired, it may prevent them from getting promoted. Even though illegal in most cases, other kinds of prejudice and discrimination may be encountered by members of all oppressed groups and may result in multiple rejections or lead to the client accepting a lower position for less money. As a result, career professionals need to be available to help culturally different clients tap into their support systems and utilize coping strategies.

For some ethnic minority clients, coping may involve a discussion of spirituality or other indigenous healing strategies. Support systems may include family and friends, as well as spiritual role models. The career professional needs to let clients discuss their religious beliefs and how these beliefs have helped them cope in the past. A career professional's knowledge and understanding of the client's religion will help make these discussions much more fruitful. For example, if a Muslim client reveals that the difficulties he experiences at his job revolve around demands that keep him too busy to say his afternoon prayers, and he has found his supervisor to be neither sympathetic nor accommodating, knowing that Muslims must pray five times a day will make this discussion more meaningful for both the client and the career professional.

Even though affirmative action has increased the number of ethnic minority groups in fields in which they were long excluded, affirmative action policies do not guarantee an individual a job. Affirmative action simply means, in many cases, that ethnic minorities have been included in the pool of applicants and perhaps interviewees. Employers simply are required to make a case for why they have not hired ethnic minority candidates. Clients need to understand that while they may get interviews, it is important to do well, including being prepared to successfully respond to any questions they may be asked. Clients also need to be briefed on the types of questions that are illegal for prospective employers to ask (such as marital status, parental status, racial/ethnic background, place of birth). The reason these kinds of questions are illegal is to prevent prospective employers from using information against clients in hiring. The career professional and client need to discuss how to handle illegal questions should they come up.

The career professional and client need to work out a strategy the client is comfortable with if a prospective employer does happen to ask an illegal question, and the client needs to rehearse the response so that the client can recite it without anger or emotional upset. Clients need to be encouraged to do research on potential employers regarding their hiring and retention of ethnic and cultural minority employees. While current federal laws protect LGBT individuals from being fired, unfortunately, there are as yet no federal restrictions preventing discrimination in hiring or being discriminated against in the workplace because of their sexual orientation or gender identity; however, at this writing, 21 states have enacted laws that protect LGBT individuals from such discrimination (Movement Advancement Project, 2019). In states without protective laws, career professionals need to discuss this distressing matter and explore ways to navigate its implications with their gay, lesbian, bisexual, or transgendered clients.

Luis is not yet ready to do a job search, but part of the planning stage was for him to determine how to approach his family about his sexuality. After much deliberation, he decides to come out to two of his cousins and siblings. He will not swear them to secrecy but will tell them that he wants to wait a while before discussing his sexuality with the older members of his family. He believes that he is prepared to accept whatever reactions his family members may have because it will be such a relief to stop deceiving them.

Stage 8: Implementing Plans

When a client obtains a job, the career counseling process is quite complex. Often a career change not only entails growth opportunities for clients, but also means clients will need to adjust to a new role within the family and community. Career professionals need to help clients prepare for these new roles. Balancing career, family, and community are important for the well-being of all individuals and the career professional's responsibility is to help clients realize an appropriate balance between these life elements. This task becomes easier when the career professional has already integrated the client's family and culture into the career decision-making process. In addition to discussing the balance among career, family, and community, career professionals need to also discuss with clients how leisure time fits into the balance. Leisure activities are influenced more by socioeconomic status and perhaps ability status than by race, ethnicity, or sexual orientation. The more money clients have, the more opportunities there are for a greater variety of leisure activities. Whatever the income level, however, it is important that clients consider leisure activities as part of the lifestyle planning process.

Luis has decided that he will go back to school full-time, which has implications for Harry's lifestyle as well as Luis', especially where their leisure time and social lives are concerned. In addition, there will be a reduction in income, an increase in expenses (tuition, books, supplies), and a change in household responsibilities.

In their last session Luis reports that he has applied to a culinary arts school that has hours that will allow him to still work part-time in his current job. His employer is willing to be flexible with his schedule while he is in school. Luis and Harry have decided to allow Harry's younger sister (who now knows about his sexual orientation) to exchange housekeeping and cooking duties for a room in their house while she attends her first year at the university. They are all happy with the solution and feel confident that it will work out well.

This concludes the illustration of the eight-stage career counseling process model. Although it is not a model that is designed exclusively for work with marginalized groups, it is easy to include the elements needed in the model.

Group Career Counseling

Group counseling can be an effective format to support career education and decision-making, job hunting, stress management, role exhaustion, and interpersonal problems that manifest themselves in the workplace. There are several reasons for the popularity of group counseling in career development. It is effective, more efficient than individual career counseling, and it meets the needs of people. Also, it is the preferred intervention for some cultures. In fact, the groups that would benefit most from a group career counseling format tend to be collectivist in nature (e.g., Latinos/as and Native Americans) or those individuals who feel particularly isolated (e.g., gays, lesbians, and bisexuals, transgender individuals, and people with disabilities) (Gladding, 2003).

The group career counseling structure is somewhat different from that of individual career counseling. Career counseling groups are typically structured groups that require pre-planning of each session and the number of sessions is usually predetermined. When organizing the group, career professionals need to be certain that multicultural groups include more than one member of any marginalized group or that there is equal representation of a number of culturally different groups. The group may be homogenous or made up of members of one specific marginalized group (e.g., Latinx, people with disabilities, LGBT individuals). One of the main purposes of a group is that the clients within the group feel as if they have something in common and that they will be able to connect. If a group is homogenous, there may be a sense of rapport, trust, and cohesion, but some of the benefits that comes from diversity can be lost. Therefore, the general consensus of group experts is that the group be heterogeneous to maximize not only the diversity of ideas, but also to promote cultural understanding among group members (DeLucia-Waak & Donigian, 2004). It may also be useful for career professionals to assess client collectivist values. Those who have the collectivist orientation would do well in a group. Otherwise individual career counseling may be more appropriate.

Once group members have been identified, group leaders typically provide a group orientation to help clients understand the group format, as recommended by many group work specialists (Bowman & DeLucia, 1993). While the orientation session can be elaborate and include activities that introduce members to group strategies, career professionals may alternately choose simply to explain the purpose, stages, and role expectations involved in group counseling. Importantly, the rules and guidelines for handling conflicts in the group need to be established. Also, it is crucial in the orientation or in the first actual group session to mention the multicultural make-up of the group, just as culture needs to be called attention to in individual counseling (DeLucia-Waak, 1996) and to model for the group appropriate behaviors for discussing differences. Since most career groups are structured, formats for career groups have been created. Pyle and Hayden's (2015) model includes four stages.

Opening Stage

In this first stage, clients get to know each other and the career professional, the rules of the group counseling process are established, and the career professional uses rapport-building skills to encourage clients to connect with one another and to create a safe environment. In a multicultural group, a challenge during this stage would be helping clients to get in touch with their similarities and differences while developing group cohesiveness. Rules will be very important during this stage, because although the group would want to talk about differences, members of the group would need to be protected from hurtful stereotypes and prejudices. In this stage, the career professional needs to get this message across to clients while simultaneously avoiding crippling client self-expression by making clients fearful of alienating one another. Career professionals must make sure they monitor the group and encourage expression of real feelings of concern and confusion yet model how to ask questions and give feedback.

Investigating Stage

In this stage, clients discover many of their own characteristics through test-taking, clients learn about careers and the barriers they may find to some careers, and the career professional encourages, supports, and self-discloses. In a multicultural group, the challenge for career professionals at this stage will be interpreting each member's test results differently, based on the available comparison groups. Also, if a client is not represented in the normative group for a particular test, then the career professional will need to decide whether or not to assign the test to the client and will need to figure out how to interpret the test results if the test is administered. The recommendation is that tests be interpreted individually, even if everything else is done as a group. This may be the best bet in a culturally diverse group.

Working Stage

In this stage, clients take in all the data presented to them and try to make sense of it, and career professionals use skills such as accurate empathy, confrontation, and feedback. This is the stage when clients discover they have either set their job prospect sights too high, or they have a wealth of choices. Group support becomes vital, and members of the group may be able to give one another a deeper understanding of their individual results. Clients are often excited about their career options. The challenge for career professionals of multicultural groups at this stage is to be sure to give information for ethnic minority organizations for the profession the clients are considering.

Decision/Operational Stage

During this final group career counseling stage, clients support each other's plans, and career professionals use termination skills, such as drawing conclusions and solidifying next steps. The challenge for career professionals of multicultural groups at this stage is that decision making can be difficult in the context of a diverse group. Not only do cultures differ in terms of what they expect from their members, but individuals within cultural groups also interpret cultural teachings in their own ways. Participants can help each other out by asking hard questions about culturally specific rules. Responding to group members will help clients articulate their ideas and, in the telling, clarify matters in their own heads.

Final Thoughts on Skills

The goals of this chapter are to assist career professionals in developing a greater understanding of the counseling process in general and, more specifically, to illustrate how to integrate the multicultural and career competencies in a counseling setting. Knowledge of cultural influences introduced in earlier chapters is essential for career professionals to integrate these competencies.

Today's career professionals need the ability to think critically and to understand the complexity of the clients they see every day. It is a difficult task, but once it is learned, integrating multicultural, social justice, and career counseling skills can be useful with all clients.

REVIEW/REFLECTION QUESTIONS

1. One of the career counseling competencies addressed in the chapter is the ability to "identify and understand social contextual conditions affecting clients' careers. Discuss the contextual conditions in Luis' life that you would personally find the most challenging if Luis were your client.
2. Discuss how personal and career issues have been intertwined in your own life—paying close attention to those times when the demands of family, culture, and career were in conflict.

References

Arbona, C. (1990). Career counseling research and Hispanics: A review of the literature. *The Counseling Psychologist, 18*, 300-323.

Arredondo, P., Toporek, M. S., Brown, S., Jones, J., Locke, D. C., Sanchez, J. & Stadler, H. (1996). Operationalization of the multicultural counseling competencies. *Journal of Multicultural Counseling and Development, 24*, 42-78.

Bingham, R. P., & Ward, C. M. (1994). Career counseling with ethnic minority women. In W. B. Walsh & S. H. Osipow (Eds.), *Career counseling for women* (pp. 165-195). Hillsdale, NJ: Lawrence Erlbaum Associates, Inc.

Blustein, D. L. (2008). The role of work in psychological health and well-being: A conceptual, historical, and public policy perspective. *American Psychologist, 63*, 228-240.

Bowman, V., & DeLucia, J. L. (1993). Preparation for group therapy: The effects of preparer and modality on group process and individual functioning. *Journal for Specialists in Group Work, 18*, 67-79.

Brammer, L. (1993). *The helping relationship: Process and skills* (5th ed.). Boston, MA: Allyn & Bacon.

Brown, D., & Brooks, L. (1991). *Career counseling techniques.* Boston, MA: Allyn & Bacon.

Campbell, R. E., & Cellini, J. V. (1981). A diagnostic taxonomy of adult career problems. *Journal of Vocational Behavior, 70*, 645-647.

Constantine, M. (1998). Developing competence in multicultural assessment: Implications for counseling psychology training and practice. *The Counseling Psychologist, 26*, 922-929.

Crites, J. O. (1981). *Career counseling: Models, methods and materials.* New York, NY: McGraw-Hill.

DeLucia-Waak, J. L., & Donigian, J. (2004). *The practice of multicultural group work: Visions and perspectives from the field.* Pacific Grove, CA: Brooks/Cole-Thomson Learning.

Evans, K. M. (1997). Wellness and coping activities of African American counselors. *Journal of Black Psychology, 23*(1), 24-35.

Evans, K. M., & Larrabee, M. J. (2002). Teaching the multicultural counseling competencies and revised career counseling competencies simultaneously. *Journal of Multicultural Counseling and Development, 30*(1), 21-39.

Fernandez, M. S. (1988). Issues in counseling South Asian students. *Journal of Multicultural Counseling and Development, 16,* 157-166.

Flores, L. Y., Spanierman, L. B., & Obasi, E. M. (2003). Ethical and professional issues in career assessment with diverse racial and ethnic groups. *Journal of Career Assessment, 11,* 76-95.

Galassi, J. P., Crace, R. K., & Martin, G. A. (1992). Client preferences and anticipations in career counseling: A preliminary investigation. *Journal of Counseling Psychology, 39,* 46-55.

Gallagher, R. P. (2012). Thirty years of the national survey of counseling center directors: A personal account. *Journal of College Student Psychotherapy, 26*(3), 172-184.

Gladding, S. T. (2003). *Group work: A counseling specialty* (3rd ed.). Upper Saddle River, NJ: Prentice-Hall.

Gold, J. M., Rotter, J. C., & Evans, K. M. (2002). Out of the box: A model for counseling in the twenty-first century. In K. M. Evans, J. C. Rotter, & J. M. Gold (Eds.), *Synthesizing family career, and culture: A model for counseling in the twenty-first century* (pp. 19-33). Alexandria, VA: American Counseling Association.

Grossman, J. M., & Porche, M. V. (2014). Perceived gender and racial/ethnic barriers to STEM success. *Urban Education, 49*(6), 698-727.

Hawks, B. K., & Muha, D. (1991). Facilitating the career development of minorities: Doing it different this time. *Career Development Quarterly, 39,* 251-260.

Helms, J. E., & Cook, D. A. (1999). *Using race and culture in counseling and psychotherapy: Theory and process.* Boston, MA: Allyn & Bacon.

Helms, J. E., & Piper, R. E. (1994). Implications of racial identity theory for vocational psychology. *Journal of Vocational Behavior, 44,* 124-138.

Herr, E. L. (1989). Career development and mental health. *Journal of Career Development, 16,* 5-18.

Herr, E. L., Cramer, S. H., & Niles, S. G. (2004). *Career guidance and counseling through the lifespan: Systematic approaches.* Boston, MA: Pearson Education.

Herring, R. D. (1990). Attacking career myths among Native Americans: Implications for counseling. *The School Counselor, 38,* 13-18.

Highlen, P. S., & Sudarsky-Gleiser, C. (1994). Co-essence model of vocational assessment for racial/ethnic minorities (CEMVA-REM): An existential model. *Journal of Career Assessment, 2,* 304-329.

Ivey, A. E., Ivey, M. B., & Zalaquett, C. P. (2018). *Intentional interviewing and counseling: Facilitating client development in a multicultural society* (9th ed.). Boston, MA: Cengage Learning.

Ivy, A. E., D'Andrea, M., Ivy, M. B., & Simek-Morgan, L. (2002). *Theories of counseling and psychotherapy: A multicultural perspective* (5th ed.). Boston, MA: Allyn & Bacon.

Krumboltz, J. D., & Coon, D. W. (1995). Current professional issues in vocational psychology. In W. B. Walsh & S. H. Osipow (Eds.), *Handbook of vocational psychology* (2nd ed., pp. 391-420). Hillsdale, NJ: Erlbaum.

Lee, C. C. (1984). Predicting the career choice attitudes of rural Black, White, and Native American high school students. *Vocational Guidance Quarterly, 32,* 177-184.

Lenz, J. G., Peterson, G. W., Reardon, R. C., & Saunders, D. E. (2010). *Connecting career and mental health counseling: Integrating theory and practice.* Retrieved from https://www.counseling.org/Resources/Library/VISTAS/2010-V-Online/Article_01.pdf

Lowman, R. L. (1993). The inter-domain model of career assessment and counseling. *Journal of Counseling and Development, 71,* 549-554.

McWhirter, J. J., McWhirter, B. T., McWhirter, E. H., McWhirter, A. C., & McWhirter, R. (2016). *At risk youth.* Boston, MA: Cengage.

Movement Advancement Project. (2019). Equality maps: State non-discrimination laws. Retrieved from: http://www.lgbtmap.org/equality-maps/non_discrimination_laws

National Career Development Association [NCDA]. (2020). *Career counseling competencies.* Retrieved from https://www.ncda.org/aws/NCDA/asset_manager/get_file/26627

Niles, S. G., & Harris-Bowlsbey, J. (2005). *Career development interventions in the 21st Century* (2nd ed.). Upper Saddle River, NJ: Pearson Merrill Prentice Hall.

Niles, S. G., & Pate, P. H., Jr. (1989). Competency and training issues related to the integration of career counseling and mental health counseling. *Journal of Career Development, 16,* 63-71.

Patterson, C. H. (1996). Multicultural counseling: From diversity to universality. *Journal of Counseling and Development, 74,* 227-235.

Pedersen, P. (1996). The importance of both similarities and differences in multicultural counseling: Reaction to C. H. Patterson. *Journal of Counseling and Development, 74,* 236-237.

Perry, J. C., & Calhoun-Butts, C. (2012). A qualitative study of urban Hispanic youth in an after-school program: Career, cultural, and educational development. *The Counseling Psychologist, 40*(4), 477-519.

Ponterotto, J. G., Rivera, L., & Sueyoshi, L. A. (2000). The career-in-culture interview: A semi-structured protocol for the cross-cultural intake interview. *Career Development Quarterly, 49,* 85-96.

Pyle, K. R., & Hayden, S. C. (2015). *Group career counseling: Practices and principles* (2nd ed.). Broken Arrow, OK: National Career Development Association.

Ridley, C. R. (1995). *Overcoming unintentional racism in counseling and therapy: A practitioner's guide to intentional intervention.* Thousand Oaks, CA: Sage.

Ridley, C. R., Li, L. C., & Hill, C. L. (1998). Multicultural assessment: Reexamination, reconceptualization, and practical application. *The Counseling Psychologist, 26*(6), 939-947.

Roysircar, G., Arredondo, P., Fuertes, J. N., Ponterotto, J. G., & Toporek, R. L. (2003). *Multicultural counseling competencies 2003: Association for multicultural counseling and development.* Alexandria, VA: Association for Multicultural Counseling and Development.

Spokane, A. R. (1991). *Career interventions.* Upper Saddle River, NJ: Prentice-Hall.

Sue, D. W., & Sue, D. (2003). *Counseling the culturally diverse: Theory and practice* (4th ed.). Hoboken, NJ: John Wiley & Sons, Inc.

Sue, D. W. & Sue, D. (2016). *Counseling the culturally diverse: Theory and Practice.* (7th ed). New York: John Wiley & Sons, Inc.

Thomas, D. A., & Alderfer, C. P. (1989). The influence of race on career dynamics: Theory and research on minority career experiences. In M. B. Arthur & T. Douglas (Eds.), *Handbook of career theory* (pp. 133-158). New York, NY: Cambridge University Press.

Walker, J. V., III, & Peterson, G. W. (2012). Career thoughts, indecision, and depression: Implications for mental health assessment in career counseling. *Journal of Career Assessment, 20*(4), 497-506.

Whaley, A. L. (2001). Cultural mistrust and mental health services for African Americans: A review and meta-analysis. *The Counseling Psychologist, 29,* 513-521.

Willis, J., & Todorov, A. (2006). First impressions: Making up your mind after a 100-ms exposure to a face. *Psychological science, 17*(7), 592-598.

Yost, E. B., & Corbishley, M. A. (1987). *Career counseling: A psychological approach.* San Francisco, CA: Jossey-Bass.

Zunker, V. (2008). *Career, work, and mental health.* Thousand Oaks, CA: Sage.

Multiculturally Competent Career Counseling Skills

CHAPTER 7

Cultural Competence in Assessment

Malachi is a seventeen-year-old, African American high school senior who has come to counseling to discuss his life after high school. He has not made any decisions about what he wants to do, and every time he has seen his high school counselor in the past, he has changed his mind about his goals. Malachi's grades are average, mainly Bs and Cs. He has taken enough of the right classes and he has gotten adequate grades to enter the local community college or a two-year technical college; however, his grades indicate that he would not be competitive at a four-year college or university. His counselor, Jim (a White male), assumes that part of his task is to help Malachi determine his career aspirations, perhaps by administering career assessments. Because he has received some training in multicultural counseling, Jim is aware that there are issues related to assessment for members of diverse groups. Therefore, he is hesitant about traditional instruments. Malachi is his first African American student, and Jim wants to be certain that he does what is best for Malachi. Jim decides that he needs more direction and guidance to work with Malachi, so he asks a colleague, who is well trained in multicultural career counseling, to supervise his work with this client.

Jim is making a culturally sensitive and ethical decision. He realizes that he lacks the expertise to serve his client in the most effective manner possible and he is seeking assistance so that he will learn more and be better prepared to handle clients like Malachi in the future. For Jim to be culturally competent in his work with Malachi, he not only will have to tap into his knowledge about cultural differences, but he will also need to learn to evaluate and interpret the instruments so that Malachi will reap the largest possible benefits from them. Jim may also need to learn alternative means of assessment which may be more appropriate for the various members of his culturally diverse clientele.

Assessment has been the cornerstone of career counseling since its inception (Gainor, 2000). In fact, skills in assessment and in providing career information are the areas of expertise that most distinguish career professionals from other counseling specialties (Niles & Martin, 2019). Traditionally, career assessment includes assessing ability and/or aptitude, along with interests, values, and personality. More recently, qualitative assessments have been used to identify clients' cognitive and affective responses that lead to making meaning from their experiences (Stoltz, Bell, & Mazahreh, 2019). Career professionals administer assessments to help clients access information about themselves that they would otherwise be unable to do in an expedient manner. The information clients learn about themselves include their needs, values, interests, abilities, and career development progress (Niles & Harris-Bowlsbey, 2005). The results of these assessments are interpreted either to diagnose client problematic areas or to assist clients with subsequent decision making (Subich, 1996; Stoltz, Bell, & Mazahreh, 2019). Therefore, career professionals take assessment courses that would typically focus on the technical qualities and the diagnostic nature of the assessments. This narrow focus can result in administering assessments without considering the holistic view of a client and may result in the ineffective or unethical evaluation and application of assessment results. The misuse of assessments has led to testing and career counseling being referred to in the past as "three sessions and a cloud of dust." The three-session practice (meet the client to choose instruments, administer the instruments, interpret the instruments), left clients more confused than helped. Today, such an approach is unlikely, given the standards for assessment and relevant ethical codes.

According to Ridley, Li, and Hill (1998), little guidance had been given to career professionals regarding multicultural assessment. They stated that "Clinicians are left to their own judgment as to what data to collect, how the data are to be collected, and how to organize and evaluate data" (p. 847). In that same year, Constantine (1998), eloquently listed the potential pitfalls of assessment with diverse populations; these include "inappropriate assessment content standardization samples, inequitable social consequences, unclear concept equivalence (i.e. whether a particular psychological construct has equivalent or similar meanings within and across various cultural groups), different predictive validity, and difference in test-taking skills" (p. 924). Since that time, there has been an effort to rectify this problem. In the 2015 edition, the National Career Development Code of Ethics Standard E 8 states:

> Career professionals use, with caution, assessment techniques that were normed on populations other than that of the client. Career professionals recognize the possible effects of age, color, culture, disability, ethnic group, gender, race, language preference, religion, spirituality, sexual orientation, and socioeconomic status on test administration and interpretation, and place test results in proper perspective with other relevant factors. Career professionals use caution when selecting assessments for culturally diverse populations to avoid the use of instruments that lack appropriate psychometric properties for the client population. (National Career Development Association [NCDA], 2015, p. 14)

Just 20 years ago, however, it was not uncommon that the standardization samples of career assessments and inventories included no people of color. Assessment developers operated under the culturally encapsulated assumption that all test takers would be similar to the White, European American, middle-class, nondisabled populations (often college students) upon which tests were normed. Because of these assumptions, not only is little known about the career development of marginalized groups, but also little is known about the applicability of career assessment to diverse populations (Ridley, Li, & Hill, 1998). Because several major test publishers have made an attempt to diversify their normative samples in recent years, the prospect of progress in this area seems brighter.

In 2012, the Association for Assessment in Counseling and Education (AACE; now the Association for Assessment and Research in Counseling, AARC) published a fourth edition of the *AACE Standards for Multicultural Assessment* (AACE, 2014). The standards cover: (a) advocacy; (b) selection of assessments: content and purpose, norming, reliability, and validity; (c) administration and scoring of assessments and (d) interpretation and application of assessment results. The introduction of the Advocacy Standard states:

> Culturally competent professional counselors recognize the importance of social justice advocacy; they integrate understanding of age, gender, ability, race, ethnic group, national origin, religion, sexual orientation, linguistic background, and other personal characteristics in order to provide appropriate assessment and diagnostic techniques. (p. 2)

In 2015, the National Career Development Association (NCDA) revised the Code of Ethics for the use of assessments with multicultural populations. Under Standard E, Evaluation, Assessment and Interpretation, Section E.8. Multicultural Issues/Diversity in Assessment states:

> Career professionals use, with caution, assessment techniques that were normed on populations other than that of the client. Career professionals recognize the possible effects of age, color, culture, disability, ethnic group, gender, race, language preference, religion, spirituality, sexual orientation, and socioeconomic status on test administration and interpretation, and place test results in proper perspective with other relevant factors. Career professionals use caution when selecting assessments for culturally diverse populations to avoid the use of instruments that lack appropriate psychometric properties for the client population. (p. 14)

Career professionals who adhere to these standards would not only serve their marginalized clients well, but would increase their effectiveness with all clients. With the guidelines from NCDA and AARC in mind, it is important for career professionals to be familiar with the benefits and liabilities of using assessments with their clients.

Cultural Issues with Assessment Instruments

For career professionals to utilize career assessment to the greatest advantage of their clients, they need to understand the societal influences that create biased instruments. Until society changes or a truly culturally fair assessment is developed, career professionals are advised to be mindful of how they select, administer and interpret the results of potentially biased assessment instruments. Culturally competent career professionals are not only aware of cultural bias in assessment, but they also do their homework to be certain that the assessments they choose are appropriate for the members of the marginalized groups they will be serving (as Jim is doing for Malachi). Without such consideration, career professionals risk perpetuating "an oppressive system that denies equal access to occupational opportunity to all (Gainor, 2000, p. 170). The discussion below outlines issues related to three different types of standardized assessments commonly used in career counseling: interest inventories, aptitude and ability tests, and personality tests.

Interest Inventories

Interest inventories are administered to help clients make career decisions by focusing on client interests rather than on existing abilities or environmental context (e.g., financial resources, family support, etc.). Career professionals usually assign interest inventories to clients to help them expand their ideas about possible careers. This expansion of choices does not always occur naturally among culturally different groups. Due to limited societal options, their perceived interests tend to cluster around a small range of career choice possibilities, and, unfortunately, interest inventories tend to confirm that tendency. As a result, marginalized groups find themselves presented with limited career options (Gainor, 2000). Several studies have been conducted, which are geared toward determining if interest inventories are appropriate to use with ethnic minority groups. Carter and Swanson (1990) state emphatically that the Strong Interest Inventory (SII) is not valid for African Americans, but subsequent research has found that Holland's hexagonal theory, which is part of the SII, is useful with ethnic minority groups (Anderson, Tracey, & Rounds, 1997; Day & Rounds, 1998; Fouad, Harmon, & Borgen, 1997). The problem is the Strong is still heavily reliant on a predominantly White reference group, and that small normative group is inappropriately applied to all clients, ethnic minority or otherwise. As with many standardized tests, the Strong was updated and re-normed in 2004. Unfortunately, the new normative sample still came up somewhat short in terms of diversity. Although the numbers for the sample overall look promising—10.3% African American females; 4.4% African American males, 6.2% Latinas, 3.8% Latinos, 4.3% Asian American females, and 2.4% Asian American males—

these marginalized groups were underrepresented in the general themes and occupational scales (Kelly, 2010). In other words, although the respondents were more representative of the general U.S. population, they were still being compared against groups that were predominantly White.

Interestingly, although the gender gap within traditional occupations has narrowed as women continue to move into occupations traditionally reserved for men, there still are enough differences between how women score items on the interest inventories to warrant continuation of separate scales for men and women (Su, Rounds, & Armstrong, 2009). When the Strong was first developed, there was a form for men and a separate form for women. Eventually, the two forms were merged, but the results for men and women were never combined. In fact, research on the Strong items found that there were differences between men and women on 97 items and that these differences were substantial enough to warrant the development of a separate scale that reflected gender differences (Harmon, Hansen, Borgen, & Hammer, 1994).

Similarly, a study on sexual orientation as it pertains to career interests by Chung and Harmon (1994) found that there are measurable patterns of career preferences for gay men that differ from those of straight men. Using the Strong (which incorporates the Holland occupational codes) research found that gay men score lower on the Realistic and Investigative occupations and higher on the Artistic and Social occupations. In fact, Croteau, Anderson, & DiStefano (2000) suggest that gay men and lesbians tend to choose nontraditional careers more often than heterosexual men and women. Unfortunately, culturally encapsulated career professionals may try to discourage their gay and lesbian clients from choosing these nontraditional careers, even though these careers may be the best for these client (Harmon et al., 1994).

DeWitt (1994) suggests that the Strong may be helpful in (a) evaluating a client's abilities and accommodating the environment to enhance abilities, (b) gaining focus in career planning, (c) reducing stereotypical occupation placements (i.e. stuffing envelopes) and encouraging a wide range of choices, and (d) facilitating re-entry into the workplace. Although the previous edition of the Strong Interest Inventory manual offered an entire section for use with clients with disabilities, unfortunately, this section was not included in the 2004 edition (Case & Blackwell, 2008; Harmon et al., 1994). Much of the research on people with disabilities, however, shows their interests do not differ from people without disabilities including the dissimilar interests of men and women. Counselor awareness of the interests of people with disabilities is likely to result in an openness to serving these clients.

Measures of Personality

Personality measures are often used in career counseling to help clients gain an understanding of how their personal characteristics fit the requirements of different professions. These instruments also show clients how much they might personally have in common with potential colleagues. Personality instruments are sometimes administered by potential employers as well to help employers reduce the risk of hiring unsuitable employees. This practice, however, has come under great scrutiny because it is difficult to prove that specific personality factors can predict job performance and employers can use such assessments to discriminate against individuals with mental disabilities and other populations (Stabile, 2001).

While there exists many personality assessments in use worldwide, for purposes of illustration, the 16PF is discussed to show both bias revelations and current cautions. The 16PF is a popular personality assessment which was re-normed in 1994. A few major changes to the fifth edition of the 16PF (Cattell, 2004) included removing racially-biased, gender-biased, and ability-status biased language from the test, and removing items that might not be easily translated by those for whom English is a second language. In addition, the 16PF added a test of general reasoning ability comparable to an IQ test. Not unlike in other ability assessments, the authors of the 16PF revision found that race was a factor in the scoring of the reasoning subtest, though gender was not. For example, they found that Asians and Whites tended to score higher on the reasoning test than Native American, African American and Latinx test-takers. That being the case, it is advised that career professionals take caution when interpreting the Reasoning scale of this instrument with client from Native American, African American and Latinx communities.

Measures of Cognitive Ability

Measures of cognitive ability include general ability (usually intelligence tests), measures of aptitude (tests of potential performance, e.g., Scholastic Aptitude Test) and tests of achievement (tests of acquired knowledge, e.g., classroom tests) (Whiston, 2012). Assessment of aptitude and general ability have received the most criticism in terms of bias. The issue is that African Americans, Latinos/as, and Native Americans routinely score lower than Whites on both achievement and intelligence tests. The reasons for ethnic differences are difficult to determine, but those differences do exist (Aiken, 2003; Helms, 2007; National Center for Educational Statistics [NCES], 2011a, 2011b; Rushton & Jensen, 2005). The fact that people of diverse backgrounds perform differently on cognitive ability measures, as well as on other career assessments, has led to caution in using these instruments on clients from diverse backgrounds. Books, articles, and other literature concerning differential test performance results have proliferated over the years, although most of the conclusions have been contradictory, often contentious, when it comes to determining the causes of the differences. Concerning racism, one faction supports the contention that culturally different individuals (primarily African Americans) tend to score lower on standardized aptitude and intelligence measures because they are innately less intelligent than Whites (Jensen, 1998). The most recent flurry of debates regarding this issue occurred with the publication of *The Bell Curve* in 1994. In this book, Herrnstein and Murray (1994) concluded that the difference in IQ scores between racial groups is genetically determined. The response from African Americans researchers and others has been that the differences in scores do not stem from innate differences in intelligence, but rather from the fact that intelligence instruments may be inherently biased against those who are culturally different and who had different environmental experiences (Whiston, 2012). Subsequent research has shown that these assessments are just as predictive for racially and culturally different individuals as they are for Whites (Reynolds & Suzuki, 2012). While psychologists debate the validity of the research and conclusions made by Herrnstein and Murray, the take-away for career professionals is that they need to be aware that acceptance of the position of innate lack of intelligence perpetuates the idea that African Americans and Latinas/os are intellectually inferior (Hilliard, 1996), which, in turn, can harm the career development and career choices of ethnic minority clients.

Studies show that aptitude measures are also as predictive for ethnic minority groups as they are for Whites (Betz, 1992). Other research more specifically reported that the instrument used mostly for college admission, the Scholastic Aptitude Test (SAT) overpredicted the grade point averages (GPAs) of African Americans, Native American, and Latinos/as, and varied in the predictions for Asian Americans. While the SAT underpredicted GPAs for women, it accurately predicted the GPAs of White men. When the SAT was revised in 1994 to address the issue of bias, scores among women and minorities increased over time. According to Freedle (2003) and the College Board, however, the SAT continues to show lower scores for ethnic minorities (College Board, 2019).

The documented lower performance by ethnic minority groups on ability measures has long-reaching effects. Steele and Aronson (1995) found that the knowledge among ethnic minorities that their group performs consistently lower on aptitude tests has a negative effect on test performance. In other words, knowing the expectations applied to them, members of ethnic minority groups do not expect to perform well on these assessments and therefore are subject to stresses that inhibit their testing abilities. Students may perceive some stigma in being a member of an ethnic minority group when it comes to test performance. This in and of itself affects test performance.

Steele and Aronson's (1995) research on test takers was designed to see if an individual's association of race and low aptitude test scores actually influences that individual's test performance. Specifically, Steele and Aronson performed a series of studies on the effect negative stereotypes may have on the test performances of African Americans. The phenomenon they were interested in was a "stereotype threat," or the fear that a negative stereotype may be applied to oneself. According to the researchers, "any test that purports to measure intellectual ability might induce stereotype threat in African American students" (Steele & Aronson, 1995, p. 404). In one of their studies, Steele and Aronson found that even the mention of race in conjunction with assessment resulted in poorer performance of African Americans as compared to Whites and Blacks in a control group. In this study, 47 undergraduates (6 Black males, 18 Black females, 11 White males, and 12 White females) were randomly assigned to one of two conditions—one that required participants to indicate their racial identity and the other that did not require racial identification. All other assessment procedures and instruments were identical. Students were asked to complete a very difficult verbal aptitude instrument and were told not to expect to do well on it. After completing the test, the students completed a questionnaire designed to determine their reactions not just to the tests, but also to the questions on stereotype threat preceding the assessment. Steele and Aronson found that the African American students who were asked to identify themselves racially performed worse than any other test participants—not only the White students, but also the African American students who were not asked to identify their race. As a result of this study and others in the series, Steel and Aronson concluded that "compared to viewing the problem of Black underachievement as rooted in something about the group or its social conditions, this analysis uncovers a social psychological predicament of race, rife in the standardized testing situation that is amenable to change" (p. 819).

It seems reasonable to conclude from various sources (Goldman, 1992; Helms, 2002; Whiston, 2009), that ability measures are a greater reflection of an oppressive society than they are of the aptitude of individuals from diverse backgrounds and these measures need to be used with caution.

Selecting Aptitude Assessments as Applied to Malachi's Situation

This chapter opened with a vignette centering on Malachi, an African American high school senior who is exploring with his school counselor, Jim, whether or not he should enter the local community college, enroll in a technical college, or directly enter the workforce following his graduation. The continuation of the vignette below reveals that Malachi has now added joining the U.S. Navy as one of his options. This vignette also illustrates how Malachi's counseling experience is impacted by the pros and cons of the types of assessments discussed above when administered to ethnic minority students.

Since Malachi was interested in learning more about how well he might compete with others going to college, as well as those going into the Navy for training, Jim suggests that Malachi take two specific aptitude measures—the SAT and the ASVAB (the Armed Services Vocational Aptitude Battery). Jim consults his colleague about her experiences in discussing and interpreting these instruments for African American students. He also does some reading on the pros and cons of these assessments regarding African Americans to help with his follow-up talk with Malachi. He learns that aptitude tests tend to be as predictive for African Americans and other minorities as they are for Whites. In other words, these measures do predict how well students will perform in the armed services or in colleges that accept their test scores. Jim will also report to Malachi the average SAT scores earned by other African American students at the high school, over the past five years, who were accepted at various colleges and universities. Jim is happy that the senior counselor has kept data on students who graduated along with the universities where they were accepted. Jim will share that information with Malachi as well.

Jim's choice to help Malachi register for both the SAT and the ASVAB is appropriate, even though African Americans score lower than Whites on these assessments. Both assessments are required either for admission by colleges (SAT) or the military (ASVAB). More important, Jim's plan to discuss Malachi's results compared to the average scores of African American graduates from his high school who have been admitted to college will help Malachi develop a realistic evaluation of his chances to being admitted to college or the military training he desires.

Cultural and Environmental Influences on Career Assessment

Cultural Influences

In addition to problems with various types of career assessments themselves, cultural and environmental factors also influence the assessment experience. A number of authors in the counseling field have reminded career professionals that they need to be secure in their own cultures before they can work with the cultural issues of clients. Further, Arredondo et al., (1996), Flores, Spanierman, and Obasi (2003), Highlen and Sudarsky-Gleiser (1994), and Ridley and colleagues (1998) have suggested that career professionals explore client cultural background deeply before moving on to the assessment stage.

The AMCD, NCDA, and the AARC have all highlighted the importance of addressing cultural differences in career assessment. Some of the cultural differences among people that may influence their assessment results (as well as the counselor's interpretation of these results) include values and beliefs, age, ethnicity, racial identity, gender, language and acculturation, sexual orientation and ability status. The cultural factors that have received the most attention in the literature are the values and beliefs, acculturation, race, and ethnicity, language, and gender. Since the implementation of the Americans with Disabilities Act (ADA), however, more consideration has been given to the needs of people with disabilities; and the cultural factors that influence the careers of gay men, lesbians, and bisexuals have received more attention recently due to a great degree to groups' own efforts to increase sensitivity to their career issues. The following sections outline ways in which values and beliefs, race/ethnicity/sexual orientation/gender, cultural/racial identity and acculturation/language affect performance and outcomes in career assessment.

Values and beliefs. An individuals' values and beliefs can determine how he or she will receive the information from assessment results. In collective cultures that value interdependence (such as Latino and Native American cultures), individual assessments rarely affect only the test taker. In these cultures, the individual is subordinate to the group. Therefore, when an individual takes an assessment, the outcome is important to the entire group (LaFramboise, Trimble, & Mohart, 1990). When one does well, this reflects positively on the group, and one's failures reflect negatively on the group. Culturally competent career professionals keep this in mind when assigning any kind of standardized assessment to people who value the collective culture (Fukuyama & Cox, 1992). While awareness of cultural collectiveness is important, career professionals also keep in mind that some individuals from these collective cultures may have adopted the Western and European American values of individuality (Ridley et al., 1998).

An intriguing example of how values and beliefs influence career assessment is that on interest inventories, certain cultural groups gravitate towards certain occupational fields. For example, on the Strong, African American males and females score high on social careers, whereas Asian Americans score high on math and science careers. Meir and Tziner (2001) have pointed out the strong influence cultures can have on the career choices of members of a cultural group. They used Hofstede's (1986) classification of cultures to outline the careers that most closely relate to the values of the cultural groups. African Americans, for example, tend to have collectivist and communal values that are most readily represented by social occupations. Asian Americans, although also collectivist, tend to avoid ambiguity and uncertainty, a choice that science and math careers tend to reflect.

Race and ethnicity. The effect of race and ethnicity on test performance has been perhaps the most hotly debated topic in the field of career counseling. The original impetus for the debate was Jensen's research on intelligence, in which Jensen concluded that African Americans are intellectually inferior to Whites

(Jensen, 1980). The reverberations of this conclusion can still be felt today. Studies have continued to show that Whites and Asians score higher on standardized aptitude measures than Latinos/as, who in turn score higher than African Americans (Hartman, McDaniel, & Whetzel, 2003). Alternate research, however, espouses that measures of aptitude are biased, because items on these tests require information more readily available in White culture (Loehlin, Lindzey, & Spuhler, 1975).

Sexual orientation and gender. For gay, lesbian and transgender clients, the Strong results may be affected by heterosexist assumptions on the part of the test developers and examiners (Whitcomb, Wettersten, & Stolz, 2006). An example is the use of heterosexual norms on the "Infrequent Response" scale of the Strong Interest Inventory. The Infrequent Response Scale was developed by creating items most people would answer a certain way. For example, if most people are asked if they would like to win a million dollars, they would say yes and if someone were to say no, that would be different from the majority of people and would be counted as an infrequent response. One assumption about this kind of response would be that the examinee may not be reading the test, but instead may be randomly filling in the test bubbles. When there are numerous infrequent responses, the results of the Strong are considered invalid. Examinees with enough nontraditional responses (such as teacher for men, construction worker for women) are in danger of having the results of their whole inventory invalidated. Career professionals need to be aware that this normative generalization is culturally encapsulated and is found not only in the Strong but, also in other career assessments. When career professionals interpret the results of the Strong for gay, lesbian, bisexual, or transgendered clients, they need to be aware that the gender-based occupational scale of the Strong needs to be accompanied by further exploration because their clients may fit certain occupational roles better than the inventory results might indicate.

Cultural and racial identity. An individual's acceptance of his or her racial or cultural identity may also have an impact on the results of standardized assessment. Subich (1996) suggests that simply noting the race of a client is insufficient when interpreting assessment results—addressing racial identity is also important to "fully appreciate individual differences" (p. 285). According to Gainor (2000), several studies have investigated the relationship between racial identity and career development and have concluded that racial identity is important to explore (Evans & Herr, 1994; Gainor & Lent, 1998). For example, individuals at the Conformity or Dissonance identity stages are more likely to experience internalized racism, which has been found to negatively affect self-efficacy and may, in turn, result in clients limiting their own career choices on interest inventories (Betz & Hackett, 1987; Highlen & Sudarsky-Gliser, 1994). Clients in the Resistance Stage may be particularly outraged by racism and may refuse to participate in testing at all.

Assessment of a client's cultural/racial identity may be conducted through an interview with the client. Career professionals familiar with the models can take educated guesses about the client's attitudes; however, there are several more formal assessment instruments that may be appropriate, for example, Parham and Helms' (1985) widely researched Racial Identity Attitude Scale (for African American clients).

Acculturation and language. Acculturation is the degree to which individuals adopt or conform to cultures different from their own. More often than not, acculturation refers to the degree to which racial and ethnic minority group members adopt the values and lifestyles of the dominant European American culture (Lee & Chuang, 2005; Lee, 1997). It is tempting for career professionals to predict how clients from particular cultures will think, behave, or emotionally react to assessment. An assessment of acculturation, however, needs to be conducted before such predictions may be applied to any specific client. Because ethnic minorities generally function within the dominant culture in their jobs or in the educational arena, they learn to maneuver between two different cultures— their own culture at home and the dominant culture at work or at school. Some individuals can separate their experiences and move in and out of the two cultures with ease. These types of people are highly acculturated because they know how to function in the dominant society without completely abandoning their own culture. Recent immigrants, on the other hand, are less likely to be acculturated and will tend to place major importance on preserving their own cultures (Berry, 1980; Levine & Padilla, 1980). In their research of an acculturation scale, Olmedo and Padilla (1978) found that language was the best predictor of acculturation— the more acculturated people are, the more likely they are to speak English. Gauging a client's level of acculturation is important in assessment selection and interpretation. The more acculturated a client is, the more helpful standardized tests will be. Conversely, many assessments may not be useful for clients whose acculturation level is low because clients may lack the fluency in English needed to perform well on the assessment, assessments translated for clients may be suspect, and assessments geared toward and normed on European American culture are not likely to provide clients with accurate information about themselves (Hanson, 1987; Highlen & Sudarsky-Gleiser, 1994).

Another important consideration is that even when assessments are translated, words do not always have equal meaning across languages, and various nuances in the original measure may be lost in translation, resulting in skewed assessment results (Hanson, 1987). The same problem may occur when career professionals use interpreters to explain assessment results to clients. In the AARC standards, instrument developers are encouraged to assess the validity of translated assessments. Assessment administrators need to review that information before deciding to administer an assessment to their clients. Additionally, career professionals with bilingual clients need to consult with their clients to determine the language where their reading skills are most proficient.

Environmental Influences on Career Assessment

In addition to cultural factors, environmental factors such as socioeconomic status, community support, or lack thereof, as well as racism and discrimination may influence career assessment results (Reynolds & Suzuki, 2012).

Socioeconomic status. As stated previously, differences in assessment scores within cultural groups can be directly related to socioeconomic status. Poverty is likely to result in poor physical health, poor nutrition, and poor cognitive development—all of which affect the results of assessments (Neisser et al., 1996). Moreover, poverty correlates with inadequate educational preparation, further affecting the assessment scores of clients from poor socio-economic backgrounds (Krane & Tirre, 2005).

Inadequate education and preparation subsequently lead to lower-level occupation options, unemployment and, for some, criminal activity. Career professionals need to be aware of any academic limitations of their clients before administering any measures. If a client's reading level is below that of an instrument, the career professional needs to obtain an appropriate form of the test, if one is available, or make other adaptations, such as employing a reader.

School districts with limited resources, such as those in impoverished areas, may not have room in the budget for a battery of assessment measures. Career professionals would do well to discover instruments at reasonable costs to the district—perhaps hand-scored instruments rather than those that are computer-scored, assessments that allow for the duplication of a certain number of forms, and/or lower-cost online assessments. Whatever the clientele, career professionals need to be creative and resourceful when they choose to use standardized assessment without sacrificing the quality of the instruments they use.

Community. The community is another environmental factor that may influence assessment outcomes. In cultures that are more collaborative than others, community support may be extensive. In a collaborative community, an individual's interest inventory or aptitude test may be either supported by the community or not. A well-used analogy compares people in a community to crabs in a barrel. The crabs on the bottom are always pulling the crabs that are crawling to the top, back down to the bottom. The negative assumption that is typically associated with crabs in a barrel carries through to Gottfredson's (1981) theory of circumscription, in which the author suggests that individuals often give up on career options that would require too much effort to achieve, or would be considered over-reaching in their communities. On the other hand, a more positive interpretation of the analogy is that the crabs at the bottom of the barrel are trying to save those climbing out of the barrel from getting thrown in a pot full of boiling water. Supportive communities, acting in unison to uplift young people, may encourage careers that students may have felt out of their reach. Some high school students, for example, attend SAT preparation courses at their churches and community centers. Career development programs sponsored by clergy, politicians, business, and so forth that are inclusive of community members have been known to have a positive effect on the career options of young people, and these young people may express wider career interests on their inventory results (D'Andrea & Daniels, 1992).

Racism and discrimination. Racism and discrimination in employment assessment is still a problem, albeit to a lesser degree than in the past, primarily due to legal constraints (Drummond & Jones, 2006). At one time, career assessments were used to eliminate individuals from jobs because of their demographic attributes, such as race, gender, age, and so forth. Nowadays, there may be more sophisticated approaches to discrimination. Over 84,000 charges of discrimination were filed in 2017 (USEEOC, 2018) and until racism and discrimination no longer exist in our society, such practice may persist, perhaps in less overtly intentional ways, but persist nonetheless via culturally encapsulated instrument creators, administrators, and career professionals.

Racism and discrimination may also influence client attitudes toward career assessment. Subich (1996) has suggested using Swanson and Tokar's (1991) Career Barriers Inventory (CBI) to help determine the degree to which clients believe they are limited in their careers as a result of racism and discrimination. Administering the CBI to multicultural populations facilitates discussion between the client and counselor and provides career professionals with greater insight into the effects of racism and discrimination on their clients. Unfortunately, as with other assessments, client perceptions of barriers may affect client willingness to complete the CBI. Some clients may have had such extensive negative experiences with testing while attending school that they "may not trust and therefore may be suspicious of the assessment process" (Gainor, 2000, p. 180).

Cultural and Environmental Factors Applied to Malachi's Situation

The following continuation of the Malachi vignette reveals Malachi's cultural and environmental situation. For his counselor, Jim, to effectively interpret Malachi's assessment results, he will need to take the cultural and environmental factors into consideration:

In terms of culture, Malachi's family and significant adults have taught him to be proud of his cultural heritage. He attends a Black church regularly and participates in the church's youth group, but this is not his primary recreation. Included in his cultural education about African Americans is sense of responsibility to give back to his community and to value good works.

Malachi and his immediate family always speak Standard English unless emphasis is needed on a particular point, in which case they may employ Black Vernacular English. Many family members outside of their household tend to switch between Standard English and Black Vernacular depending on who is being addressed. Malachi lives in an extended family household. He is the oldest of three children—he has two sisters. His father died when Malachi was nine years old, at which time his maternal grandmother (also a widow) came to live with them. About a year ago, Malachi's mother's second cousin, Aisha (two years his junior), came to live with them as well, because Aisha's mother was deployed to the Middle East. Malachi says that living with five women has not been difficult except when they hog the bathroom or badmouth Black men.

In terms of racial identity, Malachi is in the Dissonance Stage, moving toward the Resistance Stage. Malachi is just waking up to the reality of racism against African American males. He, of course had read about it, and heard about it from others and he had been taught about the history of discrimination, but until he and his friends grew to their current height, racism was an abstract concept to Malachi. Now when he walks down the street with four or five of his friends, they are eyed warily and scrutinized by other people. When they enter a store, they are stopped immediately and asked what they want to buy and then they are followed around the store. Malachi's uncle told him once about the problems of being stopped by law enforcement officers for DWB (Driving While Black), and Malachi had laughed. Now he does not think the DWB story is so funny.

Malachi lives in a working-class neighborhood that is predominantly African American. Several adolescents in the neighborhood have gone to college (most to the local community college), and Malachi is feeling the pressure to go as well. In fact, his mother is always hassling him about it. From Malachi's career genogram (career family tree), Malachi's career counselor, Jim, discovers that the men in Malachi's family traditionally have been skilled workers—mechanics, brick masons, carpenters, and so forth. The women have worked in traditional female occupations—nurses and domestic workers. Malachi's father and paternal grandfather were mechanics, but Malachi's mother is an administrative assistant at a book publishing company.

Jim uses the information about Malachi's cultural background not only to determine the appropriate assessments for Malachi, but also to interpret those assessments. If he goes to college, Malachi will be the first one in his family to do so. It is important that Jim repeatedly caution Malachi that the assessments are not infallible and in fact, because of the low percentage of individuals to compare him against, they may not give a truly accurate snapshot of Malachi. Jim must be mindful of Malachi's racial identity status because it may have a great impact on his career interests and the career decisions he makes later. Jim is aware that Malachi is in a vulnerable place right now—just beginning to develop an emotional awareness of racism. Malachi appears to be between identity stages and probably developing some anger towards Whites at this point. Jim will need to explore with Malachi how he will feel if he enters a predominantly White technical school to pursue a career. How will he cope with microaggressions and outright racism? Jim knows that Malachi has a strong support system and will use that information to help Malachi work out a strategy to overcome the sting of racism.

Jim will need to recall, when he interprets the results of the interest and ability assessments, how important family and community are to Malachi. Giving back to the community is a very significant value that will be reflected in several of Malachi's assessments. Some of these values can be fostered through a career or through volunteer work depending on how much of a commitment Malachi has to them. Finally, Jim needs to keep in mind that Malachi's male family history is overwhelmingly blue collar—a fact that may show up in Malachi's interest inventory and assessment results. Jim will need to address this phenomenon with Malachi and explore technical careers as well as college careers during interpretations as well.

Assessment Interpretation for Diverse Populations

Prior to interpreting assessment results, career professionals are culturally sensitive and diligent in selecting the appropriate assessments for their clients, and they may have already performed qualitative assessments to establish rapport, define the career problems, gather information about the client's culture and level of acculturation, and determine that formal assessment is the best option to unearth the information the client needs. Qualitative assessment may include interview questions, career stories, career fantasies, guided imagery, etc. Many authors recommend that qualitative assessment be given to all culturally different populations (Goldman, 1990; Highlen & Sudarsky-Gleiser, 1994). They argue that there are too many possible pitfalls with the use of standardized testing, and therefore qualitative assessment is a necessary step in avoiding stereotyping and labeling clients. To get a true measure of the client's possible testing pitfalls and to ensure the assessments are not interpreted in a culturally encapsulated manner, multiple qualitative assessments need to be administered. Comas-Diaz (1996) lists twenty factors that career professionals need to consider discussing with culturally different clients in a pretesting interview. In addition to the topics discussed in previous chapters such as race, racial identity, culture, religion, socioeconomic status and history, sexual orientation and physical disabilities, she also suggests discussing historical age cohorts, acculturation, experiences with trauma and abuse, marital status, and generic dispositions. Not every factor will need to be discussed with every client, however.

Taking all Comas-Diaz's factors into consideration is a daunting task. An additional daunting factor for career professionals, as Ridley, Li, and Hill (1998) point out, is that the career counseling literature consistently recommends that career professionals consider factors of culture and environment, yet rarely does the literature give guidance about how to do so. It is not surprising that beginning career professionals may feel overwhelmed with the responsibility. In an effort to help, several authors have designed models for multicultural career assessment, two of which are discussed in more detail, after the interpretation scenario between Jim and Malachi is shared. The two models that follow are the Ridley, Li, and Hill model, and the model by Flores and colleagues.

Assessment Interpretation as Applied to Malachi's Situation

The following are sections of the dialog that took place when Jim interpreted Malachi's scores. Included are the sections that address the integration of culture and environment into the interpretation. Jim has administered the SAT, the Strong Interest Inventory, and the 16PF personality assessment to Malachi.

SAT

Jim met with Malachi once all the test scores were in. The session went as follows:

Jim: Malachi, before you took the SAT, we talked about what you wanted to get from taking this test, and as I recall, you wanted to get an idea of whether you were "college material." Is that still what you want to know?

(They discuss the goals for taking this test and Malachi's reaction to the test itself.)

Jim: We also talked about some of the issues for African Americans regarding the results. You may recall that African Americans have traditionally scored lower than Whites on the SAT. There have been a great many debates as to why this occurs, but no definitive proven reasons have been found. What we do know is that the SAT is good at predicting college performance for African Americans as well as Whites. Your scores indicate that you have great potential to be successful in college. I was worried that your scores may have been negatively affected after our talk about how African Americans score lower than Whites. At least that is my understanding of what sometimes happens. But you did very well. In fact, you scored in a range that indicates you could probably have done better in high school than you have. What is your reaction to that?

(Jim goes on to explore this issue with Malachi.)

Jim: So, it seems you could be making As and Bs, but maybe you think this would make you uncool.

Malachi: Yeah, you don't want to seem too smart. I'd catch hell from my boys if they thought I was too into the books.

Jim empathizes and asks how his friends will feel about his going to college. Malachi replies that they will probably be cool with it. They have other friends who have gone to college and Malachi thinks his friends respect them for it.

Jim: So, college is cool but being a geek is not.

Jim then suggested that Malachi's family and his church would be very happy if he went to college and did well. Malachi agreed and said that it was what his mother had been pushing for this last year, but he really did not think he had a chance to get in.

Jim: Malachi, with your GPA you will probably be more competitive right now at the community college level, but we should leave the four-year college option open, because your SAT scores are good. Depending on what you intend to take as your major and how you feel about being at a more hectic and competitive four-year institution, you could perform well at a four-year college as well. Remember what I said about how SAT scores tend to over-predict performance for African American men? What that means is that you may not get as high of a grade point average as your White classmates with the same SAT scores. Tell me, what is your reaction to this information?

Malachi: If I get into college, I will not fool around like I did in high school, so I will probably have a good GPA. I will just have to work even harder to get grades as high as those White guys. It is not fair but, at least I know what I'm up against.

During this interpretation, Jim did a good job of including Malachi in the conversation about the results. He reminded Malachi of the limitations of the test for African Americans but, most important, Jim took into consideration the reactions of Malachi's family, friends and community.

Strong Interest Inventory

(Jim and Malachi first discuss the reason for taking the Strong Interest Inventory.)

Jim: Malachi, you may remember that we decided on the Strong Interest Inventory to give you some ideas about careers you may not be aware of that may interest you. I feel pretty confident about some of your results on the Strong Interest Inventory. Remember that we discussed that the Strong was researched very heavily to see how it works with African Americans. The general occupational themes tend not to vary in terms of people's ethnicity, so when I give you your results on the

General Occupational Themes (GOT), you can feel pretty certain that they are not biased against African Americans.

(Jim goes on to report on the GOT.)

Jim: The Basic Interest Scales and the Occupational Scales have not been proven scientifically to differentiate among cultural groups, so we really do not know, for example, whether you are similar to other African Americans in nuclear engineering or any other career field. What will show is how similar you are to a general population of nuclear engineers (whether they are White, Black, Asian, Latino/a or any other group). You may have similar interests as these individuals or you may not. We just do not have that kind of comparison information right now. We decided to go on with this test because we thought it would give us a better idea of the general categories of careers that you might be interested in. I think it has done that.

Jim goes on to report Malachi's results on the Basic Interest and Occupational Scales, paying particular attention to the career Malachi has shown an expressed interest in and that reflect some of his family's interest, such as mechanical engineering. Malachi may look at other engineering types of jobs as well as those related to the field that do not require four years of college.

Again, Jim is meticulous about reminding Malachi about why the test was chosen and the limitations of the test for African Americans. What is not included here is Jim's discussion of traditional careers for African Americans. Jim was concerned that Malachi's scores may be restricted to those traditional careers as researchers have found. Such a discussion is appropriate when interpreting the results from an interest inventory based on stereotypic career groupings.

16PF

Jim: Remember that this is a personality test, and it will give us some information about your personality characteristics that might be helpful in selecting a career. Some of the things in your culture that you say are important are your family, your connection with other African Americans, and the fact that you want to make both your family and the people in your community proud of you. Some of these values are reflected in this inventory. Now, the 16PF did a much better job at getting ethnic minority participation than the Strong Interest Inventory. The group you are compared against (the normative sample) is represented in proportion to their numbers in the general U.S. population. The U.S. population is 12 percent African American, and 12 percent of the people your scores are compared against are African Americans. Interestingly, researchers did not find any real differences between African Americans and other groups on most of the scales of the 16PF. However, in this latest version, there is a general reasoning scale (which is an ability measure), and African Americans score lower on that scale than Whites. We really *do not need the reasoning scale because you have already taken the SAT and that is a good indicator of your abilities. (Jim goes on to report Malachi's 16PF scores.) One more thing, remember that your score is supposed to reflect what you are like on a typical day. People change, and their test scores on personality tests are likely to be affected by those changes, but usually in personality tests, the scores are pretty stable. Even so, these tests are not 100 percent precise as compared to, say a DNA test. If you were to take the test again, for example, you might get the same score but it is more likely that your scores will fall within a certain range (higher or lower), but we can be pretty confident about that range by using a standard formula.*

Jim did a good job again reminding Malachi about the purpose and limitations of the test. He was careful to mention how Malachi's family and community helped contribute to his personality development and how that would be reflected in the test results.

This scenario is just one way that demonstrates how career professionals might interpret a client's results on assessment instruments. Each career professional needs to discover his or her own strategy to incorporate race/ethnicity, culture, age, gender, ability status, and sexual orientation. However, there is help in the form of multicultural career assessment models that outline a step by step process.

Models of Multicultural and Career Assessment

The Ridley, Li, and Hill model and the model of Flores and colleagues have been designed to assist the multicultural career counselor to synthesize cultural information and make decisions about how to use cultural information. Neither model is explicit regarding selecting, administering, and interpreting assessments; however, both of the models provide some structure for utilizing both qualitative and quantitative data.

The Ridley, Li, and Hill Model: The Multicultural Assessment Process (MAP)

Ridley, Li, and Hill (1998) offer a conceptual framework, known as the Multicultural Assessment Process, or MAP, for assessment that they say is missing from previous multicultural assessment literature. While these authors developed their MAP model to focus on assessment of psychological disorders, the model is readily adaptable for career professionals. Figure 7.1 lists MAP's ten foundational principles. These principles include not only the need to thoroughly assess culture and environments, but also to take this one step further into practical application by speaking to the complexity and subjectivity of the cultural/environmental assessment process.

Figure 7.1

The Ten Foundational Principles of MAP

1. A sound assessment is accurate and comprehensive (p. 853)
2. Assessment is a larger concept than is diagnostic classification [and]... includes prognosis, severity ratings, compilation of strengths and resources, and social supports (pp. 853-854)
3. Psychological assessment is complex (p. 854)
4. Psychological assessment is a process of progressive decision making (p. 854)
5. As a decision-making process, assessment involves considerable subjectivity (p. 855)
6. A sound assessment has clinical utility (p. 857)
7. Culture is always relevant to psychological assessment (p. 857)
8. Assessment should include dispositional and environmental factors (p. 858)
9. Sound assessment requires a systemic methodology based on a conceptually coherent framework (p. 858)
10. Psychological assessment is a challenging responsibility (pp. 853-859)

Note. The ten Foundational Principles of MAP are listed by section heading and page number, as adapted from "Multicultural Assessment: Reexamination, Reconceptualization, and Practical Application" by C. R. Ridley, L. C. Li, & C. L. Hill, 1998, *The Counseling Psychologist, 26*(6) pp. 853-859. Copyright 1998 by the American Psychological Association.

According to Ridley et al. (1998), most clinical assessment needs "a systematic methodology based on a conceptually coherent framework" (p. 858). As a result, the MAP is systemically organized into a four-phase framework: (1) identify cultural data, (2) interpret cultural data, (3) incorporate cultural data, and (4) arrive at a sound assessment decision. Ridley, Li, and Hill also provide "decision points" throughout the process—decisions that need to be made to keep the process on track. In addition, the authors include "debiasing" strategies to assist career professionals in making good decisions.

Phase 1 of MAP is to identify the client's cultural information, whether this information seems relevant or not, and Phase 2 involves interpreting and organizing the information to yield a "working hypothesis" (p. 873) about the possible origins of a client's career issue (e.g., choosing a career, changing careers, etc.) with the goal of testing this hypothesis as valid or invalid during Phase 3. In other words, Ridley et al. (1998) suggest that counselors develop a scientific attitude. They suggest that counselors "use psychological testing to test hypotheses, not to generate them" (p. 881).

This is an interesting idea in career counseling. For example, Client A comes to career counseling stating that career decision-making is complicated because of family demands. In the client's culture, the family determines each member's occupation as it is never an individual decision. If, after the discussion of cultural values with the client, the counselor hypothesizes that client A's career interests differ greatly from those that her parents wish her to pursue, the counselor would administer an interest assessment to prove or disprove that hypothesis. As a result, the interpretation of the assessment results may be more relevant to the test taker. This procedure also forces career professionals to think about and choose assessments more methodically. During this phase, the career professional needs to also be aware of biases in assessment and assessment interpretation, especially concerning statistical error and the standard error of measurement.

Finally, in Phase 4 of MAP, the counselor uses information gleaned from hypothesis testing to make final decisions or a diagnosis to help the client move forward. For example, if the results of Client A's interest inventory prove the hypothesis, suggesting that the client does, in fact, have different interests from those her parents wish her to pursue, then the next step would be to discuss these differences with the client and how such differences might affect career decision-making. It may also be an option to bring in Client A's parents to discuss these differences, if it is appropriate for that cultural group. For some clients, differences between their career ideas and their parents' may not be such an issue. Then, it would be appropriate to introduce the client to other similar-minded people, who may act as role models.

Sometimes the counselor may need to recycle through the MAP process, based on the results of hypothesis testing—for example if the hypothesis does not stand up to testing. Ridley et al., however, warn counselors not to get caught up in endless testing and re-testing cycles.

In addition, Ridley et al. (1998) recommend using "debiasing" techniques during the MAP process to ensure that assessment has not been compromised by counselor values and beliefs regarding their clients' cultures. Counselors may erroneously employ one of three possible heuristics that impede scientific judgement: (a) failing to search for further information because the answer seems obvious based on the counselor's experience with similar client problems (known as the "availability heuristic"), (b) favoring information given at the beginning of an interview and ignoring information given later on (known as the "anchoring heuristic"), and (c) relying on stereotypes when looking for norms among a client's cultural group (known as the "representativeness heuristic"). To combat these errors. Ridley and colleagues recommend the following debiasing strategies:

- Look for other explanations for client problems, such as environmental or cultural explanations, rather than relying on stereotypes or past experiences with other clients (Arkes, 1981)
- Reframe interpretations of client issues so that they speak to strengths rather than weaknesses (for example, the client with few resources due to low socioeconomic status, but who is still successful, may be referred to as resourceful rather than disadvantaged).
- Delay making a decision about client issues in order to increase objectivity. This is a process similar to holding onto an emotion-packed email for three days to cool off before sending it (Spengler, Strohmer, & Dixon, 1995).

The Flores, Spanierman, and Obasi Model: Culturally Appropriate Career Assessment Model (CACAM)

In their discussion of instrument selection, Flores, Spanierman and Obasi (2003) provide recommendations to instrument developers and researchers that will assist career professionals in administering assessments to diverse populations. Among other things, Flores et al. (2003) suggest that when assessment developers see performance differences among diverse groups, they need to scientifically construct scales to accurately measure diverse groups. In addition, Flores and colleagues stress that counselors and psychologists need to establish their own reliability and validity data for specific populations, and that more representative samples need to be used in normative data. The authors suggest that career professionals use qualitative assessment, nonstandard assessments, computers, and verbal methods; they also advocate taking career assessment out into the community to churches, community centers, and schools.

The CACAM assumes that career professionals are competent in general, career, and multicultural counseling. There are four steps in the CACAM: (1) "information gathering, (2) selection of career instruments, (3) administration of career instruments, (4) interpretation of career assessment results" (Flores et al., 2003, p. 81). The authors believe that much can be discovered from sources other than standardized testing such as interviewing the client and following up with information taken from intake forms, checklists, and inventories that measure worldview and cultural values.

Not only do Flores et al. (2003) discuss the issues of widely used standardized tests such as the Strong Interest Inventory, they also recommend that career professionals review career assessments for problems with assessment construction regarding cultural validity and equivalency (linguistic, conceptual, scale, and normative equivalence). Only after such a review is a career professional to administer an assessment. Of course, the next step would be the culturally appropriate administration of the selected assessments that requires a strong relationship with the client and an environment that is welcoming and safe to the client, and everything needs to be done to make the environment comfortable including adjusting the physical accommodations or hiring readers.

The last step is the culturally appropriate interpretation of assessments. Flores et al. (2003) are similar to Ridley et al. (1998) in that they suggest using client information to test hypotheses about client assessment needs. According to Flores and colleagues, career professionals need to look for consistencies in the data—both qualitative and quantitative—before making hypotheses. In their view, integrating cultural data with assessment data is essential, and any information communicated to clients needs to be in a format clients will readily understand.

Final Thoughts about Assessment

Assessment is a technical and complicated process that causes concern for both clients and career professionals. Although it is always inadvisable to offer cookbook solutions to complicated issues, it may help to summarize some of the research described in this chapter. With that in mind, the following are some guidelines for administering tests to culturally diverse groups in career counseling:

1. Review the purpose of the assessment collaboratively with clients to ensure that the tests utilized will meet client needs.

2. If the instrument seems to meet client needs, investigate the test by reading all available information (such as manuals, mental measurements yearbooks, research articles), about its cultural inclusiveness including information on language and reading levels. Similarly, read instrument reviews, such as those found in Stoltz and Barclay's 2019 career assessment book and online companion.

3. Pay special attention to the standardization sample. Ensure that diversity percentages are close to population numbers of diverse groups. If there are no ethnic minorities listed among the normative sample, justify the use of this particular test with a particular client (justification might include that the client is highly acculturated or the local norms exist for this test).

4. If the instrument utilizes ethnic minorities or other special populations in the normative sample, pay close attention to how close the ethnic population compares to that of the general population. Also, check to see if any analyses have been conducted comparing the responses of different cultural groups. If the ethnic populations numbers are too small and/or

there is no cultural comparison data, administration of the assessment needs to be justified, as in item 3 above.

5. If there is data concerning administrative differences between culturally different groups, note the data and make a decision as to whether or not to proceed with the assessment. If there are norms for your client's group, it is feasible to go ahead and use that instrument. If there are testing differences, but no norms for your client's cultural group, the information about the norming sample may still be used to interpret a client's results. Determine how this information will be reported to the client.

6. Always explain to clients any caveats before administering a test and again when you interpret the test for clients.

7. Provide the best interpretation of the test results you can while taking into consideration the client's race, culture, and environment. Some lead-ins that may be helpful are:

   (a) We decided to use this test because...

   (b) This test has limitations for you because...What do you think?

   (c) A few of the things that are important to you as a(n)____are...and this test ____. Am I right?

   (d) What all this means for you, according to what you have told me, is ____. Does that sound right to you?

REVIEW/REFLECTION QUESTIONS

1. Use either the Flores, Spanierman, and Obasi (2003) Model or the Ridley, Li, and Hill (1998) Model, to assess your own career development. Discuss each of the steps and how each one may be useful in helping a client like yourself who is experiencing career problems.

2. Given the criticisms of cultural relevance of assessment, how do you see psychological assessment changing in the next twenty years as the United States becomes a more diverse country?

3. Review the guidelines in the last section of the chapter. Create a list of Don'ts (things not to do) for administering and interpreting assessments with culturally different groups.

4. You have been asked to create a culturally fair math aptitude instrument based on the information in this chapter. What are some of the cultural issues you need to be aware of when creating this test? How will you solve these cultural dilemmas in your assessment?

References

Aiken, C. R. (2003). *Psychological testing and assessment.* Boston, MA: Allyn & Bacon.

Anderson, M. Z., Tracey, T. J. G., & Rounds, J. (1997). Examining the invariance of Holland's vocational interest model across gender. *Journal of Vocational Behavior, 50,* 349-364.

Arkes, H. R. (1981). Impediments to accurate clinical judgment and possible ways to minimize their impact. *Journal of Consulting and Clinical Psychology, 49,* 323-330.

Arredondo, P., Toporek, R., Brown, S. P., Jones, J., Locke, D. C., Sanchez, J., & Stadler, H. (1996). Operationalization of the multicultural counseling competencies. *Journal of Multicultural Counseling and Development, 24,* 42-78.

Association for Assessment in Counseling and Education (2014). Standards for multicultural assessment in counseling and education. Retrieved December 27, 2018 from http://aarc-counseling.org/assets/cms/uploads/files/AACE-AMCD.pdf

Berry, J. W. (1980). Acculturation as varieties of adaptation. *Acculturation: Theory, models and some new findings, 9,* 25.

Betz, N. E. (1992). Counseling uses of self-efficacy theory. *Career Development Quarterly, 41,* 22-26.

Betz, N. E., & Hackett, G. (1987). The concept of agency in educational and career development. *Journal of Counseling Psychology, 34,* 299-308.

Carter, R. T., & Swanson, J. L. (1990). The validity of the Strong Interest Inventory with Black Americans: A review of the literature. *Journal of Vocational Behavior, 36,* 195-209.

Case, J. C., & Blackwell, T. L. (2008). Review of the Strong Interest Inventory. *Rehabilitation Counseling Bulletin, 51*(2), 122-126.

Cattell, H. (2004). *16PF fifth edition technical manual.* Champaign, IL: IPAT.

Chung, Y. B., & Harmon, L. W. (1994). The career interests and aspirations of gay men: How sex-role orientation is related. *Journal of Vocational Behavior, 45*(2), 223-239.

College Board. (2019). *SAT suite of assessments annual report.* Retrieved from https://reports.collegeboard.org/pdf/2019-total-group-sat-suite-assessments-annual-report.pdf

Comas-Diaz, L. (1996). Cultural considerations in diagnosis. In F. W. Kaslow (Ed.), *Handbook on relational diagnosis and dysfunctional family patterns* (pp. 152-168). Oxford, England: John Wiley, & Sons, Inc.

Constantine, M. G. (1998). Developing competence in multicultural assessment: Implications for counseling psychology training and practice. *The Counseling Psychologist, 26*(6), 922-929.

Croteau, J. M., Anderson, M. Z., & DiStefano, T. M. (2000). Lesbian, gay, and bisexual vocational psychology: Reviewing foundations and planning construction. In R. M. Perez, K. A. DeBond, & K. J. Bieschke (Eds.). *Handbook of counseling and psychotherapy with lesbian, gay, and bisexual clients* (pp. 383-408). Washington, DC, US: American Psychological Association.

D'Andrea, M., & Daniels, J. (1992). A career development program for inner-city Black youth. *Career Development Quarterly, 40*(3), 272-280.

Day, S. X, & Rounds, J. (1998). Universality of vocational interest structure among racial and ethnic minorities. *American Psychologist, 53*(7), 728-736.

DeWitt, D. W. (1994). Using the Strong with people who have disabilities. In L. W. Harmon, J. Hansen, F. H. Borgen, & A. Hammer (Eds.), *Strong Interest Inventory: Applications and technical guide* (pp. 281-290). Stanford, CA: Stanford University Press.

Drummond, R. J. & Jones, K. D. (2006). Assessment procedures for counselors and helping professions (6th ed.). Upper Saddle River, NJ: Pearson Education Inc.

Evans, K. M., & Herr, E. L. (1994). The influence of racial identity and the perception of discrimination on the career aspirations of African American men and women. *Journal of Vocational Behavior, 44,* 173-184.

Flores, L. Y., Spanierman, L. B., & Obasi, E. M. (2003). Ethical and professional issues in career assessment with diverse racial and ethnic groups. *Journal of Career Assessment, 11,* 76-95.

Fouad, N. A., Harmon, L. W., & Borgen, F. H. (1997). Structure of interests in employed male and female members of U.S. racial-ethnic minority and nonminority groups. *Journal of Counseling Psychology, 44,* 339-345.

Freedle, R. O. (2003). Correcting the SAT's ethnic and social-class bias: A method for re-estimating SAT scores. *Harvard Educational Review, 73,* 1-43.

Fukuyama, M. A., & Cox, C. I. (1992). Asian-Pacific islanders and career development. In D. Brown & C. Minor (Eds.), *Career needs in a diverse workforce: Implication of the NCDA Gallup survey* (pp. 27-50). Alexandria, VA: National Career Development Association.

Gainor, K. A. (2000). Vocational assessment with culturally diverse populations. In L. A. Suzuki, J. G. Ponterotto & P. J. Meller (Eds.), *Handbook of multicultural assessment: Clinical, psychological, and educational application* (2nd ed., pp. 169-189). San Francisco, CA: Jossey Bass.

Gainor, K. A., & Lent, R. W. (1998). Social cognitive expectations and racial identity attitudes in predicting the math choice intentions of Black college students. *Journal of Counseling Psychology, 45,* 403-413.

Goldman, L. (1990). Qualitative assessment. *The Counseling Psychologist, 18*(2), 205-213.

Goldman, L. (1992). Qualitative assessment: An approach for counselors. *Journal of Counseling and Development, 70,* 616-621.

Gottfredson, L. S. (1981). Circumscription and compromise: A developmental theory of occupational aspirations. *Journal of Counseling Psychology (Monograph), 28(6),* 545-579.

Hanson, J. I. C. (1987) Cross-cultural research on vocational interests. *Measurement and Evaluation in Counseling and Development, 20,* 65-71.

Hartman, N., McDaniel, M.A., & Whetzel, D.L. (2003). Racial and ethnic difference in performance. In J. E. Wall & G. Walz (Eds.), *Measuring Up: Assessment Issues for Teachers, Counselors and Administrators* (pp. 99-115). CAPs Press.

Harmon, L. W., Hanson, J. C., Borgen, F. & Hammer, A. (1994). *Strong Interest Inventory: Application and technical guide.* Palo Alto, CA: Consulting Psychologists Press.

Helms, J. E. (2002). A remedy for the Black-White test score disparity. *American Psychologist, 57,* 30-35.

Helms, J. E. (2007). Implementing fairness in racial group assessment of individuals. *American Psychologist, 62,* 1083-1085.

Herrnstein, R. J., & Murray, C. (1994). *The bell curve.* New York, NY: The Free Press.

Highlen, P. S., & Sudarsky-Gleiser, C. (1994). Co-essence model of vocational assessment for racial/ethnic minorities (CEMVA-REM): An existential model. *Journal of Career Assessment, 2,* 304-329.

Hilliard, A. G. III. (1996). Either a paradigm shift or no mental measurement: The nonscience and the nonsense of the bell curve. *Cultural Diversity and Mental Health, 2*(1), 1–20. https://doi.org/10.1037/1099-9809.2.1.1

Hofstede, G. (1986). Cultural difference in teaching and learning. *International Journal of Intercultural Relations, 10,* 301-320.

Jensen, A. R. (1980). *Bias in mental testing.* New York, NY: Free Press.

Jensen, A. R. (1998). *The g factor: The science of mental ability.* Westport, CT: Praeger/ Greenwood.

Kelly, K. R. (2010). Review of the Strong Interest Inventory (newly revised). In R. A. Spies, J. F. Carlson, K. F. Geisinger (Eds.), *The eighteenth mental measurements yearbook* (pp. 894-897). Lincoln, NE: Buros Institute for Testing.

Krane, N. E. R., & Tirre, W. C. (2005). Ability assessment in career counseling. In S. D. Brown & R. W. Lent (Eds.), *Career development and counseling: Putting theory and research to work* (pp. 330-3520). Hoboken, NJ: John Wiley & Sons, Inc.

LaFramboise, T. D., Trimble, J. E., & Mohart, G. V. (1990). Counseling intervention and Native American tradition. *The Counseling Psychologist, 18,* 628-654.

Lee, C. C. (1997). Cultural dynamics: Their importance in culturally responsive counseling. In C. C. Lee (Eds.), *Multicultural issues in counseling: New approaches to deliver* (2nd ed., pp. 15-30). Alexandria, VA: American Counseling Association.

Lee, C. C., & Chuang, B. (2005). Counseling people of color. In D. Capuzzi & D. R. Gross (Eds.), *Introduction to the counseling profession* (pp. 465-483). New York, NY: Allyn & Bacon.

Levine, E. S., & Padilla, A. M. (1980). *Crossing cultures in therapy: Pluralistic counseling for the Hispanic.* Monterey, CA: Brooks/Cole.

Loehlin, J. C., Lindzey, G., & Spuhler, J. N. (1975). *Race differences in intelligence.* San Francisco, CA: Freeman.

Meir, E. I., & Tziner, A. (2001). Cross-cultural assessment of interests. In F. T. L. Leong & A. Barak (Eds.), *Contemporary models in vocational psychology* (pp.133-166). Mahwah, NJ: Erlbaum.

NCDA. (2015). *NCDA code of ethics.* Retrieved from https://www.ncda.org/aws/NCDA/asset_manager/get_file/3395

National Center on Education Statistics. (2011a). *The nation's report card: Mathematics 2011 (NCES 2012-458).* Washington, DC: Institute of Education Sciences, U.S. Department of Education.

National Center on Education Statistics. (2011b). *The nation's report card: Reading 2011 (NCES 2012-458).* Washington, DC: Institute of Education Sciences, U.S. Department of Education.

Neisser, U., Boodoo, G. L., Bouchard, T. J., Boykin, A. W., Brody, N., Ceci, S. J., Halpern, D. F., Loehlin, J. C., Perloff, R., Sternberg, R. J., & Urbina, S. (1996). Intelligence: Knowns and unknowns. *American Psychologist, 51*(2), 77-101.

Niles, S. G., & Harris-Bowlsbey, J. (2005). *Introduction to career development interventions in the 21st century* (2nd edition). Columbus, OH: Merrill Prentice Hall.

Niles, S., & Martin, C. V. (2019). Career assessment: Perspectives on trends and issues. In K. B. Stoltz & S. R. Barclay (Eds.), *A comprehensive guide to career assessment* (pp. 43-58). Broken Arrow, OK: National Career Development Association.

Olmedo, E. L., & Padilla, A. M. (1978). Empirical and construct validation of a measure of acculturation for Mexican Americans. *Journal of Social Psychology, 10,* 179-187.

Parham, T. A., & Helms, J. E. (1985). Relation of racial identity attitudes to self-actualization and affective states of Black students. *Journal of Counseling Psychology, 32,* 431-440.

Reynolds, C. R., & Suzuki, L. A. (2012). Bias in psychological assessment: An empirical review and recommendations. In J. R. Graham, J. A. Naglieri, & I. B. Weiner (Eds.), *Handbook of psychology: Assessment psychology* (p. 82–113). John Wiley & Sons, Inc.

Ridley, C. R., Li, L. C., & Hill, C. L. (1998). Multicultural assessment: Reexamination, reconceptualization, and practical application. *The Counseling Psychologist, 26*(6). 939-947.

Rushton, J. P., & Jensen, A. R. (2005). Thirty years of research on race differences in cognitive ability. *Psychology, Public Policy, and Law, 11,* 235-294.

Spengler, P. M., Strohmer, D. C., & Dixon, D. N. (1995). A scientist-practitioner model of psychological assessment: Implications for training, practice and research. *The Counseling Psychology, 23,* 506-532.

Stabile, S. J. (2001). The use of personality tests as a hiring tool: Is the benefit worth the cost. *University of Pennsylvania Journal of Business Law, 4,* 279.

Steele, C. M., & Aronson, J. (1995). Stereotype threat and the intellectual test performance of African Americans. *Journal of Personality and Social Psychology, 69,* 797-811.

Stoltz, K. B., & Barclay, S. R. (Eds.), (2019). *A comprehensive guide to career assessment.* Broken Arrow, OK: National Career Development Association.

Stoltz, K. B., Bell, S., & Mazareh, L. G. (2019). Selecting and understand career assessments. In K. B. Stoltz & S. R. Barclay (Eds.), *A comprehensive guide to career assessment* (pp. 43-58). Broken Arrow, OK: National Career Development Association.

Su, R., Rounds, J., & Armstrong, P. I. (2009). Men and things, women and people: A meta-analysis of sex differences in interests. *Psychological Bulletin, 135*(6), 859.

Subich, L. M. (1996). Addressing diversity in the process of career assessment. In M. L. Savickas & W. B. Walsh (Eds.), *Handbook of career counseling theory and practice* (pp. 277-289). Palo Alto, CA: Davies-Black.

Swanson, J. L., & Tokar, D. M. (1991). Development and initial validation of the Career Barriers Inventory. *Journal of Vocational behavior, 39,* 344-361.

USEEOC. (2018). Charge statistics (charges filed with EEOC) FY 1997 through FY 2017. Retrieved January 10, 2019 from https://www.eeoc.gov/eeoc/statistics/enforcement/charges.cfm

Whitcomb, D. H., Wettersten, K. B., & Stolz, C. L. (2006). Career counseling with gay, lesbian, bisexual and transgender clients. In D. Capuzzi & M. S. Stauffer (Eds.), *Career counseling foundations, perspectives, and applications* (pp. 386-420). Boston, MA: Allyn & Bacon.

Whiston, S. C. (2012). *Principles and application of assessment in counseling* (4th ed.). Belmont, CA: Brooks/Cole.

CHAPTER 8

Culturally Competent Career Counseling with Children and Adolescents

Harlem is a first-year graduate student in an elementary school counseling program. When she reviewed her program of study, she said to her advisor "I'm going to be an elementary school counselor. Why do I need to take a course on career development? It's not like my students are going to go out and get a job when they finish elementary school. I need a course like play therapy. A career course is just a waste of my time."

It is not uncommon to see a reaction like Harlem's to those who are new to the school counseling profession. To the general public, career development for children boils down to asking them what they want to be when they grow up, and almost no one takes those wishes and dreams seriously. Often children's aspirations are ignored by adults because they tend to change frequently. Scholars agree, however, "that children as early as grade school years, establish a worker orientation and a coherent view of the world of work" (Porfeli, Hartung, & Vondracek 2008, p. 26). In fact, researchers have found that early childhood experiences with careers and family encouragement (or discouragement) have a major impact on future decision-making.

Unfortunately, school counselors are often reluctant to offer career counseling in the elementary school. Although they may include career development in their curriculum, some school counselors may put it on hold to address other issues. The lack of priority given to early career development can be detrimental to the future of marginalized students (Solberg, Howard, Blustein, & Close, 2002).

Why Career Counseling for Elementary Schoolers?

Career theorists have helped us to understand the role childhood dreams play in a person's career development. Ginzberg, Ginsburg, Axelrad and Herma (1951) and later Super (1957) were the first theorists to mention how childhood career development works. Besides Gottfredson (1981), subsequent theorists mention childhood but are not as detailed as Super and Ginzberg et al. Unfortunately, there has been little research devoted to confirming that the other theories available are applicable to childhood career development (Flores et al., 2006).

Ginzberg et al. (1951) proposed one stage for children from birth to age 11. They legitimized the belief that career development begins in early childhood and continues over a lifetime. Super's (1957) theory mentions that the first stage of career development is Growth (birth to age 14). Growth was subdivided further into fantasy, tentative, and realistic phases. During this time, children move from dreaming about what are, most likely, unrealistic career choices, to trying on activities and making new choices, to focusing on careers they believe are the best fit for them. Ginzberg et al. and Super both suggested that during the Growth period, children fantasize about and role play different careers that may eventually lead to career interests as they get older. During this period children have the opportunity to try on some occupational tasks through extracurricular activities and later through work experiences during high school. In 1996, Super, Savickas and Super updated the stages to include four revised substages – concern (what will I be), control (can I do it), conviction (I can do it), and competence (I can do it well). These substages better depict the sequence of tasks during the developmental stages according to Super et al. (1996).

In 1981, Gottfredson (a theorist with a different developmental approach) proposed further explanations of childhood career development with her theory of compromise and circumscription. In one of her tenets, she proposed that in early childhood, children sex stereotype careers and make decisions based on occupations that correspond to their gender. It is reasonable to assume that a similar process occurs with regard to race/ethnicity, sexual orientation, and physical disabilities (Brown, 2012).

Hartung, Porfeli & Vondracek (2008) suggest that "practically all other established and emerging career theories to some extent consider at least mentioning the formative nature of the childhood period relative to vocational choice development and adjustment" (p. 67). Given all the theoretical support for including childhood in career development practice, it is surprising to find that there has been so little research to support these concepts. In 2008, Schultheiss not only suggested that more research needed to be conducted to support existing theories but also that researchers need to consider alternative explanations of childhood career development that would include families, communities and other life contexts. This kind of approach would be suited for ethnic minority children, LGBT children, children with disabilities, and children from other marginalized groups (e.g., religious minorities and immigrants) as well as others who are marginalized in the school.

School Counselor Reluctance to Offer Career Counseling in the Elementary School

Career counseling for elementary school children is the purview of the school counselor but as Knight (2015) points out, counselor preparation for offering career development in elementary school is lacking in many counselor education programs leaving school counselors unprepared for doing this work. Although the Council for the Accreditation of Counseling and Related Educational Programs (CACREP, 2016) requires that school counseling programs train students in understanding contextual dimensions and practice of career development, there is little specificity regarding that training. In a recent study, Morgan, Greenwaldt and Gosselin (2014) found that school counselors believed they lacked the competence they needed for career programming for their students. The CACREP (2016) Standards for school counseling programs that pertain to early career development state that school counseling students are required to learn:

- models of P-12 comprehensive career development
- school counselor roles in consultation with families, P-12 and postsecondary school personnel, and community agencies
- use of developmentally appropriate career counseling interventions and assessments
- strategies to facilitate school and postsecondary transitions
- strategies to promote equity in student achievement and college access.

Elementary school counselors admit that they either (a) do not have time to offer much career guidance, (b) rank career as least important for elementary children or (c) wish they knew more so they could do more (Freeman, 1994; Osborn & Baggerly, 2004). In her critique of school counselor education, Knight (2015) stated that there were few evidence-based practices for elementary counselors to refer to because of the paucity of research on this population.

Career Needs of Ethnic Minority and Marginalized Children

As of the 2015-2016 academic year, the number of non-White children enrolled in public education has risen to 51%. The breakdown is 26% Latinos/as, 15% African American, 5% Asian American, 1% Native American and 3% more than one race (National Center for Educational Statistics, 2019). The need for cultural competence is critical. However, it is not enough that counselors understand cultural differences and nuances of societal and individual oppression. It is also not enough that counselors understand cultural differences in values, traditions, and expectations. Counselors also need to be prepared for the realities of oppression. The reality is 17.5% percent of all children (regardless of race) under 18 years of age live in poverty whether in cities or rural areas. There are considerable differences across ethnic groups. According to the Children's Defense Fund (2018), 33.7% of African American children, 15.6% of Asian American/Pacific Island children, 26.2% of Latino/a children and 36.2% of Native American/Alaska Native children live in poverty as compared to 11.7% of White children. According to Holcomb-McCoy (2007) "low income students and students of color are more likely to be taught by less-experienced teachers than are White students. Researchers have cited this factor as one of the most critical variables for explaining the achievement gap" (p. 7) between White students and students of color.

Another reality is that African American and Native American Indian children are overrepresented in special education classes (16% and 17.5% respectively; Editorial Projects in Education, 2019). This over representation is problematic enough but the special education classification labels children, affects their entire future, and is a contributing factor in poverty among ethnic minority group members. Few, if any, school counseling programs offer courses preparing students to work with children in special education, much less how to prepare these children for careers. When addressing the career needs of marginalized children, career practitioners will need to take into consideration poverty, family influence, and achievement gap.

Poverty

Poverty can have devastating effects on the educational and career development for children and adolescents. Poverty can lead to poor nutrition and emotional stress which can lead to cognitive impairment and academic failure (Holcomb-McCoy, 2007; McWhirter, McWhirter, McWhirter, McWhirter, 2013). People living in poverty not only have the day to day struggles of covering basic needs, but impoverished environments can expose children to the harsh realities of unemployment, crime and violence with few positive role models of people who work in occupations they really enjoy. Unfortunately, some of the role models urban children living in poverty see may be unemployed, and some may be involved in illegal activities and violence. Children living in families who are homeless have an even greater challenge in their career development because of the barriers associated with school attendance such as residency requirements, need for school records, immunization records and birth certificates (McWhirter et al., 2013). A distressing problem for career practice with elementary children is that schools in areas of poverty often lack resources for fundamental educational requirements and are even less likely to have the resources for expanded career exploration.

Career practitioners in schools may meet challenges when children live in families whose socioeconomic status is classified as the "working poor" and the families have a negative attitude toward work. According to McWhirter et al. (2013), "working poor families influence a child's development through parents' attitudes, disposition, and behavior" (p. 30). Often the breadwinners in working poor families have low-paying blue-collar jobs or work as unskilled labor. They may work long hours for minimum wage and/or have more than one such job. Unskilled occupations are disappearing rapidly, being replaced by automation, leaving a future of unemployment for those workers. The attitudes of the struggling adults who are part of the working poor are certain to affect the children's ideas about work and success (McWhirter et al. 2013).

Family Influence

When stories are written about ethnic minority individuals, invariably family influence and support is mentioned and that has been supported by research (Flores & O'Brien, 2002; Fisher, Gushe & Cerrone, 2011; Fisher & Padmawidjaja, 1999). However, family influence has only become of interest in the career development field during the last 20 years due in part to the changes in work, the family structure, and in U.S. demographics (Chope, 2012). According to Chope, families have the most influence over attitudes toward and restrictions on career options (Miller & Brown 2005). Tyson (2007) found that among African American males, family was the number one influencer of career choice over community and the media. Family influence on culturally competent career counseling may take on major relevance for recently immigrated groups where children acculturate more quickly than the adults. Sadly, there has not been much research on family issues in the career decision-making of young people. Instead the family research on careers has been concentrated on the adults and how career decisions affect their families. Brown (2004) stated that this lack of research is problematic especially in regard to ethic minority populations that have a collectivist culture where family comes before the individual. A social justice approach based on the contextual factors that influence career choice and decision-making has brought the family of origin influence to the attention of school counselors.

Achievement Gap

One of the most impactful problems that affect marginalized children and adolescents is the achievement gap which was mentioned earlier in this chapter. Holcomb-McCoy (2007) explained the achievement gap as one that "denotes when groups of students with relatively equal abilities don't achieve in school at the same levels" (p. 5).

Research for decades has shown that children who have not learned to read by the third grade are most at risk for dropping out of school (Lloyd, 1978). This is especially true for African American and Latino/a students because they are twice as likely not to graduate as compared to their White peers with the same reading disability. What is crucial for educators to understand is that "interventions for struggling readers after third grade are seldom as effective as those in the early years" (Annie E. Casey Foundation, 2012, p. 4).

The fact that the achievement scores for African Americans, Latinos/as, and Native Americans are significantly lower than the scores of their White peers means that their future earning power and career choices will be greatly limited (Holcomb-McCoy, 2007). There is a gap between males and females as well as between poor and wealthy, between urban and suburban schools, between students with and without disabilities, between native English speakers and those for whom English is not their first language, and between LGBT students and straight students (National Education Association, [NEA], n.d.).

This is a national problem that has baffled educators for decades (Stanford Center for Education Policy, n.d.). Testing assessment bias is only one of the sources of this discrepancy. Other issues include lack of teacher experience, low expectations of teachers of marginalized students, lack of cultural competence among teachers, school counselors, and administrators in the schools, availability of resources and, of course, the higher enrollment of African American, Latino/a, and Native American students in special education, and a higher percentage of marginalized students living in poverty (Holcomb-McCoy 2007; McWhirter et al, 2013). Because of the achievement gap, these students' career opportunities are diminished just for being who they are.

Career Needs of Marginalized Adolescents

Although high school graduation rates are at an all-time high for all races of adolescents (84%), dropout rates are still higher for African American (6.2%) and Latinos (8.6%) than they are for Whites (5.2%; McFarland et al., 2018). Also, the rise in graduation rates in schools might be inflated because many low achieving students are funneled into alternative schools, which have increased in number by 33% from 2004-2014 (Atwell, Balfanz, Bridgeland, & DePaoli, 2018). Graduation rates from alternative schools rarely exceed 67% (Atwell et al., 2018). This is especially problematic for low income students who represent 56% of the students involved in alternative schools and 60% who are ethnic minority students. "Low educational achievement is associated with high unemployment, lower earnings, higher crime, and a greater dependency on welfare and other social services. The social costs of these outcomes can be staggering" (Holcomb-McCoy, 2007, p. 5).

The challenges for marginalized populations of adolescents result from years of oppression, discrimination, and microaggressions. They are confronted with obstacles due to lack of appreciation of cultural differences and institutional and individual oppression. As a result, they are at risk for dropping out of school, being retained a grade, suspended or expelled from school, and being among those who are bullied. The quality of education declines with each of these issues. While graduating from high school does not guarantee someone a job, research indicates that dropping out of high school leads to lower pay and unemployment (McFarland, Cui, Holmes, & Wang, 2019) and employment will be a perpetual struggle.

McWhirter et al., (2013) outline characteristics of adolescents who are at risk, which they define as "a set of presumed cause-effect dynamics that place an individual child or adolescent in danger of future negative outcome. At risk designates a situation that is not necessarily current…but that can be anticipated in the absence of intervention" (p. 8). They refer to at risk on a continuum from minimal on the lower end to at risk activity on the upper end. Children and adolescents may have negative experiences and influences but not all lead to engaging in risky behaviors. Such environments, though, are fertile grounds for the growth of self-destructive behavior (e.g., drug use or abuse, teen pregnancy, suicide, violence, dropping out of school). McWhirter also points out that

> risk factors are also multiplicative. A young person who is from an impoverished, dysfunctional family and who attends a poor school in an economically marginalized neighborhood is potentially further along the "at risk" continuum than children who do not experience these conditions, especially if there are additional major psychosocial stressors. (McWhirter et al., 2013, p. 10)

It is safe to say, given the achievement gap and the multiplicative factors described by McWhirter et al., that marginalized students would be classified as at risk. In schools, at risk typically refers to risk of failure or risk of dropping out. No matter the definition, the adolescent's career development is impacted and school counselors and others will need to intervene to turn these students around.

Strategies for Career Counseling Marginalized Youth

Super's (1957) theory provided the groundwork for career development standards and guidelines for elementary school children such as those in the American School Counseling Association's (ASCA) National Model (American School Counselor Association, 2005). In its second edition of the National Model, ASCA outlined specific standards for students under the career domain. When planning the guidance curriculum, school counselors can use these standards and decide how and when they will be met in terms of activities and appropriate grade level. In the third edition (ASCA, 2012), school counselors can find examples of activities used to meet the standards online and share their own examples with others. Also in the third edition, the manual refers school counselors to the National Career Development Association's Minimum Competencies for Multicultural Career Counseling and Development (2020). However this framework is not broken down into grade levels to truly assist school counselors. In 2011, the National Career Development Association released their Career Development Policy Statement that outlines specifics regarding competencies for K-12 students. Figure 8.1 is the list for elementary students (National Career Development Association, 2011). Number 6 of the elementary school activities is the most specific to marginalized groups. While all of the activities will be helpful for marginalized children, there are special challenges when school counselors are working in environments and cultures with which they are not familiar. School counselors will need to work on becoming integrated into the community by reaching out to the local clergy, community leaders and programs like boys and girls clubs, sports clubs, soup kitchens, recreation centers, as well as social workers and law enforcement. School counselors can learn to understand how each of these entities is perceived by the community and establish those relationships that will be most useful in completing the activities that will enhance the career development of their students. Working with teachers and parents as well as the rest of the school, counselors are able to meet the goals of career development for elementary children. It is the school counselor's responsibility to advocate for early career development and once counselors can help their schools understand that career development for elementary aged children is more about creating an environment and opportunities which open possibilities for their students, there will be enough enthusiasm to accomplish this goal.

Competencies

There have been a great many researchers who have studied strategies for helping children at risk for failure, dropping out of school or other destructive behavior. To be of assistance to children at risk, school counselors must be culturally competent. As seen in Appendix C, Holcomb-McCoy's (2004) School Counselor Multicultural Competence Checklist (SCMCC) outlines specific activities that multiculturally competent school counselors are able to perform. The list of competencies is long and becoming culturally competent takes time. In fact, it is a lifelong process. There is no need for school counselors to be overwhelmed about the enormity of the process because they do not need to master all these competencies to be effective with diverse students.

The most important competencies to achieve first are the awareness of school counselor biases and knowledge of clients. Once these competencies are achieved, they motivate school counselors to gain the other skills.

Figure 8.1
Career Development in Grades K-6

NCDA policy is to encourage elementary and secondary schools to form partnerships with parents...In addition, each of the following major kinds of activities is endorsed by NCDA as needed and especially appropriate for use by teachers and counselors beginning at the K-6 level:

1. Making the Classroom a Workplace. NCDA policy is to strongly support recent recommendations of both the Secretary's (of Labor) Commission on Achieving Necessary Skills (SCANS) (1991, 1992) and of the Commission on the Skills of the American Workforce (1990) for changing the classroom from one based on the "assembly line" concept of the industrial revolution to the "high skills" concept of the coming high productivity American workforce where work -- not drudgery -- of both students and educators is emphasized. This emphasis holds high potential for helping each student acquire a positive set of work values as part of his/her value system and thus for helping each pupil want to work. This must begin at the K-6 level if the total effort is to be successful.

2. Teaching/Reinforcing Productive Work Habits. NCDA policy is to encourage all teachers to emphasize and reward the practice of the kinds of work habits needed in a high productivity occupational society. These include such habits as: (a) coming to work (to school) on time, (b) doing one's best in carrying out work (school) assignments, (c) finishing assigned work tasks on schedule, (d) cooperating with other workers (pupils) in team efforts, (e) participating in problem solving and creative thinking, and (f) following directions given by supervisors (teachers). NCDA's position is that, when such habits become part of the pupil's lifestyle during the K-12 years, it is more likely he or she will possess these habits when seeking employment, after leaving school.

3. Helping Pupils Understand Career Applications of Subject Matter. NCDA policy is to encourage all teachers to help pupils to understand how the subject matter they are being asked to learn is valuable for success in a variety of occupational areas. This is especially true with regard to the basic academic skills of reading, mathematics, and oral/written communication to be learned at the K-6 level. NCDA policy is to use this kind of motivation as one among several means of encouraging pupils to learn -- not as the only one or the most important one.

4. Using Community Resource Persons To Emphasize both Work and Occupations. NCDA policy is to encourage the involvement of resource persons representing various occupations in the community as one means of helping pupils understand career applications of subject matter. Such resource persons should be selected, in part, because they are able to illustrate clearly to pupils the importance of subject matter -- and especially of basic academic skills -- in their occupations. In part, resource persons should be selected based on their commitment to work as illustrated by their commitment to the importance of what they are doing, why people need them to exist, and how people are helped through what they do. Only persons with a demonstrable commitment to work should be selected as occupational resource persons.

5. Emphasizing Career Awareness But Not Specific Occupational Choices. NCDA policy is to encourage all elementary school pupils to become aware of a wide array of occupations existing within and outside of their community. NCDA policy is to emphasize the societal contributions and natures of occupations but not to encourage specific occupational decision-making by K-6 pupils.

6. Reducing Bias and Stereotyping In Career Awareness. NCDA policy is to encourage career development facilitators and all other educators, beginning at the K-6 level, to help pupils become aware of occupations in ways that demonstrate the potential of occupations being open for choice without restrictions based on sex, race, ethnic heritage, age, sexual orientation, creed, or disability. The emphasis should be on the possibility of openness, not on the likelihood of bias and stereotyping.

> **Competency exercise.** Using the SCMCC in Appendix C, evaluate where you are on each one of those competencies in terms of whether you are still learning that skill (unmet) or have mastered that skill enough to use it effectively (met).

Social Justice School Counseling

In addition to the multicultural competencies, Holcomb-McCoy (2004) suggests that there are six key factors in social justice counseling in the school: (1) counseling and intervention planning, (2) consultation, (3) connecting schools with families and communities, (4) collecting and utilizing data, (5) challenging bias, and (6) coordinating student services and support. During counseling and intervention planning, counselors will find it beneficial to approach the student's issues from the context of the student's life and the environment the student lives in (culture, race, socioeconomic status, etc.). In consultation, counselors work with teachers and parents in the absence of the students to help them give the student the support he or she needs. When connecting schools, families and communities, counselors reach outside the school to give presentations in the community and programs in the school to address the social justice needs of the students. According to Bohan-Baker & Little (2002), the school, community, and parent partnerships have resulted in raising test scores of marginalized students. When counselors use data (e.g., drop-out statistics, discrepancies in Advance Placement enrollments, etc.) to illustrate the needs of the students, it increases the strength of their arguments and increases the possibility of policy changes that reflect social justice. Challenging the biases of others is always difficult but it is one of the most important tasks that social justice school counselors are expected to do. Institutional biases are easier to approach and document but biases of individual teachers and administrators are more likely to inflict personal pain on students. Coordinating services available in the school and in the community that help close the achievement gap is also an important school counselor task. Sometimes that may also mean creating programs that increase opportunities for students at local colleges, universities and/or service organizations.

McWhirter and colleague's (2013) recommendations for helping children and adolescents at-risk focus on how the counselor could help students thrive and survive in a hostile environment. Their five-C model is based on observations and research on the differences between low- and high-risk children. Their five Cs of competency are: (1) Critical school competencies, (2) Concept of self, self-esteem and self-efficacy, (3) Connectedness, (4) Coping Ability and (5) Control. In critical school competencies, they point out how important it is for children to not only gain basic academic skills at an early age but also to acquire basic social-behavioral skills (e.g., following directions, staying on task, getting along with others). McWhirter et al. explain the differences between self-concept, self-esteem and self-efficacy, and essentially point out how important success is to all three. Academic success leads to higher self-esteem (how much we value ourselves). Success in school, or in athletics, or any task leads to higher self-efficacy (the belief that we can successfully perform). Self-concept is positively affected by success because success contributes to our definition of ourselves. In connectedness, McWhirter et al. refer to feelings of belonging that comes from "knowing that one matters to others" (p. 137). Another crucial skill that marginalized children need is the ability to cope with the stressors in their lives. Without the ability to cope, children often "act out," or become anxious or depressed. Finally, children who feel that they have some control over their environment and their own behavior are more likely to be at low-risk for destructive or dangerous consequences of their behavior.

> **Social justice exercise.** Read the story of Sofia and respond to the prompts.
>
> *Sofia has just been hired as the only school counselor at an inner-city elementary school, where the population includes 99% ethnic minority children, with three special education classrooms, two of which are self-contained. Ninety percent of the children are on free or reduced lunch, records show low attendance rates in all grades, and student mobility is high. Sofia is 23 years old, single, and comes from a multiple-heritage background (Latina/African American). She had a choice of jobs--one was in an affluent area near where she grew up. It was staffed with both a full-time and a part-time counselor for 600 students but the school she chose had a higher student-counselor ratio, the pay was better and Sofia had interned in a similar school. What convinced her to take the job was that the principal in her new school is pro-counselor as opposed to the unsupportive principal in the school where she did her internship. The principal there felt that guidance and counseling takes away too much time from instruction, and provided little support for programs. Sofia wants to make a difference in an inner-city school and wants to focus more on career development because she thinks it is crucial for the elementary children at this school. However, she is somewhat fearful that it will be too much of a challenge to do so right out of graduate school.*
>
> If you were in Sophia's shoes, how would you approach her plan for career development for the students in your new school? Write your responses to the following questions in your notebook.
> 1. From a social justice perspective what would be the first thing you would do?
> 2. What information would you need to help your first year go smoothly?
> 3. How would you set your priorities?
> 4. How would you evaluate your performance?

Final Thoughts about Career Counseling for Marginalized Children and Adolescents

For culturally different students and those who have been marginalized (e.g., LGBT, children with disabilities) career counseling and guidance is vital. Herr, Cramer, and Niles (2004) stated that teens who drop out of school at age 16 have really dropped out, psychologically, in the third grade. As we have stated previously, a child's ability to read by the time he or she reaches the third grade is crucial to the child continuing his or her education. The higher dropout rates for Latinos/as, African Americans and Native Americans, therefore, has staggering implications for elementary teachers and school counselors. The fact that members of oppressed groups tend to limit their career choices very early in life only exacerbates the problem (Gottfredson, 1981). It is crucial, therefore, that career counseling begin as early as possible in the lives of all marginalized clients. The authors believe career development occurs from the cradle to the grave and that elementary counselors have a key role in helping children negotiate that development in the best possible way. Besides the dropout rates, these children experience discrimination, daily microaggressions from fellow students, teachers and school counselors, poverty, and lower achievement levels as compared to Whites. Elementary school counselors were placed in schools to facilitate children's growth by opening possibilities to them so that they can reach their real potential as adults. Many of the skills described in this chapter are useful for school counselors when they work with children and parents from marginalized groups.

References

American School Counselor Association. (2005). *The ASCA national model: A framework for school counseling programs* (2nd ed.). Arlington, VA: Author

American School Counselor Association. (2012). *The ASCA national model: A framework for school counseling programs* (3rd ed.). Alexandria, VA: Author.

Annie E. Casey Foundation. (2012). *Double jeopardy: How third-grade reading skills and poverty influence high school graduation.* Retrieved from https://www.aecf.org/resources/double-jeopardy/

Atwell, M. N., Balfanz, R., Bridgeland, J. DePaoli, J. (2018). *Building a grad nation: Progress and challenge in raising high school graduation rates. An annual update.* Retrieved from https://gradnation.americaspromise.org/2018-building-grad-nation-report

Bohan-Baker, M., & Little, P. M. D. (2004). *The transition to kindergarten: A review of current research and promising practices to involve families.* Retrieved from Harvard Family Research Project website: https://citeseerx.ist.psu.edu/viewdoc/download?doi=10.1.1.470.6636&rep=rep1&type=pdf

Brown, D. (2012). *Career information, career counseling, and career development.* Upper Saddle River, NJ: Pearson.

Brown, M. T. (2004). The career development influence of family of origin: Considerations of race/ethnic group membership and class. *The Counseling Psychologist, 32*(4), 587-595.

Children's Defense Fund. (September, 2018). *Child poverty in America 2017: National analysis.* Retrieved from https://www.childrensdefense.org/wp-content/uploads/2018/09/Child-Poverty-in-America-2017-National-Fact-Sheet.pdf

Chope, R. C. (2012). *Family matters: The intertwining of the family with career decision making.* Chelsea, MI: Counseling Outfitters, LLC.

Council for the Accreditation of Counseling and Related Educational Programs. (2016). *2016 Standards.* Retrieved from http://www.cacrep.org/wp-content/uploads/2018/05/2016-Standards-with-Glossary-5.3.2018.pdf

Editorial Projects in Education. (2019, December 17). Special education: Definition, statistics, and trends. *Education Week.* Retrieved from http://www.edweek.org/ew/issues/special-populations/

Fisher, L. D., Gushue, G. V., & Cerrone, M. T. (2011). The influences of career support and sexual identity on sexual minority women's career aspirations. *The Career Development Quarterly, 59,* 441–454. doi:10.1002/j.2161-0045.2011.tb00970.x

Fisher, T. A. & Padmawidjaja, I. (1999). Parental influences on career development perceived by African American and Mexican-American college students. *Journal of Multicultural Counseling and Development, 27,* 136-152.

Flores, L. Y., Berkel, L. A., Nilsson, J. E., Ojeda, L., Jordan, S. E., Ginger, L. L., & Leal, V. M. (2006). Racial/ethnic minority vocational research: A content and trend analysis across 36 years. *The Career Development Quarterly, 55,* 2-21.

Flores, L. Y., & O'Brien, K. M. (2002). The career development of Mexican American adolescent women: A test of social cognitive career theory. *Journal of Counseling Psychology, 49,* 14-27.

Freeman, B. (1994). Importance of the national career development guidelines to school counselors. *The Career Development Quarterly, 42,* 224-228. Doi:10.1002/j.2161-0045.1994.tb00937.x

Ginzberg, E., Ginsburg, S. W., Axelrad, S., & Herma, J. (1951). *Occupational choice: An approach to a general theory.* New York, NY: Columbia University Press.

Gottfredson, L. S. (1981). Circumscription and compromise: A developmental theory of occupational aspirations. *Journal of Counseling Psychology, 28*(6), 545-579.

Hartung, P. J., Porfeli, E. J., & Vondracek, F. W. (2008). Career adaptability in childhood. *The Career Development Quarterly, 57*(1), 63-74.

Herr, E. L., Cramer, S. H., & Niles, S. G. (2004). *Career guidance and counseling through the lifespan: Systematic approaches* (6th ed.). Boston, MA: Allyn & Bacon.

Holcomb-McCoy, C. (2004). Assessing the multicultural competence of school counselors: A checklist. *Professional School Counseling, 7,* 178-182.

Holcomb-McCoy, C. (2007). *School counseling to close the achievement gap: A social justice framework for success.* Thousand Oaks, CA: Sage Publications.

Knight, J. L. (2015). Preparing elementary school counselors to promote career development: Recommendations for school counselor education programs. *Journal of Career Development, 42*(2), 75-85.

Lloyd, D. N. (1978). Prediction of school failure from third-grade data. *Educational and Psychological Measurement, 38,* 1193-2000.

McFarland, J., Cui, J., Holmes, J., and Wang, X. (2019). Trends in high school dropout and completion rates in the United States: 2019 (NCES 2020-117). *U.S. Department of Education.* Washington, DC: National Center for Education Statistics. Retrieved from https://nces.ed.gov/pubsearch/pubsinfo.asp?pubid=2020117

McFarland, J., Hussar, B., Wang, X., Zhang, J., Wang, K., Rathbun, A., Barmer, A., Forrest Cataldi, E., & Bullock Mann, F. (2018). The condition of education 2018 (NCES 2018-144). *U.S. Department of Education.* Washington, DC: National Center for Education Statistics. Retrieved from https://nces.ed.gov/pubsearch/pubsinfo.asp?pubid=2018144

McWhirter, J. J., McWhirter, B. T., McWhirter, E. H., & McWhirter, R. J. (2013). *At risk youth: A comprehensive response for counselors, teachers, psychologists, and human service professionals* (5th ed.). Belmont, CA: Brooks/Cole/Cengage.

Miller, M. J., & Brown, S. D., (2005). Counseling for career choice: Implications for improving interventions and working with diverse populations. In S. Brown & R. W. Lent (Eds.), *Career development and counseling: Putting theory and research to work* (pp. 441–465). Hoboken, NJ: John Wiley and Sons.

Morgan, L. W., Greenwaldt, M. E., & Gosselin, K. P. (2014). School counselors' perceptions of competency in career counseling. *Professional Counselor, 4*(5), 481-496.

National Career Development Association. (2011), Career development: A policy statement of the National Career Development Association. Retrieved from https://ncda.org/aws/NCDA/pt/fli/4728/false

National Career Development Association. (2020). Minimum competencies *multicultural career counseling and development.* Retrieved from https://www.ncda.org/aws/NCDA/asset_manager/get_file/26627

National Center for Educational Statistics. (2019). Status and trends in the education of racial and ethnic groups. Retrieved from https://nces.ed.gov/programs/raceindicators/indicator_rbb.asp

Osborn, D., and Baggerly, J. (2004). School counsellors' perception of career counseling and career training: Preferences, priorities, and predictors. *Journal of Career Development, 31,* 45-49. doi: 10.1023/B:JOCD.0000036705.02911.d

Porfeli, E. J., Hartung, P. J., & Vondracek, F. W. (2008). Children's vocational development: A research rationale. *The Career Development Quarterly, 57*(1), 25-37.

Schultheiss, D. E. P. (2008). Current status and future agenda for the theory, research, and practice of childhood career development. *The Career Development Quarterly, 57*(1), 7-24.

Solberg, V. S., Howard, K. A., Blustein, D. L., & Close, W. (2002). Career development in the schools: Connecting school-to-work-to-life. *The Counseling Psychologist, 30*(5), 705-725.

Stanford Center for Education Policy. (n.d.). Racial and ethnic achievement gaps. Retrieved from https://cepa.stanford.edu/educational-opportunity-monitoring-project/achievement-gaps/race/

Super, D. E. (1957). *The psychology of careers*. New York, NY: Harper & Row.

Super, D. E., Savickas, M. L., & Super, C. (1996). A life-span, life-space approach to career development. In D. Brown, & L. Brooks, *Career choice and development* (3rd ed., pp. 121-178). San Francisco, CA: Jossey-Bass.

Tyson, C. T. (2007). *Social learning and the career aspirations of adolescent African American males* (Doctoral dissertation, University of South Carolina).

CHAPTER 9

Social Justice Career Counseling

Tamiko is a young Japanese American career professional who has recently married and is considering starting a family. One morning, on the way to work from her racially mixed working-class neighborhood, she notices a huge cloud of smoke coming from three or four blocks away. Not having time to investigate, she goes to work, but when she returns home that evening, she discovers that the smoke had been coming from a fire that destroyed one of the few affordable childcare agencies in her neighborhood. Several parents are interviewed about their reactions to the fire and because she has worked with clients with similar childcare concerns, Tamiko is familiar with their plight. Understanding how important the agency is to working parents, Tamiko is spurred to be one of the first volunteers for the rebuilding project. Every weekend for three weeks, she helps with the rebuilding. When it is over, she feels very proud and fulfilled. However, something the news commentator had mentioned the day of the fire has worried her the whole time she has been participating in this project: the demand for affordable day care far exceeds the number of facilities available. Tamiko decides that she needs to do more. In most of the households in her neighborhood, both parents must work to make ends meet and more expensive day care may mean losing their homes. Tamiko does some research and locates several organizations devoted to obtaining legislative intervention regarding the day care issue for families in her state. After attending her first meeting, Tamiko is satisfied that she is doing what she can do to bring about a needed change in society for working parents.

Social action is an essential component of multicultural career counseling. Tamiko's involvement in day care initiatives is a response to a core issue in career counseling—the realities of the dual-worker household. Counselors and practitioners today can no longer enjoy the luxury of sitting in an office focusing solely on the client sitting before them while outside of the office oppressive policies exist that deny large segments of the population (including the client) their dignity and rights.

In recent years, there has been a steady increase in the number of articles calling on counselors to become involved in attaining social justice. According to Medea Benjamin of Global Exchange, social justice exists in "a society where all hungry are fed, all sick cared for, the environment is treasured, and we treat each other with love and compassion" (Kikuchi, 2005, paragraph 1). Sue and Sue (2016) offered their definition of social justice counseling:

> Social justice counseling/therapy is an active philosophy and approach aimed at producing conditions that allow for equal access and opportunity; reducing or eliminating disparities in education, health care, employment, and other areas that lower the quality of life for affected populations; encouraging mental health professionals to consider micro, meso, and macro levels in the assessment, diagnosis, and treatment of client and client systems; and broadening the role of the helping professional to include not only counselor/therapist but advocate, consultant, psychoeducator, change agent, community worker, and so on. (p.134)

Counselors and practitioners can be particularly instrumental in working toward accomplishing the goal of social justice by taking social action. To define the term, social action is a commitment "to become agents of systematic change, to channel energy and skill into helping clients from marginalized or powerless groups break down institutional and social barriers to optimal development" (Lee, 1998, p. 7). Similarly, advocacy is defined by Toporek (2000) as "an action taken by a counseling professional to facilitate the removal of external and institutional barriers to clients' well-being" (p. 6). Multicultural awareness and knowledge among counselors cannot help but impact their sense of social responsibility, and this naturally leads to social action (Lee, 1998; Lewis & Arnold, 1998).

In career counseling, social justice counseling involves working toward the elimination of discrimination against all oppressed groups in the career arena, whether that involves working with clients individually, or in the community, or even national or international organizations. Social justice career counseling entails eliminating discrimination in career training, hiring, or promotion. To achieve this goal, social justice career professionals and practitioners are committed to actions such as:

- Taking action to equalize the inequities in education for poor and ethnic minorities, as well as people with disabilities
- Taking action to equalize the inequities in applicant selection for jobs and education
- Working to defeat efforts to shut down affirmative action
- Taking action to break the glass ceiling that women, men of color, and others experience in the workplace
- Speaking out and lobbying legislators to include gays, lesbians, bisexuals, and transgendered individuals under civil rights protection.

A civil rights slogan of the 1960s illustrates this point: "If you are not part of the solution, you are part of the problem." Career professionals therefore need to become advocates for social justice, which, as described by Bell (2016) is "a world in which the distribution of resources is equitable and ecologically sustainable, and all members are physically and psychologically safe and secure, recognized, and treated with respect" (p. 3).

Interestingly, the father of career counseling, Frank Parsons, set the standard for career professionals taking social action right from the start (Davis, 1969; Pope, Briddick, & Wilson, 2013). Working with immigrants to help them find jobs in a newly industrialized world, Parsons believed that the unequal distribution of wealth and power required him to be tireless in his efforts to empower the poor and working classes. He helped establish the Vocation Bureau of Boston, which among its many goals, worked to keep children from dropping out of school (Hartung & Blustein, 2002). Hartung and Blustein believe that counselor involvement in social action would bring career counseling back to the roots of its founder, Frank Parsons.

In addition to challenging the oppressive systems that exist outside of the counseling office, as many others since Parsons' time have advocated, Lewis and Arnold (1998) insist that counselors review the oppressive nature of the counseling profession itself and become activists for change within the profession. Although there has long been a call for social action among career professionals, there has at the same time been little change in the way career counseling is practiced. Fox (2003) and Vera and Speight (2003) criticize the profession for not taking the next step from awareness to action. Hartung and Blustein (2002) agree, and further point out that even the theories of career counseling do not reflect a social justice agenda. For example, Liu and Ali (2005) have suggested that career counseling is biased when it focuses on college and professional careers for everyone. Li and Ali say that counselors therefore do not demonstrate an understanding of clients who do not aspire to college, and thereby allow their own biases and classism to interfere with the counseling of the client. Fox (2003) takes this point further and states that career counseling, as a field, is so focused on counseling individuals, on objective value-free science, and on the cultivation of moderate stances for tenure and promotion that it is unlikely much will change in the field.

Social Justice Competencies

The good news is that multicultural and career counseling competencies both address advocacy and social justice, and various authors in the field have expanded upon this position. For instance, in her discussion of using multicultural counseling competencies as tools to address oppression and racism, Arredondo (1999) refers to the specific competencies that can help counselors reduce oppressive behaviors. She also points out several multicultural competencies that are particularly relevant to social activism:

- "Culturally skilled counselors are aware of institutional barriers that prevent minorities from using mental health services" (Sue, Arredondo, & McDavis, 1992, p. 482).
- "Culturally skilled counselors have knowledge of the potential bias in assessment instruments and use of procedures, and interpret findings in a way that recognizes the cultural and linguistic characteristics of the clients" (Arredondo, et al. 1996, p. 69)
- "Culturally skilled counselors should attend to as well as work to eliminate biases, prejudices, and discriminatory context in conducting evaluations and providing interventions, and should develop sensitivity to issues of oppression, sexism, heterosexism, elitism, and racism" (Sue et al., 1992, p. 483).

In 2003, ACA endorsed the Advocacy Competencies. The competencies address issues relevant to career counseling to concentrate on specific skills that are needed to be effective as agents of social justice. A summary of the competencies can be found in Appendix D.

The Multicultural Social Justice Counseling Competencies (MSJCC) (Ratts, Singh, Nassar-McMillan, Butler, & McCollough, 2016) synthesizes the multicultural and social justice competencies. Including the multicultural career counseling competencies with the already combined multicultural social justice competencies is not such a daunting task because there is a great deal of overlap among the three sets of competencies. It is just that some of the competencies are more explicit than others, providing more information to counselors and practitioners about how to best meet the requirements. The MSJCC addresses a few issues that the original competencies did not, but a great deal has changed in over two decades. The MSJCC addresses privileged and marginalized statuses and since multiculturalism now embraces differences beyond race and ethnicity, individuals in almost all groups can identify with privilege and marginalization. Relatedly, the MSJCC bring intersectionality of multiple identities into focus as well. Because one individual may identify with more than one group, he or she may experience both privilege and marginalization which brings complexity to his or her identity. Where social justice and social action comes into play with the MSJCC is that Ratt et al. (2016) have added "action" as a fourth competency to the original Arredondo, et al. (1996) competencies of awareness, knowledge, and skill.

"Action" in the area of self-awareness refers to how career professionals seek out their blind spots, biases and assumptions and immerse themselves "in their communities to learn how poverty, privilege, and oppression influence their experience" (Ratts et al., 2016, p. 39). "Action" in client worldview requires that career professionals immerse themselves in the client's community to understand how poverty, privilege, and oppression influence worldview and experiences of clients. In the counseling relationship, action requires that career professionals get together with other professionals and the community to learn more effective ways to help clients. By doing so, career professionals understand issues of poverty, privilege and oppression that may affect the counseling relationship (Ratts et al., 2016).

Committing to Social Action and Social Justice

Social justice is thought by many to be the natural next step in multicultural competence. As one author put it, the career professional committed to social justice "seeks to transform the world, not just understand the world" (Vera & Speight, 2003, p. 261). Fox (2003), however, is pessimistic about the career counseling field ever fully embracing social action and taking on a more radical stance because career counseling students are not often encouraged to take social action during their training programs.

Fox (2003) further suggests that resistance to social advocacy and social action occurs at times because it is a difficult task to change the deep-seated mindsets that come with any profession. Some professionals prefer to separate their politics from their work, while some are not sure how to combine work and politics. Additionally, one important theme that recurs throughout the literature on social actions is that social action often involves risks that many are unwilling to take or that may be too costly for the career professional. If career professionals decide to take stands on issues or become actively involved in protesting or supporting unpopular causes, they risk ridicule and harassment from others, both in the workplace and in the community (Fickling, 2016; Lee, 1998; Toporek, 2018). They may also gain reputations as troublemakers and may alienate people who may be able to assist them. Blustein, McWhirter, and Perry (2005) also mention that true involvement in social justice may interfere with earning a livable income. Still, while Grieger and Ponterotto (1998) acknowledge that social advocacy may come with risks, they believe it is a necessary task. According to Gainor (2005), "understanding the resistance to change is, ironically, necessary for change to proceed" (p. 185).

Though Blustein and colleagues (2005) suggest that career professionals have a moral imperative to become active in social justice because they are a privileged, educated group, Gainor (2005) argues that such an "awesome responsibility" may seem unattainable (p. 182). She suggests that even when privileged individuals want to change their passive behaviors to actively oppose oppression, they often resist doing so, not only because changing the system is a monumental task, but also because changing the system might mean losing privileged positions.

Even so, Gainor (2005) believes that losing privilege is a risk well worth taking, and using Evans' (1996) framework for implementing change, Gainor outlines the steps for career professionals to follow in the process of becoming activists:

1. Career professionals must develop a strong enough sense of moral outrage that the outrage will overcome the fear of trying to change conditions faced by oppressed clients. The idea at work here is that career professionals will be so upset about the state of affairs in society that to do nothing is a far more frightening prospect than to do something. One example is the people who took to the streets by the thousands in protest all over the world in 2016 when Donald Trump was inaugurated as the 45th president of the United States. Since then, people who were outraged about the presidential agenda have remained politically active and actively protesting – many of whom never were engaged in politics before (Jordan & Clement, 2018). Gainor suggests that the values outlined by Blustein and colleagues (2005) that come into play during this step are:

   > (a) self-determination, or the power to foster in oneself and others the ability to attain mutually acceptable goals; (b) caring and compassion, not just for clients but, for marginalized people who may not present themselves for mental health services; (c) collaboration and democratic participation, or the equitable opportunity for citizens to have peaceful and respectful input into their own lives; (d) human diversity, or the respect for and recognition and appreciation of diverse social identities; and (e) distributive justice, or the fair distribution of goods and opportunities among all social groups. (Blustein et al., 2005, pp. 150-151)

2. In this step, career professionals move from a sense of loss to a sense of commitment. Gainor (2005) suggests that career agencies can facilitate this step by allowing career professionals to embark on the change in their own time and in their own way rather than by mandate. She suggests that perhaps frank discussions of possible loss of privilege involved may facilitate acceptance and movement toward social action.

3. Career professionals gain competence in their new social action skills. Gainor (2005) suggests that this process should begin in preservice-level training. Students should be taught social advocacy skills in their career development courses as well as in specific courses on social justice.

4. The last two of Gainor's (2005) steps toward becoming socially active are less focused on how to assist individual career professionals, but rather focused on how the counseling profession can change. Step 4 is to "address the uncertainty and confusion that arises during the early stages of institutional reform" (p. 184).

5 Step 5 is to engage a critical mass of supporters to "exert pressure and appropriately use power [to]…assist in implementing a social justice agenda" (p. 184).

Social Justice Training

Once career professionals are committed to actively pursuing social justice in their work with oppressed clients, and once the agency is also committed, social action training should naturally follow. There is little evidence that social advocacy training is widely practiced in counselor education. Although most professional counseling organizations advise career professionals to become advocates, Blustein and colleagues (2005) point out that, although social justice has been discussed in the counseling literature by many, the majority of textbooks used by students and practitioners still focus heavily on one-on-one career services, not social justice or advocacy. In fact, Fox (2003) argues that because the counseling field is so tied to existing institutions (schools, government agencies, hospitals), there is little chance that widespread social justice training will occur in the foreseeable future. Others are doubtful because counseling has traditionally focused on the specific issues of the individual while leaving community interventions to social workers and other professions (Albee, 2000; Vera & Speight, 2003). A recent study of 19 career counselors (Fickling, 2016) asked about the importance of advocacy in their work and two factors emerged as important. The first was empowering their clients and teaching them self-advocacy. The second factor was the burden of multiple roles career counselors must play and how it keeps them from doing more advocacy beyond the client level.

Goodman, Liang, Helms, Latta, Sparks, and Weintraub (2004), however, have designed a training program to integrate social justice into training professionals. The program strives to assist

> students to (a) gain an awareness of systemic factors impacting mental health, psychological growth, and career development, (b) experience collaboration across the profession, (c) do collaborative work, advocacy or indirect service with underserved populations, and (d) engage in the design, delivery and/or evaluation of preventive interventions. (p. 808)

In designing the program, Goodman and colleagues required first-year doctoral students to spend six hours per week working in both urban and rural communities as well as courts, detention centers, community organizations, and agencies, and public health departments to gain exposure to diverse groups. Through such exposure, students developed "skills in prevention, interprofessional collaboration, and advocacy" (Goodman et al., 2004, p. 808).

Before beginning this program, Goodman and colleagues (2004) reviewed multicultural family literature for evidence of discussion of social justice and found that it was indeed discussed and the following themes were most integral to bringing about social justice: "(a) ongoing self-examination, (b) sharing the power, (c) giving voice, (d) facilitating consensus, (e) building on strengths, and (f) leaving the client with tools" (p. 793). The program was therefore designed to provide students with opportunities to develop these skills.

According to Buckley (1998), there are three qualities of social justice: (1) the affective dimension, or the awareness of and sensitivity to the suffering that occurs under oppression, (2) the intellectual dimension, or the understanding of the causes and effects of oppression, and (3) the pragmatic dimension, or the practice of bringing about social justice. Counselor training texts typically address the first two dimensions, the affective and intellectual, while overlooking the pragmatic dimension. The activities that the student participated in and immersed themselves in during the project of Goodman and colleagues did address the pragmatic dimension. The students gained so much insight from the project that Goodman and colleagues (2004) recommend that more programs integrate social advocacy and social action into existing courses.

Keep in mind, however, while learning projects such as that of Goodman and colleagues (2004) bring social awareness into the forefront, and social awareness can be helpful in treating the symptoms of social problems, awareness is not the same as social advocacy or social action. Of course, awareness is a great place to start. Serving soup to the hungry may go a long way in helping career professionals and students gain a greater understanding of the plight of those living poverty, but such an activity does not change the fact that there are very poor people in the first place. Social advocacy is about doing something to change the institutions that, through their policies, cause these problems. For example, to reduce homelessness, students and practitioners can learn to challenge the policies for early release of patients from mental hospitals, raising the minimum wage to a living wage, and educating employers about the benefits of hiring people with mental and physical disabilities as well as people who have been incarcerated.

Collison et al. (1998) have also outlined steps to train career professionals for social action. They suggest first determining whether or not career professionals want to engage in social activism and, if so, determining each individual's style. They offer the following pivotal steps in learning social advocacy:

(a) reading advocacy materials and other materials about social and organizational change
(b) understanding the law
(c) keeping track of changes that affect oppressed persons
(d) becoming a part of an existing advocacy group, either a larger, long-standing group such as the NAACP or the Southern Poverty Law Center or a locally-based affiliate of such organizations devoted to promoting the welfare of the poor, the homeless, ethnic minority groups, gay, lesbian, bisexual and transgendered people, and/or people with disabilities.

Some counselors may be interested in global participation in social action and advocacy. Marsella (2013) encourages social justice education and training for all future professionals across the college curriculum that prepares students for the global era. Several of Marsella's suggestions can translate from the college environment to career professionals. For example, career professionals and students can:

1. Read the United Nations "Universal Declaration of Human Rights" (United Nations, 1948)
2. Position social justice art, statements, comments, poetry, and photographs at conspicuous locations in the workplace
3. Develop electronic materials as resources on social justice
4. Develop community outreach programs for marginalized individuals
5. Create a justice orientation for current and new employees
6. Support projects concerned with the study of application of justice (e.g., travel, research, and teaching support).

Social Action Skills Categories for Career Professionals

Social action has been recommended by many as a practice in which all career professionals should engage. For career professionals in particular, there are specific social action skills that are of importance. The remainder of this chapter is organized into eight categories of social action skills for career professionals, with the organization informed by the work of Lee and Walz (1998).

Commit to promoting greater access and competence in the use of information technologies. Casey (1998) explains that the use of technology is something that most workers take for granted; however, a technology gap divides the social classes. Upper-and-middle-class people have more access to technology and more control over the technology they use, while those in the lower classes tend not to have as much access to technology, and when they do have access, they are burdened by the technology. Casey (1998) provides an example of an upper-class White male who uses technology to make his work life more convenient (e.g., interactive calendars, GPS systems, teleconferencing), while a working-class mother is unable to do her work without a computer and headset. Technology is needed to do the job, it does not make the job more convenient. Moreover, lack of convenient access to technology in the home and at school affects the education of the woman's children and limits her family's access to career information. While it is true public schools in existence today typically provide computer access to students, such access is limited to the school building and there is a "homework gap" between students who do not have access to the internet at home and those who do. The Pew Research Center released a report in 2017 (Anderson, 2017) on what they call the digital divide—the technology gap between the poor and the more affluent. The survey revealed that 30% of families with incomes $30,000 and below do not even own a smart phone, half of those families do not own a computer or have internet access at home, and the majority of low-income families do not have tablets. Of those who have smart phones, most were smart phone-only users (Anderson, 2017). This is problematic not only to school children but, also to parents who are likely to use their smart phones to find and apply for jobs.

Sampson (1998) challenges career professionals to identify websites that are specific to the client's career development needs and to create self-help programs that can be used to track career development milestones. In all, the call is for counselors professionals to push for more up-to-date technology in underserved schools, more computer training for underserved clients, and access to computers in more locations (such as in housing development offices).

Acquire and use multiple assessment procedures. The enactment of No Child Left Behind Act (2001) resulted in a decade long focus on ability and achievement assessment for poor and underserved school districts. There were high stakes involving the loss of federal funding when the average test scores in school districts did not meet goals. Social action on the part of parents, teachers, administrators and school districts has been instrumental in changing this system in many states. Because most ability and achievement assessments have been proven to have racial and cultural bias, using only this kind of testing is discriminatory. Career professionals in states where it still exists have an opportunity to make a difference through social justice counseling and social action within their community.

Instead of relying on questionable standardized tests, multiple assessments should be used to assist career decision-making with clients. Qualitative assessments such as self-estimates of abilities, card sorts, and assessments of actual performance would all be options career professionals should consider using (Wilkins-Yel, Chung, Cheng, Li, 2019).

Assign a higher priority for social advocacy in counselor education programs. The fact that so few students have received training in social action is unfortunate, but it is a reflection of how recently the desire for this competency has developed. The good news is that both Council for the Accreditation of Counseling and Related Educational Programs (CACREP) and the American Psychological Association (APA) now require advocacy training for students, so a foundation for social advocacy skills among counselors has been set (CACREP, 2015; APA, 2015).

Until such standards are more pervasive in educational institutions as well as in the above-mentioned organizations, counselor educators can push to include social justice counseling as a part of the required career counseling course. Social justice counseling is particularly relevant to career development, because many of the oppressive conditions endured by clients are determined by their careers. Individual instructors should act as role models for social action by becoming knowledgeable about social action strategies and policies that impede social justice. They can start by taking a public stance on issues important to career counseling, such as affirmative action, bias in job and college placement testing, and/or bilingual education (Vera & Speight, 2003). Ibrahim and Heuer (2016) also recommend having students engage service learning with social justice and advocacy focus.

Intervene into client environments to promote positive changes in those environments. Most of the strategies suggested by authors of social justice literature fall under this category. Although the list of activities and behaviors that entail intervention is very long, only those most relevant to career counseling and development are discussed here.

Grieger and Ponterotto (1998) have provided a number of suggestions for advocacy intervention on behalf of the client, including:

- Defend causes for social justice in schools and in the workplace.
- Advocate for a zero-tolerance policy against discriminatory and harassing behaviors in the workplace.
- When necessary, engage in formal protests against discriminatory policies.

Other actions counselors might consider include soliciting the assistance of appropriate community organizations to oppose injustices and becoming involved with community groups and individuals who are "fighting for change on their own behalf" (Lewis & Arnold, 1998, p. 59). Several authors suggest that counselors join forces with outside professional organizations to assist in facilitating social change (Brabeck, Wash, Kenny, & Comilang, 1997; Hartung & Blustein, 2002). Career professionals, therefore, would not only be joining forces with other helping professionals but, also getting business industries, and professional organizations run by ethnic minority and other disenfranchised groups involved in social advocacy.

To ensure that interventions further a social advocacy agenda, Prilleltensky and Prilleltensky (2003) suggest that counselors ask themselves (and others) the following questions:

- "Do interventions educate participants on the timing, components, targets, and dynamics of best strategic actions to overcome oppression?" (p. 200). In other words, do clients and others know the who, when, what, and how of the plan?
- "Do interventions empower participants to take action to address political inequities and social injustice within their relationships, settings, communities, states, and at the international level?" (p. 200).
- "Do interventions promote solidarity and strategic alliances and coalitions with groups facing similar issues?" (p. 200)
- "Do interventions account for the subjectivity and psychological limitations of the agents of change?" (p. 200). The intervention should be appropriate for those advocating for change.

Help empower clients to advocate for themselves. Career professional may begin the process of empowering clients to act on their own behalf by helping them recognize that the career challenges they experience often have a social cause. Empowering clients to act on their own behalf is a basic social advocacy skill career professionals need to develop. In fact, empowering client advocacy seems to be the strategy used most according to Fickling (2016). Clients are to be encouraged to initiate grievance processes when they experience discrimination on the job, and career professionals support them through this process. Also, clients need to be supplied with the information regarding resources and policies needed to take on such challenges. Support not only includes providing information but also providing emotional assistance when clients become frustrated with the systems they are fighting. In addition, clients could be encouraged to get involved with (or establish if none is available) diversity-positive groups at their jobs, in their schools, or in their neighborhoods (Brabeck et al., 1997; Gainor, 2005; Geiger & Ponterroto, 1998; Hartung & Blustein, 2002; Herr & Niles, 1998). Although counselors seem to focus on individual career counseling for social justice, Fickling, 2016 and Ibrahim & Heuer, 2016) advocate for group career counseling as opposed to individual counseling. They state that it is the best way to effect change because the system affects many, not just one.

The following scenario illustrates the importance of client empowerment:

Margarita, a career counseling intern, has a White female client, Susan, who is enrolled in the civil engineering program. Susan sadly informs Margarita that she is going to drop out of the program because she cannot stand the negative attitudes of the students and faculty. Both students and professors either ignore or ridicule her ideas, fellow students leave her out of study groups, professors typically do not call on her in her upper-level engineering classes, and she hates the condescending way the teaching assistant looks at her every time she has a question during her laboratory classes. Susan says that it really is not worth the hassle, and there are other areas of engineering she can pursue without having to put up with this "old boy" stuff.

When Margarita suggests to Susan that she is being sexually harassed, Susan insists that no one has made a pass at her or anything remotely like that. Margarita explains that the hostile environment she is experiencing is, in fact, sexual harassment. Susan then gets really angry. Margarita and Susan discuss harassment further and Susan decides that she wants to do something about it. They work out a process for Susan to collect data by recording the time, place, and specifics about each incident over the next couple of weeks. She will then file a complaint. Although Susan had thought she would not change her mind about getting out of civil engineering, she now thinks pursuing both her degree and a sexual harassment claim will be positive moves not just for her but also for the next woman who wants to enter the civil engineering program.

Work to improve policies with respect to human welfare and development. Regarding the skill of improving policies, it is probably most expedient for career professionals to begin by exploring policies that are working well and those that are detrimental in their own places of work before going on to explore the policies in place at other organizations. The types of actions career professionals should take regarding improving policies include the following:

- Getting involved at the policy-making level, such as being on a committee that makes policy decisions on hiring, retaining, and promotion of employees. In such a role, career professionals can also help resist the pressure from privileged groups to retreat from multiculturalism.

- Getting involved in the evaluation of the organization's performance with diverse groups and being involved with developing an improvement plan if needed (Geiger & Ponterroto, 1998).

Career professionals who do not want to take on the entire organization to eliminate policies may be willing to ensure that their own departments or programs are culturally diverse and sensitive (Geiger & Ponterroto, 1998). When working to improve policies outside of their own organizations, career professionals may want to start by examining a local policy that affects their clients. For example, advocating for updating technology in an inner-city or rural school so that children can have better access to career information, or doing as Tamiko did in this chapter's opening scenario and finding an issue that is important in career development, even if one does not have a client with such an issue at that time, are ways to improve policies.

Advocate at all levels of government. According to Herr (2003), career counseling has been closely aligned with governmental policy making throughout history, and as such, career counseling has affected a great many governmental changes that have had positive effects on the career development of individuals from diverse backgrounds. Some governmental policy changes that have been put into place largely through the efforts of career professionals include, but are not limited to, the School to Work Opportunities Act, the North American Free Trade Act, and the Workforce Investment Act. Herr notes that career professionals have failed to effectively convince governmental agencies to expand their notion of appropriate client base and types of problems for career counseling. Instead, only certain clients (such as unemployed, high school seniors, or displaced workers) are being funded, and only certain career issues are addressed. Because of their long-standing history of influencing governmental policies, Herr (2003) challenges career professionals to "take the lead for advocating for career counseling issues to policy makers at all levels" and "where there are voids in legislative provisions that affect particular subpopulations, career professionals should advocate for amended policies and legislation" (p. 15). The NCDA Government Relations Committee has taken up this challenge and has as part of its agenda "to work collaboratively to identify and support legislation and policies that are of primary concern to NCDA including the areas of elementary and secondary education, veterans support, workforce development, career and technical education, and higher education" (NCDA, n.d., para. 1).

Final Thoughts

A career professional may assist clients in choosing a career that seems "perfect" in terms of their personality, interests, and abilities, and may prepare those clients to meet the cultural challenges such careers may present to them but such a career professional has only completed half the task. The task is not complete until society is confronted with changing its oppressive policies so that someday any child can be told truthfully, "You can be anything you want to be when you grow up." Therefore, career professionals are encouraged to develop competencies in social action, commit to becoming involved in social action and social justice, and promote training in social action for counseling students. To quote Derald Sue's presidential address to the APA's Division of Counseling Psychology, "How can we possibly live our lives, day in and day out, with the knowledge of our complicity in the dehumanization of [disenfranchised persons]? And how can we possibly sit at home and do nothing about it?" (Sue, 2005, p. 112).

REVIEW / REFLECTION QUESTIONS

1. Refer to the list of Advocacy Competencies in Appendix D, and discuss how being a culturally competent career professional (using all the knowledge and skills discussed in this text) will or will not prepare you for acting on social justice issues.

2. Think of an injustice that exists in your community (such as overcrowded urban schools, lack of day care, limitations on mass transit, a legislature that has no representation by females or men of color). Discuss how these injustices influence career development of workers and future workers. Discuss how you would go about getting involved in social action at each level (client, organization, community, nationally) to change the status quo.

3. Several authors mention resistance to social action. List some of the reasons that were stated that career professionals might resist involvement in social action. Discuss your reactions to each of these reasons in terms of your own participation in social action. If you find yourself feeling resistant, what might you do to reduce that resistance?

References

Albee, G. W. (2000). The Bolder model's fatal flaw. *American Psychologist, 55,* 247-248.

American Psychological Association. (2015). *Commission of accreditation: Implementing regulations.* Retrieved from https://irp-cdn.multiscreensite.com/a14f9462/files/uploaded/Section%20C_1.15.2020%20update.pdf

Anderson, M. (2017). Digital divide persists even as lower-income Americans make gains in tech adoption. *Pew Research Center.* Retrieved from https://www.pewresearch.org/fact-tank/2019/05/07/digital-divide-persists-even-as-lower-income-americans-make-gains-in-tech-adoption/

Arredondo, P. (1999). Multicultural competencies as tools to address oppression and racism. *Journal of Counseling and Development, 77,* 102-108.

Arredondo, P., Toporek, R., Brown, S. P., Jones, J., Locke, D. C., Sanchez, J., & Stadler, H. (1996). Operationalization of the multicultural counseling competencies. *Journal of Multicultural Counseling and Development, 24,* 42-78.

Bell, L. A. (2016). Theoretical foundations for social justice education. In M. Adams, L. A. Bell, D. J. Goodman, & K. Y. Josh (Eds.), *Teaching for diversity and social justice,* (3rd edition, pp. 3-26). New York, NY: Routledge.

Blustein, D. L., McWhirter, E. H., & Perry, J. C. (2005). An emancipatory communitarian approach to vocational development theory, research, and practice. *The Counseling Psychologist, 33*(2), 141-179.

Brabeck, M., Wash, M. E., Kenny, M., & Comilang, K. (1997). Interprofessional collaboration for children and families: Opportunities for counseling psychology in the 21st century. *The Counseling Psychologist, 25,* 615-636.

Buckley, M. J. (1998). *The Catholic university as promise and project: Reflections in a Jesuit idiom.* Washington, DC: Georgetown University Press.

Casey, J. A. (1998). Technology: A force for social action. In C. C. Lee & G. R. Walz (Eds.), *Social action: A mandate for counselors* (pp. 199-212). Alexandria, VA: American Counseling Association.

Collison, B. B., Osborne, J. L., Gray, L. A, House, R. M., Firth, J., & Lou, M. (1998). Preparing counselors for social action. In C. C. Lee & G. R. Walz (Eds.), *Social action: A mandate for counselors* (pp. 263-277). Alexandria, VA: American Counseling Association.

Council for Accreditation of Counseling and Related Educational Programs [CACREP]. (2015). 2016 CACREP Standards. Retrieved from: http://www.cacrep.org/wp-content/uploads/2017/08/2016-Standards-with-citations.pdf

Davis, H. V. (1969). *Frank Parsons: Prophet, innovator, counselor.* Carbondale, IL: Southern Illinois University Press.

Evans, R. (1996). *The human side of school change: Reform, resistance, and the real-life problems of innovation.* San Francisco, CA: Jossey-Bass.

Fickling, M. J. (2016). An exploration of career counselors' perspectives on advocacy. *Professional Counselor, 6*(2), 174-188.

Fox, D. R. (2003). Awareness is good, but action is better. *The Counseling Psychologist, 31*(3), 299-304.

Gainor, K. A. (2005). Social justice: The moral imperative of vocational psychology. *The Counseling Psychologist, 33*(2). 180-188.

Goodman, L. A., Liang, B., Helms, J. E., Latta, R. E., Sparks, E., & Weintraub, S. R. (2004). Training counseling psychologists as social justice agents: Feminist and multicultural principles in action. *The Counseling Psychologist, 32*(6), 793-837.

Grieger, I., & Ponterotto, J. G. (1998). Challenging intolerance. In C. C. Lee & G. R. Walz (Eds.), *Social action: A mandate for counselors* (pp. 17-50). Alexandria, VA: American Counseling Association.

Hartung, P. J., & Blustein, D. L. (2002). Reason, intuition, and social justice: Elaborating on Parsons' career decision-making model. *Journal of Counseling and Development, 80,* 41-47.

Herr, E. L. (2003). The future of career counseling as an instrument of public policy. *Career Development Quarterly, 52,* 8-17.

Herr, E. L., & Niles, S. G. (1998). Career: Social action in behalf of purpose, productivity and hope. In C. C. Lee & G. R. Walz (Eds.), *Social action: A mandate for counselors* (pp. 117-136). Alexandria, VA: American Counseling Association.

Ibrahim, F. A., & Heuer, J. R. (2016). *Cultural and social justice counseling*. Geneva: Springer.

Jordan, M., & Clement, S. (2018). Rallying nation: In reaction to Trump, millions of Americans are joining protests and getting political. Retrieved from: https://www.washingtonpost.com/news/national/wp/2018/04/06/feature/in-reaction-to-trump-millions-of-americans-are-joining-protests-and-getting-political/?utm_term=.16315c8bc6d5

Kikuchi, D. (2005). What is "social justice?" A collection of definitions. Retrieved from https://shop.reachandteach.com/defining-social-justice-what-social-justice

Lee, C. C. (1998). Counselors as agents of social change. In C. C. Lee & G. R. Walz (Eds.), *Social action: A mandate for counselors* (pp. 117-136). Alexandria, VA: American Counseling Association.

Lee, C. C., & Walz. G. R. (1998). A summing up and call to action. In C. C. Lee & G. R. Walz (Eds.), *Social action: A mandate for counselors* (pp. 307-312). Alexandria, VA: American Counseling Association.

Lewis, J. A., & Arnold, M. S. (1998). From multicultural to social action. In C. C. Lee & G. R. Walz (Eds.), *Social action: A mandate for counselors* (pp. 52-65). Alexandria, VA: American Counseling Association.

Liu, W. M., & Ali, S. R. (2005). Addressing social class and classism in vocational theory and practice: Extending the emancipatory communitarian approach. *The Counseling Psychologist, 33*(2), 189-196.

Marsella, A. J. (2013). All psychologies are indigenous psychologies: Reflections on psychology in a global era. *Psychology International, 24*(4), 5-7.

NCDA. (n.d.). *Legislative goals and objectives*. Retrieved from https://ncda.org/aws/NCDA/pt/sp/govtrelations_legagenda

No Child Left Behind PL 107-110 (2001). Retrieved from https://www.congress.gov/bill/107th-congress/house-bill/1

Pope, M., Briddick, W. C., & Wilson, F. (2013). The historical importance of social justice in the founding of the National Career Development Association. *The Career Development Quarterly, 61*(4), 368-373.

Prilleltensky, I., & Prilleltensky, O. (2003). Synergies for wellness and liberation in counseling psychology. *The Counseling Psychologist, 31*, 273-281.

Ratts, M. J., Singh, A. A., Nassar-McMillan, S., Butler, S. K., & McCullough, J. R. (2016). Multicultural and social justice counseling competencies: Guidelines for the counseling profession. *Journal of Multicultural Counseling and Development, 44*(1), 28-48.

Sampson, Jr., J. P. (1998). The internet as a potential force for social change. In C. C. Lee & G. R. Walz (Eds.), *Social action: A mandate for counselors* (pp. 213-225). Alexandria, VA: American Counseling Association.

Sue, D. W. (2005). Racism and the conspiracy of silence: Presidential address. *The Counseling Psychologist, 33,* 100-114.

Sue, D. W., Arredondo, P., & McDavis, R. J. (1992). Multicultural competencies and standards: A call to the profession. *Journal of Counseling and Development, 70,* 477-486.

Sue, D. W., & Sue, D. (2016). *Counseling the culturally diverse: Theory and practice* (7th edition). Hoboken, NJ: John Wiley & Sons.

Toporek, R. L. (2000). Developing a common language and framework for understanding advocacy in counseling. In J. Lewis & L. Bradley (Eds.), *Advocacy in counseling: Counselors, clients, and community* (pp. 5-14). Greensboro, NC: CAPS Publications.

Toporek, R. L. (2018). Strength, solidarity, strategy and sustainability: A counseling psychologist's guide to social action *The European Journal of Counselling Psychology, 7*(1), 90–110. doi:10.5964/ejcop.v7i1.153

United Nations. (1948). *United Nations universal declaration of human rights.* Retrieved from https://www.un.org/en/universal-declaration-human-rights/

Vera, E. M., & Speight, S. L. (2003). Multicultural competence, social justice, and counseling psychology: Expanding our roles. *The Counseling Psychologist, 31*(3), 253-272.

Wilkins-Yel, C. G., Chung, Y. B., Cheng, J, Li, Y (2019). Multicultural considerations in career assessment. In K. B. Stoltz & S. R. Barclay (Eds.), *A comprehensive guide to career assessment* (pp. 59-73). Broken Arrow, OK: National Career Development Association.

APPENDICES

Appendix A

Association for Multicultural Counseling and Development (AMCD) Cross-Cultural Competencies

I. Counselor Awareness of Own Cultural Values and Biases

A. Attitudes and Beliefs
1. Culturally skilled counselors believe that cultural self-awareness and sensitivity to one's own cultural heritage is essential.
2. Culturally skilled counselors are aware of how their own cultural background and experiences have influenced attitudes, values, and biases about psychological processes.
3. Culturally skilled counselors are able to recognize the limits of their multicultural competency and expertise.
4. Culturally skilled counselors recognize their sources of discomfort with differences that exist between themselves and clients in terms of race, ethnicity and culture.

B. Knowledge
1. Culturally skilled counselors have specific knowledge about their own racial and cultural heritage and how it personally and professionally affects their definitions and biases of normality/abnormality and the process of counseling.
2. Culturally skilled counselors possess knowledge and understanding about how oppression, racism, discrimination, and stereotyping affect them personally and in their work. This allows individuals to acknowledge their own racist attitudes, beliefs, and feelings. Although this standard applies to all groups, for White counselors it may mean that they understand how they may have directly or indirectly benefited from individual, institutional, and cultural racism as outlined in White identity development models.
3. Culturally skilled counselors possess knowledge about their social impact upon others. They are knowledgeable about communication style differences, how their style may clash with or foster the counseling process with persons of color or others different from themselves based on the A, B and C, Dimensions, and how to anticipate the impact it may have on others.

C. Skills
1. Culturally skilled counselors seek out educational, consultative, and training experiences to improve their understanding and effectiveness in working with culturally different populations. Being able to recognize the limits of their competencies, they (a) seek consultation, (b) seek further training or education, (c) refer out to more qualified individuals or resources, or (d) engage in a combination of these.
2. Culturally skilled counselors are constantly seeking to understand themselves as racial and cultural beings and are actively seeking a non-racist identity.

II. Counselor Awareness of Client's Worldview

A. Attitudes and Beliefs
1. Culturally skilled counselors are aware of their negative and positive emotional reactions toward other racial and ethnic groups that may prove detrimental to the counseling relationship. They are willing to contrast their own beliefs and attitudes with those of their culturally different clients in a nonjudgmental fashion.
2. Culturally skilled counselors are aware of their stereotypes and preconceived notions that they may hold toward other racial and ethnic minority groups.

B. Knowledge
1. Culturally skilled counselors possess specific knowledge and information about the particular group with which they are working. They are aware of the life experiences, cultural heritage, and historical background of their culturally different clients. This particular competency is strongly linked to the "minority identity development models" available in the literature.
2. Culturally skilled counselors understand how race, culture, ethnicity, and so forth may affect personality formation, vocational choices, manifestation of psychological disorders, help seeking behavior, and the appropriateness or inappropriateness of counseling approaches.
3. Culturally skilled counselors understand and have knowledge about sociopolitical influences that impinge upon the life of racial and ethnic minorities. Immigration issues, poverty, racism, stereotyping, and powerlessness may impact self-esteem and self-concept in the counseling process.

C. Skills
1. Culturally skilled counselors should familiarize themselves with relevant research and the latest findings regarding mental health and mental disorders that affect various ethnic and racial groups. They should actively seek out educational experiences that enrich their knowledge, understanding, and cross-cultural skills for more effective counseling behavior.
2. Culturally skilled counselors become actively involved with minority individuals outside the counseling setting (e.g., community events, social and political functions, celebrations, friendships, neighborhood groups, and so forth) so that their perspective of minorities is more than an academic or helping exercise.

III. Culturally Appropriate Intervention Strategies

A. Beliefs and Attitudes
1. Culturally skilled counselors respect clients' religious and/ or spiritual beliefs and values, including attributions and taboos, because they affect worldview, psychosocial functioning, and expressions of distress.
2. Culturally skilled counselors respect indigenous helping practices and respect help~giving networks among communities of color.
3. Culturally skilled counselors value bilingualism and do not view another language as an impediment to counseling (monolingualism may be the culprit).

B. Knowledge
1. Culturally skilled counselors have a clear and explicit knowledge and

understanding of the generic characteristics of counseling and therapy (culture bound, class bound, and monolingual) and how they may clash with the cultural values of various cultural groups.
2. Culturally skilled counselors are aware of institutional barriers that prevent minorities from using mental health services.
3. Culturally skilled counselors have knowledge of the potential bias in assessment instruments and use procedures and interpret findings keeping in mind the cultural and linguistic characteristics of the clients.
4. Culturally skilled counselors have knowledge of family structures, hierarchies, values, and beliefs from various cultural perspectives. They are knowledgeable about the community where a particular cultural group may reside and the resources in the community.
5. Culturally skilled counselors should be aware of relevant discriminatory practices at the social and community level that may be affecting the psychological welfare of the population being served.

C. Skills

1. Culturally skilled counselors are able to engage in a variety of verbal and nonverbal helping responses. They are able to send and receive both verbal and nonverbal messages accurately and appropriately. They are not tied down to only one method or approach to helping, but recognize that helping styles and approaches may be culture bound. When they sense that their helping style is limited and potentially inappropriate, they can anticipate and modify it.
2. Culturally skilled counselors are able to exercise institutional intervention skills on behalf of their clients. They can help clients determine whether a "problem" stems from racism or bias in others (the concept of healthy paranoia) so that clients do not inappropriately personalize problems.
3. Culturally skilled counselors are not averse to seeking consultation with traditional healers or religious and spiritual leaders and practitioners in the treatment of culturally different clients when appropriate.
4. Culturally skilled counselors take responsibility for interacting in the language requested by the client and, if not feasible, make appropriate referrals. A serious problem arises when the linguistic skills of the counselor do not match the language of the client. This being the case, counselors should (a) seek a translator with cultural knowledge and appropriate professional background or (b) refer to a knowledgeable and competent bilingual counselor.
5. Culturally skilled counselors have training and expertise in the use of traditional assessment and testing instruments. They not only understand the technical aspects of the instruments but are also aware of the cultural limitations. This allows them to use test instruments for the welfare of culturally different clients.
6. Culturally skilled counselors should attend to as well as work to eliminate biases, prejudices, and discriminatory contexts in conducting evaluations and providing interventions, and should develop sensitivity to issues of oppression, sexism, heterosexism, elitism and racism.
7. Culturally skilled counselors take responsibility for educating their clients to the processes of psychological intervention, such as goals, expectations, legal rights, and the counselor's orientation.

Reference

Arredondo, P., Toporek, R., Brown, S. P., Jones, J., Locke, D.C., Sanchez, J., & Stadler, H. (1996). Operationalization of the multicultural counseling competencies. *Journal of Multicultural Counseling and Development, 24,* 42-78.

Appendix B

Minimum Competencies for Multicultural Career Counseling and Development
(developed in 2009 to replace the Career Counseling Competencies)
(updated September 2020)

Introduction

The purpose of the multicultural career counseling and development competencies is to ensure that all individuals practicing in, or training for practice in, the career counseling and development field are aware of the expectation that we, as professionals, will practice in ways that promote the career development and functioning of individuals of all backgrounds. Promotion and advocacy of career development for individuals is ensured regardless of age, culture, mental/physical ability, ethnicity, race, nationality, religion/spirituality, gender, gender identity, sexual orientation, marital/partnership status, military or civilian status, language preference, socioeconomic status, any other characteristics not specifically relevant to job performance, in accordance with NCDA and ACA policy. Further, they will provide guidance to those in the career counseling and development field regarding appropriate practice about clients of a different background than their own. Finally, implementation of these competencies for the field should provide the public with the assurance that they can expect career counseling and development professionals to function in a manner that facilitates their career development, regardless of the client's/student's background.

If you believe that you need assistance with performing at these minimum levels, or would like to further develop your skills in these areas, please visit the NCDA website www.ncda.org for contact information regarding sources for increasing your competence in dealing with individuals with different cultural backgrounds than yourself.

For those seeking a credential to prove their mastery, NCDA offers career development credentials. See the NCDA Credentials section for more information.

The multicultural career professional:

CAREER DEVELOPMENT THEORY:
- understands the strengths and limitations of career theory and utilizes theories that are appropriate for the population being served.

INDIVIDUAL AND GROUP COUNSELING SKILLS:
- is aware of his/her own cultural beliefs and assumptions and incorporates that awareness into his/her decision-making about interactions with clients/students and other career professionals.
- continues to develop his/her individual and group counseling skills in order to enhance his/her ability to respond appropriately to individuals from diverse populations.
- is cognizant when working with groups of the group demographics and monitors these to ensure appropriate respect and confidentiality is maintained.

INDIVIDUAL/GROUP ASSESSMENT:
- understands the psychometric properties of the assessments he/she is using to effectively select and administer assessments and interpret and use results with the appropriate limitations and cautions.

INFORMATION, RESOURCES, & TECHNOLOGY:
- regularly evaluates the information, resources, and use of technology to determine that these tools are sensitive to the needs of diverse populations amending and/or individualizing for each client as required.
- provides resources in multiple formats to ensure that clients/students are able to benefit from needed information.
- provides targeted and sensitive support for clients/students in using the information, resources, and technology.

PROGRAM PROMOTION, MANAGEMENT AND IMPLEMENTATION:
- incorporates appropriate guidelines, research, and experience in developing, implementing, and managing programs and services for diverse populations.
- utilizes the principles of program evaluation to design and obtain feedback from relevant stakeholders in the continuous improvement of programs and services, paying special attention to feedback regarding specific needs of the population being served.
- applies his/her knowledge of multicultural issues in dealings with other professionals and trainees to ensure the creation of a culturally-sensitive environment for all clients.

COACHING, CONSULTATION, AND PERFORMANCE IMPROVEMENT:
- engages in coaching, consultation, and performance improvement activities with appropriate training and incorporates knowledge of multicultural attitudes, beliefs, skills and values.
- seeks awareness and understanding about how to best match diverse clients/students with suitably culturally sensitive employers.

SUPERVISION:
- gains knowledge of and engages in evidence-based supervision, pursues educational and training activities on a regular and ongoing basis inclusive of both counseling and supervision topics. Further, is aware of his/her limitations, cultural biases and personal values and seeks professional consultative assistance, as necessary.
- infuses multicultural/diversity contexts into his/her training and supervision practices, makes supervisees aware of the ethical standards and responsibilities of the profession, and trains supervisees to develop relevant multicultural knowledge and skills.

ETHICAL/LEGAL ISSUES:
- continuously updates his/her knowledge of multicultural and diversity issues and research and applies new knowledge as required.
- employs his/her knowledge and experience of multicultural ethical and legal issues within a professional framework to enhance the functioning of his/her organization and the image of the profession.
- uses supervision and professional consultations effectively when faced with an ethical or legal issue related to diversity, to ensure he/she provides high-quality services for every client/student.

RESEARCH/EVALUATION:
- designs and implements culturally appropriate research studies with regards to research design, instrument selection, and other pertinent population-specific issues.

NCDA Headquarters
305 N. Beech Circle
Broken Arrow, OK 74012
918/663-7060
Fax: 918/663-7058
www.ncda.org

Reference

National Career Development Association. (2009). Minimum Competencies for Multicultural Career Counseling and Development. Retrieved from: https://ncda.org/aws/NCDA/pt/fli/12508/true

Appendix C

School Counselor Multicultural Competence Checklist

COMPETENCE   Met   Unmet

I. Multicultural Counseling
1. I can recognize when my attitudes, beliefs, and values are interfering with providing the best services to my students.
2. I can identify the cultural bases of my communication style.
3. I can discuss how culture affects the help-seeking behaviors of students.
4. I can describe the degree to which a counseling approach is culturally inappropriate for a specific student.
5. I use culturally appropriate interventions and counseling approaches (e.g., indigenous practices) with students.
6. 1 can list at least three barriers that prevent ethnic minority students from using counseling services.
7. I can anticipate when my helping style is inappropriate for a culturally different student.
8. I can give examples of how stereotypical beliefs about culturally different persons impact the counseling relationship.

II. Multicultural Consultation
9. I am aware of how culture affects traditional models of consultation.
10. I can discuss at least one model of multicultural consultation.
11. I recognize when racial and cultural issues are impacting the consultation process.
12. I can identify when the race and/or culture of the client is a problem for the consultee.
13. I discuss issues related to race/ethnicity/culture during the consultation process, when applicable.

III. Understanding Racism and Student Resistance
14. I can define and discuss White privilege.
15. I can discuss how I (if European American/White) am privileged based on my race.
16. I can identify racist aspects of educational institutions.
17. I can define and discuss prejudice.
18. I recognize and challenge colleagues about discrimination and discriminatory practices in schools.
19. I can define and discuss racism and its impact on the counseling process.
20. I can help students determine whether a problem stems from racism or biases in others.
21. I understand the relationship between student resistance and racism.
22. I include topics related to race and racism in my classroom guidance units.

| COMPETENCE | Met | Unmet |

IV. Understanding Racial and/or Ethnic Identity Development
23. I am able to discuss at least two theories of racial and/or ethnic identity development.
24. I use racial/ethnic identity development theories to understand my students' problems and concerns.
25. I have assessed my own racial/ethnic development in order to enhance my counseling.

V. Multicultural Assessment
26. I can discuss the potential bias of two assessment instruments frequently used in the schools.
27. I can evaluate instruments that may be biased against certain groups of students.
28. I am able to use test information appropriately with culturally diverse parents.
29. I view myself as an advocate for fair testing and the appropriate use of testing of children from diverse backgrounds.
30. I can identify whether or not the assessment process is culturally sensitive.
31. I can discuss how the identification of the assessment process might be biased against minority populations.

VI. Multicultural Family Counseling
32. I can discuss family counseling from a cultural/ethnic perspective.
33. I can discuss at least two ethnic group's traditional gender role expectations and rituals.
34. I anticipate when my helping style is inappropriate for an ethnically different parent or guardian.
35. I can discuss culturally diverse methods of parenting and discipline.

VII. Social Advocacy
36. I am knowledgeable of the psychological and societal issues that affect the development of ethnic minority students.
37. When counseling, I consider the psychological and societal issues that affect the development of ethnic minority students.
38. I work with families and community members in order to reintegrate them with the school.
39. I can define "social change agent."
40. I perceive myself as being a "social change agent."
41. I can discuss what it means to take an "activist counseling" approach.
42. I intervene with students at the individual and systemic levels.
43. I can discuss how factors such as poverty and powerlessness have influenced the current conditions of at least two ethnic groups.

Reference

Holcomb-McCoy, C. (2004). Assessing the multicultural competence of school counselors: A checklist. *Professional School Counseling, 7,* 178-182.

Appendix D

Advocacy Competencies Based on the Competencies Endorsed by the American Counseling Association (ACA)

DOMAIN	COUNSELOR COMPETENCY
Client/Student Empowerment An advocacy orientation involves not only systems change but also the implementation of empowerment strategies in direct counseling. Client empowerment is focused on helping the client identify systemic barriers, learning approaches to address those barriers, helping them to evaluate those approaches as well as facilitating their reflective processing of their advocacy experiences.	• Identify strengths and resources of clients and students. • Identify the social, political, economic, and cultural factors that affect the client/student. • Recognize the significance of counselor's own cultural background and sociopolitical position in relation to power, privilege and oppression and in relation to the client or client communities. • Recognize signs indicating that an individual's behaviors and concerns reflect responses to systemic or internalized oppression. • At an appropriate developmental level and cultural perspective, help the individual identify the external barriers that affect his, her or their development. • Share resources and tools that are appropriate for the client/student's developmental level and issue. • Train students and clients in self-advocacy skills. • Help students and clients develop self-advocacy action plans. • Assist students and clients in carrying out action plans.

Client/Student Advocacy	Client/Student Advocacy Counselor Competencies
Client/student advocacy refers to actions a counselor takes to advocate on behalf of an individual client, student or family. This may be appropriate in situations where the counselor has access to systems or processes that the client may not have, or in ways the client may not. This may also be appropriate when the client chooses not to engage in advocacy due to fear of retribution, concerns about communication or cognitive challenges, or other factors. Counselors engaging in client/student advocacy directly address the system in which the barrier or problem exists or where a solution can be found. Often, this type of advocacy involves addressing systemic issues within the counselor's own organization or school but may also include advocacy within broader systems of care on behalf of a specific client or student.	• Identify barriers to the well-being of clients and students with attention to issues facing vulnerable groups. • Recognize the significance of counselor's own cultural background and sociopolitical position in relation to power, privilege and oppression and in relation to the client or client communities. • Identify potential allies for confronting the barriers including those within the organization as well as those who have cultural expertise relevant to the client's issue. • Develop an initial plan of action for confronting these barriers in consultation with client and ensuring plan is consistent with client's goals. • Communicate plan with client including rationale, and possible outcomes of advocacy. • Negotiate relevant services and education systems on behalf of clients and students. • Help clients and students gain access and create a plan to sustain needed resources and supports. • Carry out the plan of action and reflect/evaluate effectiveness of advocacy efforts.

Community Collaboration

In community collaboration, the counselor works with a group or community to identify and address systemic barriers and issues. The role of the counselor in this type of advocacy is primarily one of ally and contributor of professional skills such as interpersonal relations, group facilitation, communications, training and research. In community collaboration, the community is viewed as the leader and expert with regard to the issue of concern. The counselor supports the community efforts and helps them to examine the issue, determine courses of action, and reflect on that action. The extent of contribution the counselor makes often varies depending on the expertise and resources held by the community.

Community Collaboration Counselor Competencies

• Identify environmental factors that impinge upon students' and clients' development.

• Alert community or school groups with common concerns related to the issue.

• Develop alliances with groups working for change and explore what has already been done to address the issue. Understand counselor's sociocultural position in relation to the issue, the client group, and allies.

• Use effective listening skills to gain understanding of the group's goals and help facilitate examination of causes and possible avenues for advocacy.

• Facilitate understanding of group dynamics, cultural and sociopolitical variations in group members, and how that may affect group decisions as well as variable repercussions for different group members.

• Identify the strengths and resources that the group members bring to the process of systemic change and communicate recognition of and respect for these strengths and resources.

• Identify and offer the skills that the counselor can bring to the collaboration as well as any ethical limitations they might have as a professional.

• Facilitate the group in considering possible outcomes of action, both favorable and unfavorable, and support them in preparing for possible resistance or other challenges.

• Integrate considerations of the ecological and political context in which the advocacy actions will be taking place.

• Assess the effectiveness of counselor's collaborative efforts with the community.

Systems Advocacy	Systems Advocacy Counselor Competencies
Systems advocacy reflects counselors advocating on behalf of groups of clients or students within a school, organization or community. Existing groups may come to counselors for assistance regarding an issue, for example a student club. In other cases, counselors' ongoing work with people gives them a unique awareness of recurring themes. Counselors are often among the first to become aware of specific difficulties in the environment. When counselors identify systemic factors that act as barriers to their students' or clients' development, they often wish that they could change the environment and prevent some of the problems that they see every day. Systems level advocacy may take place within the organization systems in which the counselor works and may engage the counselor in arenas where client groups may not have access, for example, staff committees. Regardless of the specific target of change, the processes for altering the status quo have common qualities. Change is a process that requires vision, persistence, leadership, collaboration, systems analysis, and strong data. In many situations, a counselor is the right person to take leadership.	• Identify environmental factors impinging on students' or clients' development. • Understand the cultural, political, developmental and environmental contexts of the clients or client groups. • Understand the counselor's own cultural identity in relation to the group and the target of advocacy including privilege, oppression, communication, values, and intentions. • Investigate the issue, population and possible allies and stakeholders. • Provide and interpret data as well as share research and expertise to show the urgency for change. • In collaboration with other stakeholders, develop a vision to guide change. • Analyze the sources of political power and social influence within the system. • Develop a step-by-step plan for implementing the change process, attending to possible ethical issues. • Develop a plan for dealing with probable responses to change. • Recognize and deal with resistance. • Assess the effect of counselor's advocacy efforts on the system and constituents.

Appendices

Collective Action

Collective action (formerly Public Information) refers to advocacy in which the counselor collaborates with groups to address issues that exist on a broad scale or that can be remedied through changing public perception or policies. Collective action refers to advocacy in which the counselor collaborates with groups to address such large scale issues. The counselor contributes as a group member and lends their knowledge and skill to the process of advocacy. This may include group facilitating, research, and communication skills as needed by the group. Advocacy strategies in the public arena may involve increasing public awareness about an issue, lobbying decision making bodies for legislative or policy change, or other such actions. In collective action, the counselor's role is as collaborator with the group or community affected by the issues who have chosen to engage in advocacy.

• Recognize the impact of oppression, other barriers, and environmental factors that interfere with healthy development.

• Identify factors that are protective of healthy development as well as various avenues for enhancing these protective factors through the public arena.

• Share research and professional expertise with partner client groups and community members in developmentally and culturally appropriate ways.

• Determine appropriate role within community initiative such as facilitator, researcher, negotiator, etc. aligned with professional and personal skill set.

• Understand counselor's own cultural identity including positionality related to power, privilege, and oppression and how that influences the ways they work with the community and the targets of advocacy (e.g., decision makers).

• Participate with and/or facilitate community partners in identifying the source of problems, setting goals, developing an action plan, considering possible outcomes, and implementing the action plan.

• Prepare written and multimedia materials that provide clear explanations of the role of specific environmental factors in human development in consultation with engaged community or client groups.

• Communicate information in ways that are ethical and appropriate for the target population.

• Disseminate information through a variety of media appropriate for the target audience.

• Collaboratively prepare and present materials and information to influence decision makers, legislators, and policy makers, ensuring that the community's voice is central.

• Facilitate the community group in assessing the influence of their public information and advocacy strategies.

Social/Political Advocacy	Social/Political Advocacy Counselor Competencies
Counselors regularly act as change agents in the systems that affect their own students and clients most directly. This experience often leads toward the recognition that some of the concerns they have addressed affect people in a much larger arena. When this happens, counselors use their skills to carry out social/political advocacy on behalf of client or student populations. In this domain, counselors engage in advocacy strategies often independent of specific clients or client groups to address issues they observe. This may include examples such as writing advocacy briefings regarding an issue, invitations to testify at hearings, appearing in mass media (e.g., talk shows, podcasts) to raise awareness of issues, and other actions where the counselor speaks on behalf of an issue.	• Identify the communities affected by this issue including who makes up the community and whether the community is engaged in advocacy around the issue. • Consult with communities affected by the issue to understand their views and experiences, with attention to economic, social and cultural perspectives. • Distinguish those problems that can best be resolved through using the counselor's expertise and where the community may have limited access. • Identify ways the community may have input into the advocacy process. • Identify and collaborate with other professionals as well as other allies who are involved in disseminating public information and may be interested in or already engaging in policy advocacy. • Identify appropriate mechanisms and avenues for addressing these problems and distinguish the role of public awareness, legislative, policy and judicial action. • Understand counselor's own cultural identity including positionality related to power, privilege, and oppression and how that influences the ways they work with the community and the targets of advocacy (e.g., decision makers). • Support existing alliances for change through providing information, support, and expertise. • With allies, prepare convincing data and rationales for public awareness campaigns or to lobby legislators and other policy makers. • Maintain open dialogue with communities and clients to ensure that the social/political advocacy is consistent with the initial goals.

Reference

American Counseling Association. (2018). Advocacy competencies. Retrieved from https://www.counseling.org/docs/default-source/competencies/aca-advocacy-competencies-may-2020.pdf?sfvrsn=85b242c_4

SUBJECT INDEX

A

AACE, *(see Association for Assessment in Counseling and Education)*
ACA, *(see American Counseling Association)*
access, 45, 48, 50, 59, 68, 69, 72, 93, 96, 117, 130, 135, 148, 150, 179, 194, 201-202, 205
accreditation 4, 6, 7, 8, 179, 203
acculturation 21, 73, 130, 131, 156, 158, 162-163
ACES, *(see Association for Counselor Education and Supervision)*
ADA, *(see Americans with Disabilities Act)*
advocacy 8, 34, 36, 149, 194-195, 197-201, 203-204
Affirmative Action, 32, 51, 54. 55, 57, 81-83
agency environment, 121-123, 140, 151, 155, 159, 160, 163, 170
AMCD, *(see Association for Multicultural Counseling and Development)*
American Counseling Association (ACA), 5, 9-11, 120
"American" culture, 20
American Psychological Association (APA), 4-7, 9, 203, 206
American School Counselor Association (ASCA), 6, 183
Americans with Disabilities Act of 1990 (ADA), 80, 82, 156
anchoring heuristic, 168
APA, *(see American Psychological Association)*

aptitude tests, 5, 153, 154
Armed Services Vocational Aptitude Battery (ASVAB), 155
assessment, 8, 13, 24, 54, 70, 98, 109, 118-119, 127-129, 134, 147-150, 152-164, 166-171, 179, 182, 194, 196, 202
Association for Adult Development and Aging (AADA), 6
AGLBIC, *(see Association for Gay, Lesbian, and Bisexual Issues in Counseling)*
Association for Assessment in Counseling and Education (AACE), 149
Association for Counselor Education and Supervision (ACES), 6
Association for Gay, Lesbian, and Bisexual Issues in Counseling (AGLBIC), 6
Association for Multicultural Counseling and Development (AMCD), 5-7, 12, 117, 118, 119, 155
Association for Specialist in Group Work (ASGW), 6
associative learning, 101-102
assumptions, 2, 22, 24, 41, 51, 82, 85, 94, 133, 136-137, 148-149, 157, 159, 196
Autonomy Status, 33
availability heuristic, 168
aversive racism, 47, 51, 55, 62

B

Bell Curve, The (Hernstein, Murray), 153
Benjamin, Medea, 193

bias, 2, 3, 10, 13, 34, 41-44, 46-66, 67, 94, 101, 120, 128, 129, 133, 134, 137, 150, 152, 153, 157, 165, 167, 168, 182, 184-186, 195-196, 202, 203, 211-213, 217-219
bilingual counselors, 109, 122, 213

C

CACREP, (*See Council for Accreditation of Counseling & Related Education Programs*)
Career Barriers Inventory, 160
career development theories, 91-92, 94-124
Culturally Appropriate Career Counseling Model, 109, 169
Career-in-Culture Interview protocol, 130
Career Pattern Study, 95
certification, 8
circumscription, 103-104, 159, 178
Civil Rights Act of 1964 and 1991, 80, 81, 83, 84
class privilege, 61
Clinton, Bill, 83
CoBRA. (*See color blind racial attitudes*)
collective identity model, 28
collective racism, 48-49
collectivist cultures, 131
Color Blind Racial Attitudes (CoBRA), 51-52, 55
community, 1, 3, 12, 20, 33, 58, 72, 83, 86, 104, 110, 119, 121, 130, 138, 147, 154, 159, 160-162, 164, 165, 166, 169, 179, 181, 184, 185, 186, 194, 197, 199, 200, 201, 202, 203
competition, 133
compromise, 103, 104, 168, 178
confidentiality, 10, 12, 126

Conformity Stage of identity development, 29, 30, 33, 35, 76, 77, 78, 79, 157
Contact Status, 32, 35, 77
coping strategies, 27, 28, 62, 70-71, 132, 137
Council for Accreditation of Counseling & Related Educational Programs (CACREP), 4, 179, 203
counseling relationship types, 2, 6, 17, 52, 71, 74, 75, 77, 78, 80, 86, 119, 120, 197
credibility, 3, 74, 76, 79, 86, 120, 122, 123, 126
crossed relationships, 77
cultural accommodation, 94
cultural encapsulation, 41, 94
Culturally Appropriate Career Counseling Model (CACCM), 109
cultural mistrust, 67, 70, 71, 72, 120
culture, 2, 6, 8, 17-36, 41, 43, 46, 48, 55-57, 59, 68-79, 86, 96-97, 102-103, 105, 107, 109, 119-123, 125-126-133, 135-136, 138-141, 148-149, 155-159, 161-163, 165-168, 171, 181, 184, 186

D

debiasing techniques, 168
decision-making styles, 136
developmental model for career counseling, 103
discrimination, 4, 23, 29, 31, 48, 51, 54-55, 58-60, 67, 70-71, 79, 81-84, 93, 95, 97, 99, 101, 103, 119, 120, 128-129, 131-134, 136-138, 159-161 *See also* racism
disengagement stage of career development, 95

Subject Index

Disintegration Status, 32, 35, 78
Dissonance Stage of racial identity development, 29, 33, 35, 76, 78, 157, 161

E

education and training, 201
Equal Pay Act of 1963, 80, 84
establishment stage of career development, 95
ethics, 2, 9, 10, 99, 120, 148, 149
exercises
    career stereotypes, 44
    on class privilege, 61
    counseling relationship dyads, 78
    cultural exposure, 54
    cultural investigation, 19
    cultural mistrust, 72
    different world, 18-20
    immersion, 55-56
    locus of control/responsibility, 24
    non-traditional career path exploration, 44
    overcoming stereotyping, 43
    personal assessment, 54-56
    recording values and traditions, 19
    for unearthing cultural heritage, 18-19
    value orientation, 25
    visual, 56
    within-group differences, 75
expectations, 18, 19, 20, 22, 25-27, 42, 67, 72-75, 80, 105, 109, 130, 133, 140, 153, 179, 182
exploration stage of career development, 95

F

family, 12, 17, 18-21, 25-26, 34, 41, 43, 46, 58, 62-63, 67-68, 70, 72-73, 105, 109, 118, 119, 121, 122, 124, 126, 129-131, 135-138, 150, 161-162, 164-166, 168, 177, 180-181, 183, 193, 200, 202
Family Leave Act, 84

G

gay, lesbian, bisexual, transgendered clients, 83, 126, 131, 133, 138, 157, 201
glass ceiling, 132, 194
Global Exchange, 193
goals, 105, 109, 141, 147, 163, 184, 195, 198, 202
group counseling, 117, 131, 139, 140

H

healing strategies, 137
hexagonal theory, 150

I

identity, 6, 8, 18, 26-31, 33-36, 53, 60, 67, 71, 75-79, 86, 95, 97, 109-110, 125, 129-130, 134, 138, 154, 156-158, 161-162, 196
Immersion Status, 33, 35, 77
individual racism, 48, 49, 51
initial assessment stage of counseling, 118, 119, 127, 134
institutional racism, 48, 120
instrumental learning, 102
intake forms, 124, 169
Integrative Awareness Stage of racial identity development, 29-30, 34
interest inventories, 99, 150-151, 156-157
internalization status, 36
internalized racism, 48, 49, 157

International Association of Marriage and Family Counseling (IAMFC), 6
Internet, 19, 69-70, 202
internships, counselor, 4-5
Interpersonal Cultural Grid, 26
intervention strategies, 27
Introspection Stage of racial identity development, 30, 36

J
job interviews, 122
job search skills, 136-138

L
language, 6, 8-9, 17-18, 21, 55-57, 59, 75, 93, 122, 124, 130, 148-149, 152, 156, 158-159, 170, 182
learning, 4, 18, 33, 42, 50, 62, 68-69, 74, 101-106, 132, 135, 155, 186, 200, 203
legal issues, 8
legislation, 20, 84-85, 206
life space, 95-96
life span, career development and, 95-97
locus of control/ responsibility, 22-24, 78-79, 86

M
maintenance stage of career development, 95
Malcolm X, 67
MAP (*See Multicultural Assessment Process*)
media, prejudicial attitudes in, 41, 46, 49, 84, 181
melting pot metaphor, 20

minorities, 27-28, 31, 33, 46, 51, 58, 67, 71, 73, 82, 85-86, 93-96, 99, 103-105, 124, 129, 131, 133, 137, 153, 155, 158, 170, 178, 194, 196,
Minority Identity Development model, 28
Multicultural Assessment Process (MAP), 166-168

N
National Career Development Association (NCDA), 8-12, 45, 54, 99, 117-119, 149, 155, 185, 206
National Model, 183
National Vocational Guidance Association (NVGA), 8
Negro-to-Black conversion model, 28
norms, *See also* testing
North American Free Trade Agreement (NAFTA), 206

O
O*NET, 93
oppression, 4, 23, 27-36, 41-42, 45, 47-56, 58-63, 68-71, 79-81, 86, 91, 93, 99, 130-131, 179-180, 183, 195-197, 200, 204
orientation sessions, 139
outcome expectations, 105

P
parallel relationships, 77
People of Color model, 28
personal counseling, 117-118, 128
personality tests, 150, 166
personality type and work environment theory, 92, 98, 108
Person/Environment Fit, 93
planned happenstance, 102

Subject Index

political climate, 67, 80
poverty, 28, 45, 51-52, 61, 82, 85-86, 95-96, 106, 119, 159, 180, 182, 188, 197, 200-201
pragmatic dimension of social justice, 200
prejudice, 2-3, 27, 41-43, 45-47, 49-56, 61-62, 134, 137, 140, 196
privilege, 21, 27, 31-33, 35-36, 42, 45, 47, 51-53, 56-62, 80-81, 96, 121-122, 196-198, 205
process models for multicultural groups, 108-109
professionalism, 126
progressive relationships, 77
Pseudo-Independence Status, 32, 35, 77-78

R

Race Is a Nice Thing to Have: A Guide to Being a White Person or Understanding the White Person in Your Life (Helms), 34
racial/cultural identity, 26-28, 30-32, 35-36, 75-77, 79, 86, 134
Racial/Cultural Identity Development Model (RCIDM), 27-28, 35
Racial Identity Attitude scale, 158
racism, 4, 23, 27-28, 31-32, 34-35, 41-42, 45, 47-56, 59, 62, 77-78, 80, 106, 120, 128, 130-132, 153, 157, 159-162, 195-196
rapport building, 123-124, 127, 140
regressive relationships, 77
Reintegration Status, 32, 35
relativism, cultural, 21-22
representativeness heuristic, 168
research and evaluation, 8
Resistance Stage of racial identity development, 29, 35, 76, 157, 161

responsibility. *See* locus of control/
role induction, 127
role models, 50, 103, 106, 132, 136-137, 168, 180, 203

S

Scale to Assess Worldview, 24
Scholastic Aptitude Test (SAT), 152-153
School to Work Opportunities Act, 206
self-concept, in Super's career development theory, 95-97, 108
Self-Directed Search (SDS), 98
self-efficacy, 105-106, 186-187
self-understanding stage of counseling, 118, 129, 134
sequential concept framework, 109
sexual harassment, 84, 205
16PF test, 152, 163, 165-166
social action, 34, 193-203, 206
Social Cognitive Career Theory (SCCT), 104-106
social context, 107
social learning theory of career development, 101, 106
Society for the Psychological Study of Ethnic Minority Issues, 7
sociopolitical influences, 27, 99, 129
spirituality, 8, 132, 137, 148-149
Standards for Multicultural Assessment, 149
stereotypes, 42-45, 49, 52, 61, 69, 74, 98, 100, 110, 120, 132-134, 140, 154, 168-169
stereotype threat, 154
Strong Interest Inventory (SII), 92, 98, 100, 150-151, 157, 163-165, 169,
supervision, 7-8, 120, 127

T

task approach skills, 102
technology, 8, 201-202, 205
testing, 11, 17, 93-94, 130, 148, 153-154, 158, 160, 162, 167-169, 182, 202-203
Texaco oil company, racism in, 48
trait and factory theory, 92-94

V

values, 9-10, 13, 18-19, 21-22, 24, 26-27, 33-34, 36, 41-63, 67, 69, 71-75, 92, 100, 120-121, 129-130, 133-134, 136, 139, 147-148, 156, 158, 162, 165, 168, 169, 179, 185, 198,
victim role, 80
Vocational Preference Inventory (VPI), 98
Vocation Bureau of Boston, 195

W

Welfare Reform Bill of 1996, 80, 84-85
white racial identity model, 31
within-group differences, 27, 74-75
women, 28, 45, 52, 57-58, 67-68, 71, 75, 81-82, 84, 86, 93, 99, 103-104, 106, 128-129, 132-133, 151, 153, 157, 161, 194
work environments, 98
Workforce Investment Act, 206
workforce issues, 59, 67, 78, 80, 83, 85-86, 102, 128, 132-133, 197
worldview, 10, 13, 21-26, 59, 67-87, 169, 197

NAME INDEX

A

Adams, M., 36, 47, 54
Albee, G. W., 199
Alderfer, C.P., 133
Alexander, C.M., 28-29, 31, 54
Alford, B., 83
Ali, S.R., 105, 195
Allport, G.W., 41, 45
American Psychological Association (APA), 4, 7, 9, 203
American School Counselor Association (ASCA), 6, 183
Ancis, J.R., 60
Anderson, M., 202
Anderson, M.Z., 150-151
Annie E. Casey Foundation, 182
Arbona, C., 136
Arkes, H.R., 169
Arnold, D., 4
Arnold, M.S., 194-195, 203
Aronson, J., 153
Arredondo, P., 6-7, 17, 34, 56, 67, 117, 129, 155, 195-196
Association for Assessment and Research in Counseling (AARC), 149
Association for Assessment in Counseling and Education (AACE), 149
Association for Multicultural Counseling and Development (AMCD), 5-6, 117
Atkinson, D.R., 22, 23, 28, 31
Atwell, M.N., 182
Axelrad, S., 177
Axelson, J.A., 19-20, 23-24, 42, 48, 49, 60-61
Ayers, L., 82

B

Balfanz, R., 182
Baggerly, J., 179
Bandura, A., 101, 104-105
Barmer, A., 182
Baron, R.S., 71
Bell, L.A.E., 36, 47, 54, 147-148, 195
Bell, S., 147-148
Bennett, S.K., 31
Berkel, L.A., 181
Berry, J.W., 158
Betz, N.E., 98, 104, 153, 157
Bibbins, V.E., 7
Bingham, R., 109
Bingham, R.P., 12, 123
BlackPast, 67
Blustein, D.L., 118, 177, 195, 197-199, 203-204
Bohan-Baker, M., 186
Bolden, M.A., 48-49
Boodoo, G., 159
Borgen, F.H., 92, 150-151
Borodowsky, L.G., 34
Bouchard, T.J., 159
Boudrot, K., 96
Bowman, V., 139
Boykin, A.W., 159
Brabeck, M., 203-204
Brammer, L., 123
Briddick, W.C., 195
Bridgeland, J., 182
Brody, N., 159
Brooks, L., 124-125, 127
Brown, C.F., 48-49
Brown, D., 92, 102, 124-125, 127, 156, 178
Brown, M.T., 91, 96, 99, 181
Brown, S., 70-71

Brown, S.D., 5, 104-105, 159, 181
Brown, S.P., 2, 6-7, 17, 34, 56, 67, 117, 129, 155
Bucceria, J., 53
Buchtel, E.E., 74
Buckley, M.J., 200
Buckley, T.R., 55
Bullock-Mann, F., 182
Bureau of Labor Statistics, 85
Burgess, M.L., 71
Burkard, A., 4
Burton, S., 103
Busacca, L.A., 108
Butler, S.K., 7, 196
Byars, A.M., 106

C
Calhoun-Butts, C., 131
Campbell, R.E., 128
Card, N., 103
Carney, C.G., 31
Carter, R., 55
Carter, R.T., 2, 5, 98, 150
Casali, S.L., 71
Casas, J.M., 2, 5, 54
Casey, J.A., 201-202
Cass, V.C., 28
Cates, J.T., 4
Ceci, S.J., 159
Celinska, 4
Cellini, J.V., 128
Cerrone, M.T., 181
Chang, D.F., 4
Chao, C.S., 93
Chen, E.C., 4, 5, 84
Cheng, J., 202
Chesler, M.A., 57
Chinn, P.C., 18
Chope, R.C., 181
Chuang, B., 158
Chung, Y.B., 151, 202
Clement, S., 198

Close, W., 177
Cochran, D.B., 104
Cohen, L.L., 27, 71
Coleman, H.L.K., 71
College Board, 153
Collison, B.B., 200
Comas-Diaz, L., 162
Constantine, M.G., 123, 148
Cook, D.A., 28, 32, 48-49, 76, 120, 127, 133
Coon, D.W., 83, 129, 132
Corbishley, M.A., 118, 124, 134
Cordova, D.I., 70, 82
Council for the Accreditation of Counseling and Related Educational Programs (CACREP), 4, 179, 203
Cox, C.I., 156
Crace, R.K., 127
Cramer, S.H., 8, 92, 95, 122, 136, 188
Creamer, J.F., 85
Crenshaw, K., 82
Crews, C., 104
Crites, J.O., 128
Crosby, F., 70, 82
Cross, W., 27-28
Croteau, J.M., 151
Crowfoot, J.E., 57
Crumlish, J.P., 83
Cui, J., 183
Cusick, M.E., 105

D
D'Andrea, M., 42, 51, 61, 123, 160
Daniels, J., 42, 51, 61, 160
Danner, M., 47
Das, A.K., 2
Davis, H.V., 195
Day, S.X, 99
DeLucia, J.L., 139
DeLucia-Waak, J.L., 139-140
DePaoli, J., 182

Name Index

DeWitt, D.W., 151
Dings, J.G., 36
Distefano, T.M., 151, 161
Dixon, D.N., 169
Donigian, J., 139
Dovidio, J.F., 45, 51
Downing, N.E., 28
Drummond, R.J., 160
Durant, C., 104

E

Elmslie, S., 104
Engels, D.W., 8
Erikson, E., p. 28
Espelage, D.L., 4
Evans, K.M., 5, 54, 85, 118, 120, 132, 157, 198

F

Falender, C.A., 36
Falicov, C.J., 4, 36
Fawcett, M.L., 54
Feagin, J.R., 58
Federal Bureau of Investigation (FBI), 50
Ferdman, B.M., 28
Fernandez, M.S., 131
Fickling, M.J., 197, 199, 204
Firth, J., 200
Fisher, L.D., 181
Fisher, T.A., 181
Fitzgerald, L.F., 98
Fitzpatrick, M.E., 4
Flores, L.Y., 105, 123, 155, 169-171, 177, 181
Forrest-Cataldi, E., 182
Fouad, A., 2, 5
Fouad, N.A., 4, 92-93, 98-99, 106, 109
Fox, D.R., 195, 197, 199
Freedle, R., 28
Freedle, R.O., 153

Freeman, K., 179
Fuertes, J.N., 5, 117
Fukuyama, M.A., 156

G

Gaertner, S.L., 45
Gainor, K.A., 147, 150, 157, 160, 197-199
Galassi, J.P., 127
Gallagher, R.P., 118
Gallardo, M.E., 31
Gallegos, P.V., 28
Gallup, 82
Ginger, L.L., 181
Ginsberg, S.W., 177
Ginzberg, E., 177
Gladding, S.T., 139
Gold, J.G., 95, 96
Gold, J. M., 120
Gollnick, D.M., 18
Gonzalez, G.M., 93
Goodman, D.J., 36, 47, 54, 199-200
Gordon, A., 58
Gosselin, K.P., 179
Gottfredson, L., 104
Gottfredson, L.S., 91, 103-104, 159, 177-178, 188
Gray, L.A., 200
Greenwaldt, M.E., 179
Grethchen, D., 31
Grieger, I., 197, 203
Gring-Pemble, L., 84
Groen, M., 4
Grossman, J.M., 136
Grothaus, T., 47
Gushue, G.V., 181
Gysbers, N.C., 91, 107

H

Hackett, G., 104, 106, 157
Haley, A., 19
Hall, W.S., 28, 82

Halpern, D.F., 159
Hammer, A., 92, 151
Haney, C., 57
Hansen, J.I., 92, 151
Hanson, J.C., 158
Hanson, J.I.C., 158
Hardiman, R., 31
Harmon, L., 92
Harmon, L.W., 150-151
Harris-Bowlsbey, J., 123, 126, 148
Hartman, N.S., 157
Hartung, P.J., 109, 177-178, 195, 203-204
Hauslohner, A., 51
Hawks, B.K., 132
Hays, P.A., 58
Helms, J.E., 28, 32, 48-49, 76, 120, 127, 133, 199
Helwig, A.A., 104
Henderson, S., 104
Heppner, M.J., 91, 107
Herlihy, B.R., 84
Herma, J., 177
Herr, E.L., 8, 92, 95, 118, 122, 136, 157, 188, 204, 206
Herring, R.D., 136
Herrnstein, R.J., 153
Hesketh, B., 104
Hess, S., 4, 103
Highlen, P.S., 128-130, 155, 157-158, 162
Hilliard, A.G. III., 153
Hill, C.L., 103, 120, 148-149, 163, 166, 167, 171
Hines, A., 26
Hofstede, G., 156
Holcomb-McCoy, C., 180-182, 184, 186
Holland, J.L., 98-100
Holmes, J., 183
Horse, P.G., 28
Howard, K.A., 177

Howard, K.A.S., 177
House, R.M., 200
Hurtado, A., 57
Hussain, S., 103
Hussar, B., 182
Hyers, L.L., 27, 71

I
Ibrahim, F.A., 24-25, 203-204
Imel, Z.E., 53
Inda, M., 105
Ivers, N.N., 104
Ivey, A., 31
Ivey, A.E., 2, 5, 119, 135
Ivey, M.B., 119, 135

J
Jackson, B., 28
Jackson, B.W., 28
Jackson, R., 56
Jacobs, S., 51
Jenal, S.T., 4
Jensen, A.R., 2, 5, 152-153, 157
Johnson, L.E., 104
Johnston, J., 91, 107
Jones, C.P., 49
Jones, J.M., 49
Jones, K.D., 160
Jordan, M., 198
Jordan, S.E., 181
Joshi, , K.Y., 36, 47, 54
Jun, H., 54

K
Kahn, H., 24-25
Kahn, K.B., 31
Kaldor, W., 104
Kanchewa, S., 103
Kao, C.F., 71
Kantamneni, N., 4, 98
Kawakami, K., 45

Kelly, K.R., 151
Kikuchi, D. 194
Kluckhohn, F.R., 24-25
Knight, J.L., 179
Knox, S., 4
Kohli, R., 49
Kohut, H., 28
Kollar, M., 85
Krane, N.E.R., 159
Krumboltz, J.D., 101-102, 104, 129, 132
Kupersmidt, J., 103

L

LaFramboise, T.D., 2, 5, 156
Lapan, R.T., 104
Larrabee, M.J., 5, 118
Latta, R.E., 199
Lau, B.D., 83
Leal, V.M., 181
Lee, C.C., 131, 158, 194, 197, 201
Lee, D., 21
Lee, H.S., 105
Lee, S.J., 83
Lent, R.W., 2, 5, 104-105, 157
Lenz, J.G., 118
Leong, F.T.L., 91, 93-94, 96, 99, 109
Levine, E.S., 158
Lewis, J.A., 194-195, 203
Li, L.C., 21, 120-123, 148-149, 155, 156, 163, 166-167, 168, 170-171, 202
Liang, B., 199
Like, K., 103
Lin, 53
Lindzey, G., 157
Little, P.M.D., 186
Liu, W.M., 195
Lloyd, D.N., 182
Locke, D.C., 2, 6-7, 17, 34, 56, 67, 117, 129, 155, 196
Loehlin, J.C., 157, 159

Loehr-Lapan, S.J., 104
Lou, M., 200

M

Manese, J.E., 2, 5
Marsella, A.J., 201
Martin, G.A., 127
Matlin, N., 97
Maxie, A., 4
Mazareh, L.G., 147-148
McAuliffe, G.J., 47
McCullough, J.R., 7, 196
McDaniel, M.A., 157
McDavis, R.J., 6, 196
McFarland, J., 182-183
McGrath, P., 20, 60-61
McIntosh, P., 57, 59-60
McNamara, K., 28
McWhirter, A.C., 131, 180-183, 186-187
McWhirter, B.T., 131, 180-183, 186-187
McWhirter, E.H., 131, 180-183, 186-187,197
McWhirter, J.J., 131, 180-183, 186-187
Meir, E.I., 156
Menke, K.A., 105
Miller, M.J., 105, 181
Milsom, A., 104
Minor, C.W., 8, 173
Mitchell, L.K., 102
Mohart, G.V. 156
Morgan, L.W., 179
Morten, G., 22, 23, 28
Muha, D., 132
Murray, C., 153
Murray, P., 95-96

N

Nadal, 53
Nassar-McMillan, S., 7, 196

National Career Development Association (NCDA), 8-12, 54, 99, 117-119, 148-149, 155, 185, 206
National Vocational Guidance Association (NVGA), 8
Neira, P.M., 83
Neisser, U., 159
Newsome, D.W., 104
Neville, H.A., 51-52, 59, 62, 91
Niles, S., 147
Niles, S.G., 8, 92, 95, 118, 122-123, 126-127, 136, 148, 188, 204
Nilsson, J.E., 181

O
O'Brien, K.M., 181
Obasi, E.M., 123, 155, 169, 171
Ochs, N., 55
Ojeda, L., 181
Olkin, R., 28
Olmedo, E.L., 158
Osborn, D., 179
Osborne, J.L., 200
Osipow, S.H., 109
Ottavi, T.M., 36
Owen, J., 53

P
Padilla, A.M., 158
Padmawidjaja, I., 181
Parham, T.A., 70-71, 158
Parker, W.M., 19, 34, 54
Parsons, F., 92
Pate, P.H., Jr., 118
Patterson, C.H., 123
Pedersen, P., 17-18, 26, 123
Pedersen, P.B., 2, 31, 46, 49
Pena, J.V., 105
Penn, L.T., 105
Peralta, E., 81
Perez, M., 4

Perez, P., 7
Perloff, R., 159
Perry, J.C., 131, 197
Peterson, G.W., 118, 128
Piper, R.E., 132
Ponterotto, J.G., 2, 5, 31, 46, 49, 54, 117, 130, 197, 203
Pope-Davis, D.B., 36
Pope, M., 195
Porche, M.V., 136
Porfeli, E.J., 177-178
Prilleltensky, I., 204
Prilleltensky, O., 204
Prince, J.P., 93
Pryor, R., 104
Pyle, K.R., 140

R
Rank, M.R., 85
Raposa, E.B., 103
Rathbun, A., 182
Ratts, M.J., 7, 196
Reardon, R.C., 118
Reents, E., 95-96
Rehfuss, M., 108
Reynolds, C.R., 153, 159
Rhodes, J., 103
Rickard, K.M., 28
Ridley, C.R., 4, 21, 45, 50, 52, 74, 80, 120, 123, 128-129, 148-149, 155-156, 163, 166-168, 170-171
Roberts, T., 95-96
Rodolfa, E., 53
Rodriquez, C., 105
Rotter, J.C., 5, 95-96, 120
Rounds, J., 99, 150-151
Roush, N.E., 28
Rowe, W., 31
Roysircar, G., 7, 117
Rubinstein, K.J., 4
Rushton, J.P., 152
Ruiz, A.S., 28

Name Index

S

Sabnani, H.B., 31, 34
Sacchetti, M., 51
Sammons, C., 4
Sampson, J.P., Jr., 202
Sampson, J.P., 8
Sanchez, J., 6-7, 17, 34, 56, 67, 117, 129, 155, 196
Sandhu, D.S., 7
Saunders, D.E., 118
Savickas, M.L, 96, 108
Schultheiss, D.E.P., 178
Schaefle, S.E., 4
Schwartz, S., 103
Semega, J., 85
Serafica, F.C., 93-94
Shafranske, E.P., 36
Sharf, R.S., 92, 97, 99, 103
Sheu, H.B., 105
Shrider, E.A., 85
Simek-Morgan, L., 123
Singh, A.A., 7, 196
Sire, J., 22
Smith, E., 82
Smith, E.J., 96
Soeprapto, E., 103
Solberg, V.S., 177
Spanierman, L.B., 51, 123, 155, 169, 171
Sparks, E., 199
Speight, S.L., 4, 7, 195, 197, 199, 203
Spengler, P.M., 169
Splete, H.H., 8
Spokane, A.R., 127
Spuhler, J.N., 157
Stabile, S.J., 152

Stadler, H., 6-7, 17, 34, 56, 67, 117, 129, 155, 196
Stams, G.J.J., 103
Starishevsky, R., 97
Steele, C.M., 153-154

Steele, S., 82
Stephenson, M., 4
Stevenson, S.J., 104
Sternberg, R.J., 159
Stoltz, K.B., 147-148, 170
Stolz, C.L., 157
Strodtbeck, F.L., 24-25
Strohmer, D.C., 169
Su, R., 151
Subich, L.M., 148, 157, 160
Sudarsky-Gleiser, C., 128-130, 155, 157-158, 162
Sue, D., 4, 21-25, 27-30, 33-35, 48, 52-54, 78-80, 120, 122-123, 126, 128, 136, 194
Sue, D.W., 2, 4-6, 21-25, 27-30, 33-35, 48, 52-54, 78-80, 120, 122-123, 126, 128, 136, 194, 196, 206
Super, D., 95-97, 108, 177-178, 183
Suzuki, L.A., 28, 31, 54, 153, 159
Swaney, K., 99
Swanson, J.L., 98, 105-106, 109, 150, 160
Swazo, R., 4
Swigonski, M., 58
Swim, J.K., 27, 71
Sykes, L.A., 103
Szymanski, D.M., 60

T

Tao, K., 53
Taylor, M.E., 82
Terry, R.W., 31
Thomas, D.A., 133
Thompson, D.E., 4
Tirre, W.C., 159
Todorov, A., 122
Tokar, D.M., 160
Tomlinson-Clark, S., 4
Tonno, 53, 57
Toporek, R., 6-7, 17, 34, 56, 67, 117, 129, 155, 194-197

Totenberg, N., 83
Torino, G.C., 53
Tourandji, P., 103
Tracey, T.J.G., 150
Trimble, J.E., 50, 156
Truax, K., 70, 82
Truong, N.N., 105
Tuffin, A., 104
Tupper, T.W., 104
Tyson, C.T., 103
Tziner, A., 156

U
U.S. Census Bureau, 2-3
USEEOC, 160
Uemura, A.K., 93
Urbina, S., 159
Utsey, S.O., 31, 48, 49

V
Vazquez-Nuttall, E., 2, 5, 28
Vera, E.M., 7, 195, 197, 199, 203
Vera, H., 58
Vespia, K.M., 4
Vondracek, F.W., 177-178
Vontress, C.E., 28

W
Walker, J.V. III, 128
Wall, J.E., 157
Walsh, W.B., 96, 101, 102, 109
Walz, G., 157
Walz, G.R., 131, 158, 194, 197, 201
Wampold, B.E., 53, 71
Wang, E.W., 104
Wang, K., 183
Wang, V.O., 4
Wang, X., 182
Ward, C.M., 12-13, 123
Watson, Z.P., 84
Weintraub, S.R., 199

Wettersten, K.B., 157
Whaley, A.L., 71, 120, 127
Whetzel, D.L., 157
Whiston, S.C., 152-154
Whitcomb, D.H., 157
Wilking-Yel, C.G., 202
Williams, E.N., 103
Willis, J., 122
Williamson, L., 95-96
Wilson, F., 195
Wood, A., 70, 82
Worthington, R.L., 51
Wrenn, C.G., 41
Wright, E., 70, 82

Y
Yoon, P., 4
Yost, E.B., 118-119, 124, 134

Z
Zhang, J., 4, 183
Zuniga, X., 36
Zunker, V., 118

Authors

Kathy M. Evans, Ph.D., LPC, CCCE, Professor Emerita of the Counselor Education Program at the University of South Carolina was President of NCDA 2019-2020. She has published widely in career counseling with over twenty publications devoted to career issues, including two books: Synthesizing family, career, and culture: A model for counseling in the twenty-first century and Gaining Cultural Competence in Career Counseling. She created the first graduate certificate program in career development for the University of South Carolina and supervised the fieldwork of the students in the program. Dr. Evans was the 2016 recipient of the Association for Counselor Education and Supervision's Lifetime Achievement Award. From 2015-2017, she served as the Trustee for Counselor Educators and Researchers for NCDA.

Aubrey L. Sejuit, Ph.D., LMSW, LCAS, MEd, CASAC-2, CCSP, Assistant Professor of Social Work and a Counselor for the Sib Collins Counseling Center at Limestone University is a Co-Founder and former Ethics & Bylaws Committee Chair for the South Carolina Career Development Association (SCCDA). Prior to working at Limestone University, she served as an Assistant Professor of Counseling and as the Counseling Program Coordinator for Lenoir-Rhyne University's Center for Graduate Studies of Columbia, SC. She is also an adjunct instructor in the Clinical Mental Health Counseling (CMHC) program at South University and in the Human Services (HS) program at Midlands Technical College, both in Columbia, SC. Dr. Sejuit is an Operation Iraqi Freedom (OIF) veteran who served with the 203D MI BN in Baghdad, Iraq as an Intelligence Analyst and earned the Joint Service Achievement Medal (JSAM) among other awards. She is also a Co-Founder of the Veterans Alumni Council (VAC) at the University of South Carolina, where she earned her Ph.D. in Counselor Education & Supervision and served under the mentorship of Dr. Kathy M. Evans. Dr. Sejuit was the 2019 recipient of the South Carolina Counseling Association's Distinguished Professional Service Award. A native of Shamokin, Pennsylvania, she is a proud graduate of Penn State University (Phi Mu Alumna), Syracuse University, the University of South Carolina, and Cochise College.

Dr. Evans and Dr. Sejuit would like to give a special thank you to the hard work of two Limestone University graduates, Ms. Kelly Smoak and Ms. Bethany Nemeth, who worked tirelessly, helping with this book.